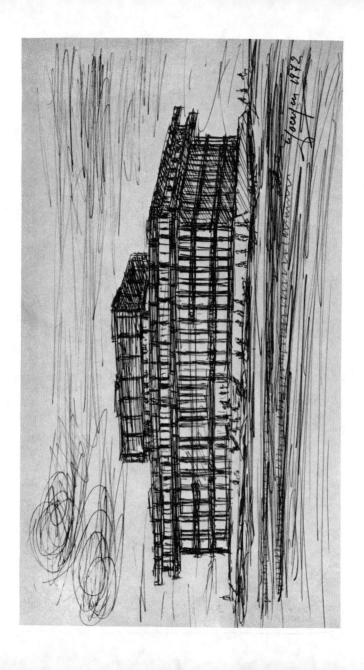

MODERN LEGAL STUDIES

THE COURT OF JUSTICE
OF THE
EUROPEAN COMMUNITIES

by

L. NEVILLE BROWN
*Solicitor; Professor of Comparative Law
at the University of Birmingham*

and

FRANCIS G. JACOBS
*Barrister; Professor of European Law
at the University of London*

LONDON
SWEET & MAXWELL
1983

First Edition 1977
Second Impression 1979
Second Edition 1983

Published by
Sweet & Maxwell Limited of
11 New Fetter Lane, London.
Computerset by Promenade Graphics, Cheltenham.
Printed in Great Britain by
Page Bros. (Norwich) Ltd.

British Library Cataloguing in Publication Data

Brown, L. Neville
   The Court of Justice of the European Communities
   —2nd ed.—(Modern Legal Studies)
   1. European Court
   I. Title   II. Jacobs, Francis G.
   III. Series
   341.7'8

   ISBN 0-421-31400–1
   ISBN 0-421-31410–9 Pbk

1350562

©
L. N. Brown
F. G. Jacobs
1983

PREFACE

The six years which have passed since our first edition represent a significant span in the short history of the European Communities. Considerable re-writing has been necessary as we have sought to bring up to date this account of the life and work of the Court of Justice, without losing sight of its origins and evolution.

We are grateful to many readers and reviewers whose constructive comments on the first edition have helped us in our task, and also to Mr. H. C. Adamson of the Law Society for comments on drafts of part of Chapter 12.

Our joint working sessions took place in London, at Teddington, and finally at Wolverhampton, where we were able to sign this preface after witnessing the success of another object of our mutual concern, Wolverhampton Wanderers Football Club.

North Bank
Molineux
January 3, 1983

L.N.B.
F.G.J.

PREFACE TO THE FIRST EDITION

In teaching the elements of Community law to English undergraduates, each of us felt the need for a fuller account of the Court of Justice than is normally included in the standard textbooks on Community law. Yet, for the readership we had in mind, the large practice books on the Court were not appropriate.

When we found that our ideas for a short monograph were running along parallel lines, we decided to collaborate in the present work. Our primary aim has been to provide a study of the composition, jurisdiction and practice of the Court, a subject which we believe to be essential for the student or practitioner seeking to understand the Community legal system and its substantive law. But we also believe that the Court deserves study in its own right as a remarkable judicial institution of modern times. On either count, our book was able, much to our satisfaction, to be included in *Modern Legal Studies*.

Although each of us undertook the first draft of particular chapters, our many meetings in London and Birmingham led to so much rewriting that the final text may truly be described as an amalgam of our several labours. As such, its imperfections must be our joint responsibility.

Platform 6   L. Neville Brown
Euston   Francis G. Jacobs
June 1977

CONTENTS

	Page
Preface	v
Preface to the first edition	vii
Table of Cases before the Court of Justice	xiii
(in alphabetical order)	
Table of Cases before the Court of Justice	xxi
(in numerical order)	
Table of Cases before other courts	xxvii
Table of Community Treaties	xxviii
Table of Community legislation	xxxi

1   General Introduction   1

PART ONE: ORGANISATION AND
COMPOSITION   13
2   Court Organisation   15
3   Judges   30
Appendix   46
Judgment of the Court
4   Advocates General   54
Appendix   64
Opinion of the Advocate General

PART TWO: FUNCTIONS AND JURISDICTION   71
5   Actions against Member States   75
6   Judicial review of Community Acts   91
7   Plenary Jurisdiction   118
Appendix   142
Methods to challenge the validity of a Regulation
8   Staff Cases   143
9   Preliminary Rulings   151
10   Opinions: External Relations   179
Appendix   185
Judicial Statistics

PART THREE: PROCEDURE AND PRACTICE   193
11   Procedure and Practice   197
Appendix   218
Notes for the guidance of Counsel at oral hearings
12   Lawyers in the Court   221

PART FOUR: THE COURT AS LAW-MAKER   233
13   Methods of Interpretation   237
14   General Principles of Law   260
15   Precedent and the Court   275
16   Future of the Court: Conclusions   286

Select Bibliography   299
Index   301

OTHER BOOKS IN THE SERIES

Anatomy of International Law (Second Edition), by J. G. Merrills

Compensation and Government Torts, by C. Harlow

Constructive Trusts, by A. J. Oakley

Council Housing (Second Edition), by D. C. Hoath

Development Control, by J. Alder

Drugs and Intoxication, by David Farrier

Economic Torts (Second Edition), by J. D. Heydon

Exclusion Clauses in Contracts (Second Edition), by David Yates

The Family Home, by W. T. Murphy and Hilary Clarke

Homelessness, by D. C. Hoath

Human Rights and Europe (Second Edition), by Ralph Beddard

Immigration Law (Second Edition), by John Evans

Mortgages (Second Edition), by P. B. Fairest

Natural Justice (Second Edition), by Paul Jackson

The Protection of Privacy, by Raymond Wacks

Registered Land (Third Edition), by David J. Hayton

Remedies for Breach of Contract, by Hugh Beale

Small Businesses (Second Edition), by Michael Chesterman

Squatting, by A. Pritchard

Strict and Vicarious Liability, by L. H. Leigh

Taxation and Trusts, by G. W. Thomas

The publishers would like to thank the artist, Mr. Edmond Goergen of Luxembourg, for his kind permission in allowing us to reproduce his drawing of the Court building.

TABLE OF CASES
BEFORE THE COURT OF JUSTICE

(in alphabetical order)

AM & S Europe Limited v. Commission (155/79) [1982] 2 CMLR
264..205, 212, 253, 294
ASSIDER (3/54) [1954–1956] ECR 63................................244, 252
Adlerblum v. Caisse Nationale d'Assurance Vieillesse des Travail-
leurs Salariés (93/75) [1975] ECR 2147 161
Alcan v. Commission (69/69) [1970] ECR 385 101
Algera and Others v. Assembly (7/56 & 3–7/57) [1957 and 1958]
ECR 39..131, 145, 149, 253
Alvis v. Council (32/62) [1963] ECR 49................................ 147, 253
Amylum and Tunnel Refineries v. Council and Commission (116 &
124/77) [1979] ECR 3497 128
Apples cases: see International Fruit Company and Others v.
Commission (41–44/70) [1971] ECR 411....................... 99, 100
Associazione Industrie Siderurgiche Italiane (ASSIDER) v. High
Authority (3/54) [1954–1956] ECR 63.........................244, 252

B.R.T. v. S.A.B.A.M. (127/73) [1974] ECR 51 216
Bakels v. Oberfinanzdirektion München (14/70) [1970] ECR
1001 277
Bayerische HNL v. Council and Commission (83 & 94/76, 4, 15, &
40/77) [1978] ECR 1209...127, 128
Becher v. Hauptzollamt München (13/67) [1968] ECR 187 215
Becker v. Finanzamt Münster (8/81) [1982] ECR 53 .... 41, 277
Belgische Radio en Televisie v. SABAM and Fonior (127/73) [1974]
ECR 51 216
Bellintani v. Commission (116/78) [1980] ECR 23 213
Bergmann v. Grows-Farm GmbH (114/76) [1977] ECR 1211 127
Bock v. Commission (62/70) [1971] ECR 897 .... 98, 102, 266
Bollmann Paul G. v. Hauptzollamt Hamburg-Waltershof (62/72)
[1973] ECR 269 217
Bonsignore v. Oberstadtdirektor der Stadt Köln (67/74) [1975] ECR
297 151
Borker (138/80) [1980] ECR 1975 165
Bosch (13/61) [1962] ECR 45 ....60, 157, 161
Bouchereau, R. v. (30/77) [1977] ECR 1999 243
Brack v. Insurance Officer (17/76) [1976] ECR 1429 ....9, 165, 252
Bresciani v. Amministrazione Italiana delle Finanze (87/75) [1976]
ECR 129 163

British Beef Co. *v.* Intervention Board for Agricultural Produce (146/77) [1978] ECR 1347 9
Broekmeulen *v.* Huisarts Registratie Commissie (246/80) [1981] ECR 2311.. 166, 167
Brunner *v.* Hauptzollamt Hof (9/72) [1972] ECR 961 248

C.A.M., SA *v.* Commission (100/74) [1975] ECR 1393 99
C.I.L.F.I.T. (283/81) (not yet reported) 172
CNTA *v.* Commission (74/74) [1975] ECR 533 .... 130, 131, 266
Cement-Convention (8–11/66) [1967] ECR 75 .... 93, 105
Centrafarm BV and de Peijper *v.* Sterling Drug Inc. and Winthrop BV (15 & 16/74) [1975] ECR 1147 and 1183 152
Chasse (15/57) [1957 and 1958] ECR 211 263
Cimenteries CBR and Others *v.* Commission (8–11/66) [1967] ECR 75 .... 93, 105
Coenen and Others *v.* Sociaal-Economische Raad (39/75) [1975] ECR 1547 224
Colditz *v.* Caisse d'Assurance Vieillesse des Travailleurs Salariés de Paris (9/67) [1967] ECR 229 257
Commission *v.* Belgium (156/77) [1978] ECR 1881 116
—— *v.* Council (22/70) [1971] ECR 263 .... 60, 94, 95, 96, 180, 181, 240, 249, 255
—— *v.* —— (81/72) [1973] ECR 575 .... 4, 96, 110, 266
—— *v.* —— (70/74) [1975] ECR 795 .... 96, 97
—— *v.* French Republic (6 & 11/69) [1969] ECR 523 104
—— *v.* —— (26/69) [1970] ECR 565 80
—— *v.* —— (167/73) [1974] ECR 359 .... 81, 86, 281
—— *v.* —— (Mutton and Lamb) (232/78) [1979] ECR 2729 .... 77, 87
—— *v.* —— (24/80 R & 97/80R) [1980] ECR 1319 87
—— *v.* —— (24/80) (not yet reported) 77
—— *v.* —— (97/80) (not yet reported) 77
—— *v.* Germany (70/72) [1973] ECR 813 85
—— *v.* Ireland (61/77) [1978] ECR 417 89
—— *v.* Italian Republic (7/61) [1961] ECR 317 .... 78, 94
—— *v.* —— (7/68) [1968] ECR 423 77
—— *v.* —— (24/68) [1969] ECR 193 251
—— *v.* —— (48/71) [1972] ECR 527 77
—— *v.* Luxembourg and Belgium (2 & 3/62) [1962] ECR 425 .... 80, 241, 249, 250
—— *v.* —— (90 & 91/63) [1964] ECR 625 .... 80, 249
—— *v.* Luxembourg (58/81) [1982] 3 CMLR 482 81
—— *v.* United Kingdom (31/77R & 53/77R) [1977] ECR 921 ..... 84, 88
—— *v.* —— (231/78) [1979] ECR 1447 .... 78, 89
Compagnie Continentale France *v.* Council (169/73) [1975] ECR 117 132

Compagnie d'Approvisionnement v. Commission (9 & 11/71) [1972]
    ECR 391 .... 127, 132
Compagnie des Hauts Fourneaux de Chasse v. High Authority
    (15/57) [1957 and 1958] ECR 211 263
Compagnie Française Commerciale et Financière v. Commission
    (64/69) [1970] ECR 221 .... 99, 100, 251
Consten and Grundig v. Commission (56 & 58/64) [1966] ECR
    299 .... 97, 109
Continental Can (6/72) [1973] ECR 215 .... 60, 97, 241, 243, 255, 258
Costa v. ENEL (6/64) [1964] ECR 585 .... 41, 158, 167, 168, 175,
                                                     176, 177, 215, 216, 249
Council v. Parliament (72/82) (discontinued) 95

DGV Deutsche Getreideverwertung und Rheinische Kraftfutter-
    werke GmbH and Others v. Council and Commission (241,
    242 & 245–250/78) [1979] ECR 3017 .... 128, 131
Da Costa en Schaake NV and Others v. Nederlandse Belastingad-
    ministratie (28–30/62) [1963] ECR 31 .... 173, 282
Dairy Products Case: Commission v. Luxembourg and Belgium (90
    & 91/63) [1964] ECR 625 .... 80, 249
Dalmas e Figli v. High Authority (21/64) [1965] ECR 175 114
Dautzenberg v. Court of Justice (2/80) [1980] ECR 3107 145
De Franceschi S.p.a. Monfalcone v. Council and Commission
    (51/81) [1982] ECR 117 129
Defrenne v. Sabena (43/75) [1976] ECR 455 .... 151, 173–175,
                                                            225, 257, 277
De Geus v. Bosch (13/61) [1962] ECR 45 .... 60, 157, 161
De Peijper (104/75) [1976] ECR 613 .... 152, 264
Donington, Lord Bruce of (208/80) [1981] ECR 2205 165
Du Pont (234/81) (not yet reported) 226
Deutsche Bakels GmbH v. Oberfinanz-direktion München (14/70)
    [1970] ECR 1001 277
Dietz v. Commission (126/76) [1977] ECR 2431 140
—— v. —— (126/76–Costs) [1979] ECR 2131 209
Dumortier and Others v. Council (64 & 113/76, 167 & 239/78, 27, 28
    & 45/79) [1979] ECR 3091 .... 128, 131
Dyestuffs cases (48 etc./69) [1972] ECR 619 280

EMI v. CBS (51, 86 & 96/75) [1976] ECR 811 152
ERTA Case: *See* Commission v. Council (20/70) ECR 263 60,
                                     94, 95, 96, 180, 181, 240, 249, 255
Elz v. Commission (56/75–rev.) [1977] ECR 1617 213
Einfur- und Vorratsstelle für Getreide- und Futtermittel v. Mack-
    prang (2/75) [1975] ECR 607 266
Eunomia di Porro v. Italian Ministry of Education (18/71) [1971]
    ECR 811 77

Europemballage Corporation and Continental Can Co. Inc. *v.*
    Commission (6/72) [1973] ECR 215 ...... 60, 97, 241, 243, 255, 258
Export Credits case: Opinion 1/75 [1975] ECR 1355 .... 181, 183

Fédéchar *v.* High Authority (8/55) [1954–1956] ECR 245 ... 60, 107, 108,
                                                    243, 258, 262
Foglia *v.* Novello (104/79) [1980] ECR 745 .... 159, 216
—— *v.* —— (244/80) [1981] ECR 3045 .... 160, 216
Fournier *v.* Commission (39/69) [1970] ECR 267 149
French Republic *v.* High Authority (1/54) [1954–1956] ECR 1 108
—— *v.* Italy (42/82R) [1982] ECR 841 210
—— *v.* United Kingdom (141/78) [1979] ECR 2923 83
Frilli *v.* Belgian State (1/72) [1972] ECR 457 264

GEMA *v.* Commission (125/78) [1979] ECR 3173 111
Geitling and Others *v.* High Authority (36–38 & 40/59) [1960] ECR
    423 269
Germany *v.* Commission (24/62) [1963] ECR 63 106
—— *v.* (34/62) [1963] ECR 131 258
Gingerbread Case: *See* Commission *v.* Luxembourg and Belgium
    (2 & 3/62) [1962] ECR 425 .... 80, 241, 249, 250
Granaria *v.* Hoofdproduktschap voor Akkerbouwprodukten (Skim-
    med milk powder) (116/76) [1977] ECR 1247 127
Groupement des Industries Sidérurgiques Luxembourgeoises *v.*
    High Authority (7 & 9/54) [1954–1956] ECR 175 .... 60, 102

Haegeman *v.* Belgian State (181/73) [1974] ECR 449 163
—— *v.* Commission (96/71) [1972] ECR 1005 .... 138, 139, 278
Hauer *v.* Land Rheinland-Pfalz (44/79) [1979] ECR 3727 273
Hoogovens *v.* High Authority (14/61) [1962] ECR 253 261
Humblet *v.* Belgian State (6/60) [1960] ECR 559 .... 242, 246

IBM *v.* Commission (60/81) [1981] ECR 2639 94
I.C.I. and Others *v.* Commission (48, 49, 51–57/69) [1972] ECR
    619 280
Importazione Bestiame Carni *v.* Commission (46/75) [1976] ECR
    65 138
Import Gadgets, S.a.r.l., Paris *v.* L.A.M.P. S.p.A., Pavia (22/76)
    [1976] ECR 1371 .... 8, 37–40, 46–53,
                            57, 64–69, 159, 215, 217, 242, 248, 277
International Fruit Company and Others *v.* Commission (41–44/70)
    [1971] ECR 411 .... 99, 100
Internationale Handelsgesellschaft *v.* Einfuhr- und Vorratsstelle für
    Getreide und Futtermittel (11/70) [1970] ECR 1125 107,
                                                    270, 273, 274

Interquell Stärke-Chemie and Diamalt *v.* Council and Commission
    (261 & 262/78) [1979] ECR 3045...............................128, 131
Ireks-Arkady *v.* Council and Commission (238/78) [1979] ECR
    2955...128, 131
Italy *v.* Council and Commission (32/65) [1966] ECR 389 116
—— *v.* High Authority (20/59) (1960) ECR 325 258

Japanese Ball-Bearings cases: Toyo Bearing Co. and Others *v.*
    Council and Commission (113 & 118–121/77) [1979] ECR
    1185 101

KSH *v.* Council and Commission (143/77) [1979] ECR 3583 128
Kampffmeyer and Others *v.* Commission (5, 7 & 13–24/66) [1967]
    ECR 245..124, 127, 130, 138
—— *v.* Commission and Council (56–60/74) [1976] ECR 711 131
Kenny *v.* Insurance Officer (1/78) [1978] ECR 1489 151
Kergall *v.* Common Assembly (1/55) [1954–1956] ECR 151 121
Koninklijke Scholten-Honig *v.* Council and Commission (143/77)
    [1979] ECR 3583 128
Koschniske *v.* Raad van Arbeid (9/79) [1979] ECR 2717 244
Kramer and Others (3, 4 & 6/76) [1976] ECR 1279 182

LTU *v.* Eurocontrol (29/76) [1976] ECR 1541 253
Lamb War cases: Commission *v.* France (24/80R & 97/80R) [1980]
    ECR 1319 87
Lee *v.* Minister for Agriculture (152/79) [1981] ECR 1495........229, 230
Leonesio *v.* Italian Ministry for Agriculture and Forestry (93/71)
    [1972] ECR 287 151
Lesieur Cotelle S.A. and Others *v.* Commission (67–85/75) [1976]
    ECR 391 138
Lord Bruce of Donington (208/80) [1981] ECR 2205 165
Lütticke *v.* Commission (48/65) [1966] ECR 19 111
—— *v.* —— (4/69) [1971] ECR 325................................125, 131, 278
Luxembourg *v.* European Parliament (230/81) (not yet reported) ... 95

Mackprang *v.* Commission (15/71) [1971] ECR 797 111
—— (2/75) [1975] ECR 607 266
Maizena *v.* Council (139/79) [1980] ECR 3393.................106, 110, 212
Manghera (59/75) [1976] ECR 91.......................................249, 256
Manzoni *v.* Fonds National de Retraite des Ouvriers Mineurs
    (112/76) [1977] ECR 1647 277
Markus & Walsh *v.* Hauptzollamt Hamburg-Jonas (14/69) [1969]
    ECR 349 248
Matisa-Maschinen GmbH *v.* Hauptzollamt Berlin-Packhof (35/75)
    [1975] ECR 1205 277
Meijer *v.* Department of Trade (118/78) [1979] ECR 1387 ....78, 89

Merkur v. Commission (43/72) [1973] ECR 1055....................130, 278
Meroni v. High Authority (9/56) [1957 and 1958] ECR 133 .....105, 114,
                                                               127, 243
Metro v. Commission (26/76) [1977] ECR 1875 ....100, 102
Meyer-Burckhardt v. Commission (9/75) [1975] ECR 1171.......121, 171
Milchkontor v. Hauptzollamt Saarbrücken (29/68) [1969] ECR
    165   172
Mills v. European Investment Bank (110/75) [1976] ECR 955   148
Minister for Fisheries v. Schoenenberg (88/77) [1978] ECR 473   89
Muller-Collignon v. Commission (4/67) [1967] ECR 365   130

Nederlandse Spoorwegen v. Minister van Verkeer en Waterstaat
    (36/73) [1973] ECR 1299   165
Netherlands v. High Authority (6/54) [1954–1956] ECR 103   96,
                                                               109, 246
—— v. —— (25/59) [1960] ECR 355   258
—— v. Ruffer (814/79) [1980] ECR 3807...............................244, 253
Niemann v. Bundesversicherungsanstalt für Angestellte (191/73)
    [1974] ECR 571   154
Nold v. Commission (4/73) [1974] ECR 491 ....107, 272, 273
—— v. High Authority (18/57) [1957 and 1958] ECR 121   280
Nordsee v. Nordstern (102/81) [1982] ECR 1095   166

Officier van Justitie v. van Haaster (190/73) [1974] ECR 1123   249
Opinion 1/76 Draft Agreement establishing laying-up fund for
    inland waterway vessels [1977] ECR 741   182
—— 1/78 concerning the International Agreement on National
    Rubber [1979] ECR 2811   182

Pellegrini v. Commission (23/76) [1976] ECR 1807   120
Petroni v. ONPTS (24/75) [1975] ECR 1149   154
Pigmeat Case: Commission v. Italy (7/61) [1961] ECR 317..........78, 94
Pig Producers Case: Commission v. United Kingdom (31/77R &
    53/77R) [1977] ECR 921...84, 88
Pigs Marketing Board v. Redmond (83/78) [1978] ECR 2347   228
Pioneer Electronic and Pioneer High Fidelity v. Commission (102 &
    103/80) (not yet reported)   294
Plaumann v. Commission (25/62) [1963] ECR 95 ... 41, 98, 100, 129, 278
Polydor Ltd. v. Harlequin Record Shops Ltd. (270/80) [1982] ECR
    329   163
Portelange v. Smith Corona Marchant International and Others
    (10/69) [1969] ECR 309   159
Prais v. Council (130/75) [1976] ECR 1589.............................150, 292
Providence Agricole de la Champagne and Others v. ONIC (4, 109
    & 145/79) [1980] ECR 2823 ....174, 175

Pubblico Ministero *v.* Manghera and Others (59/75) [1976] ECR
    91 ....249, 256
—— *v.* Ratti (148/78) [1979] ECR 1629 41

R. *v.* Bouchereau (30/77) [1977] ECR 1999 243
—— *v.* Henn and Darby (34/79) [1979] ECR 3795 152
—— *v.* Secretary of State for Home Affairs *ex p.* Santillo (131/79)
    [1980] ECR 1585..244, 259
Racke *v.* Hauptzollamt Mainz (98/78) [1979] ECR 69 266
Ratti (148/78) [1979] ECR 1629 41
Razanatsimba (65/77) [1977] ECR 2229 165
Rewe Handelsgesellschaft Nord and Rewe Markt Steffen *v.*
    Hauptzollamt Kiel (158/80) [1981] ECR 1805 213
Reyners *v.* Belgian State (2/74) [1974] ECR 631 223
Rey Soda *v.* Cassa Conguaglio Zucchero (23/75) [1975] ECR
    1279 249
Rheinmühlen *v.* Einfuhr- und Vorratsstelle für Getreide und
    Futtermittel (6/71) [1971] ECR 719 284
—— *v.* —— (146 & 166/73) [1974] ECR 33 and 139..............155, 157,
                                                                       159, 171, 283, 284
Richez-Parise *v.* Commission (19, 20, 25 & 30/69) [1970] ECR
    325 126
Roquette *v.* Council (138/79) [1980] ECR 3333................106, 110, 212
Royal Scholten-Honig (Holdings) and Tunnel Refineries *v.* In-
    tervention Board for Agricultural Produce (103 & 145/77)
    [1978] ECR 2037 265
Rüffer (814/79) [1980] ECR 3807...244, 253
Rutili *v.* Minister for the Interior (36/75) [1975] ECR 1219.......272, 273

SNUPAT *v.* High Authority (42 & 49/59) [1961] ECR 53 ....107, 114
Saar Tubes *v.* High Authority (1 & 14/57) [1957 and 1958] ECR
    105 93
Sabbatini *v.* European Parliament (20/71) [1972] ECR 345 114,
                                                                              146, 265
Santillo (131/79) [1980] ECR 1585 ....244, 259
Sayag (5/68) [1968] ECR 395 ....135, 136
—— *v.* Leduc (9/69) [1969] ECR 329......................................135, 136
Schots-Kortner and Others *v.* Council and Commission (15–33 etc.
    /73) [1974] ECR 177 ....130, 147, 265
Sgarlata *v.* Commission (40/64) [1965] ECR 215 ....262, 269
Simmenthal (106/77) [1978] ECR 629 176
—— *v.* Commission (92/78) [1979] ECR 777 113
Simon *v.* Court of Justice (15/60) [1961] ECR 115 145
Société des Grands Moulins des Antilles *v.* Commission (99/74)
    [1975] ECR 1531 138
Sotgiu *v.* Deutsche Bundespost (152/73) [1974] ECR 153 249

Staff salaries cases (81/72 and 70/74)...................... 4, 96, 97, 110, 266
Stauder *v.* Ulm (29/69) [1969] ECR 419 ....107, 244, 270
Stork *v.* High Authority (1/58) [1959] ECR 17 269
Suiker Unie and Others *v.* Commission (40–48 etc./73) [1975] ECR
    1663 ....212, 294

Tither *v.* Commission (175/80) [1981] ECR 2345.....................228, 229
Toepfer *v.* Commission (106 & 107/63) [1965] ECR 405 .... 98, 100,
                                                                                                                 101, 124
Torrekens (28/68) [1969] ECR 125 252
Toyo Bearing Co. and Others *v.* Council and Commission (113 &
    118–121/77) [1979] ECR 1185 101
Transocean Marine Paint Association *v.* Commission (17/74) [1974]
    ECR 1063... 97, 107, 267, 277

United Brands *v.* Commission (27/76R) [1976] ECR 425 ....210, 213

Vaassen-Göbbels *v.* Beambtenfonds voor het Mijnbedrijf (61/65)
    [1966] ECR 261 163
van Binsbergen *v.* Bestuur van de Bedrijfsvereniging voor de
    Metaalnijverheid (33/74) [1974] ECR 1299 223
van Duyn *v.* Home Office (41/74) [1974] ECR 1337..............9, 241, 242
van Gend en Loos *v.* Nederlandse Administratie Belastingen
    (26/62) [1963] ECR 1 .... 8, 41, 60, 89, 162, 173, 175, 243, 277
van Haaster (190/73) [1974] ECR 1123 249
Vloeberghs *v.* High Authority (9 & 12/60) [1961] ECR 197 ......127, 134
von Lachmüller *v.* Commission (43, 45, & 48/59) [1960] ECR 463 ... 121

Watson and Belmann (118/75) [1976] ECR 1185 ....225, 272
Wöhrmann and Lutticke *v.* Commission (31 & 33/62) [1962] ECR
    501 114

Zuckerfabrik Schöppenstedt *v.* Council (5/71) [1971] ECR 975 41,
                                                                                                      126, 127, 128, 130

TABLE OF CASES
BEFORE THE COURT OF JUSTICE

(in numerical order)

1/54 French Republic v. High Authority 108
3/54 ASSIDER v. High Authority 244, 252
6/54 Netherlands v. High Authority 96, 109, 246
7 & 9/54 Groupement des Industries Sidérurgiques Luxem-
    bourgeoises v. High Authority 60, 102
1/55 Kergall v. Common Assembly 121
8/55 Fédéchar v. High Authority 60, 107, 108, 243, 258, 262
7/56 & 3–7/57 Algera and Others v. Assembly...........131, 145, 149, 253
9/56 Meroni v. High Authority.................................105, 114, 127, 243
1 & 14/57 Saar Tubes v. High Authority 93
15/57 Compagnie des Hauts Fourneaux de Chasse v. High Autho-
    rity 263
18/57 Nold v. High Authority 280
1/58 Stork v. High Authority 269
20/59 Italy v. High Authority 258
25/59 Netherlands v. High Authority 258
36–38 & 40/59 Geitling and Others v. High Authority 269
42 & 49/59 SNUPAT v. High Authority............................. 107, 114
43, 45 & 48/59 von Lachmüller v. Commission 121
6/60 Humblet v. Belgian State..................................... 242, 246
9 & 12/60 Vloeberghs v. High Authority 127, 134
15/60 Simon v. Court of Justice 145
7/61 Commission v. Italian Republic 78
13/61 De Geus v. Bosch.................................... 60, 157, 161
14/61 Hoogovens v. High Authority 261
2 & 3/62 Commission v. Luxembourg and Belgium...... 80, 241, 249, 250
24/62 Germany v. Commission 106
25/62 Plaumann v. Commission........................ 41, 98, 100, 129, 278
26/62 van Gend en Loos v. Nederlandse Administratie Belas-
    tingen.............................. 8, 41, 60, 89, 162, 173, 175, 243, 277
28–30/62 Da Costa en Schaake NV and Others v. Nederlandse
    Belastingadministratie..............................173, 282
31 & 33/62 Wöhrmann and Lütticke v. Commission 114
32/62 Alvis v. Council 147, 253
34/62 Germany v. Commission 258
90 & 91/63 Commission v. Luxembourg and Belgium............... 80, 249
106 & 107/63 Toepfer v. Commission 90, 100, 101, 124
6/64 Costa v. ENEL......... 41, 158, 167, 168, 175, 176, 177, 215, 216, 249

21/64 Dalmas e Figli *v.* High Authority 114
40/64 Sgarlata *v.* Commission 262, 269
56 & 58/64 Consten and Grundig *v.* Commission..................... 97, 109
32/65 Italy *v.* Council and Commission 116
48/65 Lütticke *v.* Commission 111
61/65 Vaassen–Göbbels *v.* Beambtenfonds voor het Mijnbedrijf 163
5, 7 & 13–24/66 Kampffmeyer and Others *v.* Commission 124, 127,
130, 138
8–11/66 Cimenteries CBR and Others *v.* Commission 93, 105
4/67 Muller–Collignon *v.* Commission 130
9/67 Colditz *v.* Caisse d'Assurance Vieillesse des Travailleurs
Salariés de Paris 257
13/67 Becher *v.* Hauptzollamt München 215
5/68 Sayag 135, 136
7/68 Commission *v.* Italy 77
24/68 Commission *v.* Italian Republic 251
28/68 Caisse régionale de sécurité sociale du nord de la France *v.*
Torrekens 252
29/68 Milchkontor *v.* Hauptzollamt Saarbrücken 172
4/69 Lütticke *v.* Commission...125, 131, 278
6 & 11/69 Commission *v.* French Republic 104
9/69 Sayag *v.* Leduc 135, 136
10/69 Portelange *v.* Smith Corona Marchant International and
Others 159
14/69 Markus & Walsh *v.* Hauptzollamt Hamburg-Jonas 248
19, 20, 25 & 30/69 Richez-Parise *v.* Commission 126
26/69 Commission *v.* French Republic 80
29/69 Stauder *v.* Ulm 107, 244, 270
39/69 Fournier *v.* Commission 149
48, 49, 51–57/69 I.C.I and Others *v.* Commission 280
64/69 Compagnie Française Commerciale et Financière *v.* Commission...99, 100, 251
69/69 Alcan *v.* Commission 101
11/70 Internationale Handelsgesellschaft *v.* Enifuhr- und Vorratsstelle für Getreide und Futtermittel...............107, 270, 273, 274
14/70 Deutsche Bakels GmbH *v.* Oberfinanzdirektion München 277
22/70 Commission *v.* Council (ERTA Case)..................60, 94, 95, 96,
180, 181, 240, 249, 255
41–44/70 International Fruit Company and Others *v.* Commission...99, 100
62/70 Bock *v.* Commission 98, 102, 266
5/71 Zuckerfabrik Schöppenstedt *v.* Council 41, 126, 127, 128, 130
6/71 Rheinmühlen *v.* Einfuhr- und Vorratsstelle für Getreide und
Futtermittel 284
9 & 11/71 Compagnie d'Approvisionnement *v.* Commission.....127, 132
15/71 Mackprang *v.* Commission 111

18/71 Eunomia di Porro *v.* Italian Ministry of Education 77
20/71 Sabbatini *v.* European Parliament.........................114, 146, 265
48/71 Commission *v.* Italy 77
93/71 Leonesio *v.* Italian Ministry for Agriculture and Forestry 151
96/71 Haegeman *v.* Commission...................................138, 139, 278
1/72 Frilli *v.* Belgian State 264
6/72 Europemballage Corporation and Continental Can Co. Inc. *v.*
    Commission...................................... 60, 97, 241, 243, 255, 258
9/72 Brunner *v.* Hauptzollamt Hof 248
43/72 Merkur *v.* Commission 130, 278
62/72 Bollmann *v.* Hauptzollamt Hamburg-Waltershof 217
70/72 Commission *v.* Germany 85
81/72 Commission *v.* Council...................................... 96, 110, 266
4/73 Nold *v.* Commission 107, 272, 273
15–33 etc./73 Schots-Kortner and Others *v.* Council and Commis-
    sion 130, 147, 265
36/73 Nederlandse Spoorwegen *v.* Minister van Verkeer en Water-
    staat 165
40–48 etc./73 Suiker Unie and Others *v.* Commission.............212, 294
127/73 B.R.T. *v.* SABAM 216
146 & 166/73 Rheinmühlen *v.* Einfuhr, etc. 155, 157, 159, 171,
                                                      283, 284
152/73 Sotgiu *v.* Deutsche Bundespost....................................... 249
167/73 Commission *v.* French Republic.............................81, 86, 281
169/73 Compagnie Continentale France *v.* Council 132
181/73 Haegeman *v.* Belgian State 163
190/73 Officier van Justitie *v.* van Haaster 249
191/73 Niemann *v.* Bundesversicherungsanstalt für Angestellte 154
2/74 Reyners *v.* Belgian State 223
15 & 16/74 Centrafarm BV and de Peijper *v.* Sterling Drug Inc. and
    Winthrop BV 152
17/74 Transocean Marine Paint Association *v.* Commission...... 97, 107,
                                                      267, 277
33/74 van Binsbergen *v.* Bestuur van de Bedrijsfsvereniging voor de
    Metaalnijverheid 223
41/74 van Duyn *v.* Home Office 9, 241, 242
56–60/74 Kampffmeyer and Others *v.* Commission and Council 131
67/74 Bonsignore *v.* Oberstadt-direktor der Stadt Köln 151
70/74 Commission *v.* Council...96, 97
74/74 CNTA *v.* Commission 130, 131, 266
99/74 Société des Grands Moulins des Antilles *v.* Commission 138
100/74 C.A.M., SA *v.* Commission 99
2/75 Einfuhr- und Vorratsstelle für Getreide- und Futtermittel *v.*
    Mackprang 266
9/75 Meyer-Burckhardt *v.* Commission 121, 171
23/75 Rey Soda *v.* Cassa Conguaglio Zucchero 249

24/75 Petroni v. ONPTS 154
35/75 Matisa-Maschinen GmbH v. Hauptzollamt Berlin-Packhof ... 277
36/75 Rutili v. Minister for the Interior 272, 273
39/75 Coenen and Others v. Sociaal-Economische Raad 224
43/75 Defrenne v. Sabena 151, 173–175, 225, 257, 277
46/75 Importazione Bestiame Carni v. Commision 138
51, 86 & 96/75 EMI v. CBS 152
56/75–rev. Elz v. Commission 213
59/75 Pubblico Ministero v. Flavia Manghera and Others......... 249, 256
67–85/75 Lesieur Cotelle SA and Others v. Commission 138
87/75 Bresciani v. Amministrazione Italiana delle Finanze 163
93/75 Adlerblum v. Caisse Nationale d'Assurance Vieillesse des
        Travailleurs Salariés 161
104/75 De Peijper.. 152, 264
110/75 Mills v. European Investment Bank 148
118/75 Watson and Belmann.. 225, 272
130/75 Prais v. Council 150, 292
Opinion 1/76 Draft Agreement establishing laying-up fund for
        inland waterway vessels 182
3, 4 & 6/76 Kramer and Others 182
17/76 Brack v. Insurance Officer...................................... 9, 165, 252
22/76 Import Gadgets v. L.A.M.P. 8, 37–40, 46–53,
                                        57, 64–69, 159, 215, 217, 242, 248, 277
23/76 Pellegrini v. Commission 120
26/76 Metro v. Commission... 100, 102
27/76 United Brands v. Commission 213
27/76R United Brands v. Commission 210
29/76 LTU v. Eurocontrol 253
64 & 113/76, 167 & 239/78, 27, 28 & 45/79 Dumortier and Others v.
        Council 128, 131
83 & 94/76, 4, 15 & 40/77 Bayerische HNL v. Council and
        Commission... 127, 128
112/76 Manzoni v. Fonds National de Retraite des Ouvriers
        Mineurs 277
114/76 Bergmann v. Grows-Farm GmbH 127
116/76 Granaria v. Hoofdproductschap voor Akkerbouwproduk-
        ten 127
126/76 Dietz v. Commission 140
126/76–Costs: Dietz v. Commission 209
31/77R & 53/77R Commission v. United Kingdom 84, 88
61/77 Commission v. Ireland 89
65/77 Razanatsimba 165
88/77 Minister for Fisheries v. Schonenberg 89
103 & 145/77 Royal Scholten-Honig (Holdings) and Tunnel Re-
        fineries v. Intervention Board for Agricultural Produce 265
106/77 Simmenthal 176

116 & 124/77 Amylum and Tunnel Refineries *v.* Council and Commission 128

143/77 Koninklijke Scholten-Honig *v.* Council and Commission 128

146/77 British Beef Co. *v.* Intervention Board for Agricultural Produce 9

156/77 Commission *v.* Belgium 116

Opinion 1/78 concerning the International Agreement on National Rubber 182

1/78 Kenny *v.* Insurance Officer 151

83/78 Pigs Marketing Board *v.* Redmond 228

92/78 Simmenthal *v.* Commission 113

98/78 Racke *v.* Hauptzollamt Mainz 266

116/78 Bellintani *v.* Commission 213

118/78 Meijer *v.* Department of Trade.................................78, 89

125/78 GEMA *v.* Commission 111

141/78 French Republic *v.* United Kingdom 83

148/78 Pubblico Ministero *v.* Ratti 41

231/78 Commission *v.* United Kingdom 78, 89

232/78 Commission *v.* French Republic.................................77, 87

238/78 Ireks-Arkady *v.* Council and Commission 128, 131

241, 242 & 245–250/78 DGV and Others *v.* Council and Commission..128, 131

261 & 262/78 Interquell Stärke-Chemie and Diamalt *v.* Council and Commission...128, 131

4, 109 & 145/79 Providence Agricole de la Champagne and Others *v.* ONIC..174, 175

9/79 Koschniske *v.* Raad van Arbeid 244

34/79 R. *v.* Henn and Darby 152

44/79 Hauer *v.* Land Rheinland-Pfalz 273

104/79 Foglia *v.* Novello 159, 216

131/79 R. v. Secretary of State for Home Affairs, *ex p.* Santillo 244, 259

138/79 Roquette *v.* Council 106, 110, 212

139/79 Maizena *v.* Council 106, 110, 212

152/79 Lee *v.* Minister for Agriculture 229, 230

155/79 A.M. & S. Europe Limited *v.* Commission......205, 212, 253, 294

814/79 Netherlands *v.* Ruffer 244, 253

2/80 Dautzenberg *v.* Court of Justice 145

24/80 Commission *v.* France 77

24/80R & 97/80R Commission *v.* France 87

97/80 Commission *v.* France 77

158/80 Rewe Handelsgesellschaft Nord and Rewe Markt Steffen *v.* Hauptzollamt Kiel 213

175/80 Tither *v.* Commission 228, 229

208/80 Lord Bruce of Donington 165

244/80 Foglia *v.* Novello 160, 216

246/80 Broekmeulen *v.* Huisarts Registratie Commissie...........166, 167

270/80 Polydor Ltd. *v.* Harlequin Record Shops Ltd. 163
8/81 Becker *v.* Finanzamt Münster....................................... 41, 277
51/81 De Franceschi S.p.A. Monfalcone *v.* Council and Commis-
    sion 129
60/81 IBM *v.* Commission 94
102/81 Nordsee *v.* Nordstern 166
230/81 Luxembourg *v.* European Parliament 95
234/81 Du Pont 226
283/81 CILFIT 172
72/82 Council *v.* Parliament 95

TABLE OF CASES BEFORE OTHER COURTS

Buchanan (James) & Co. *v.* Babco Forwarding and Shipping (U.K.)
    [1978] A.C. 141 (H.L.) 296
Bulmer *v.* Bollinger [1974] Ch. 401 .... 167, 170, 237

Concorde Express Transport *v.* Traffic Examiner, Metropolitan
    Area [1980] 2 CMLR 221 171

Garland *v.* British Rail Engineering [1982] 2 CMLR 174 170

Heydon's Case (1584) 3 Co.Rep. 7a 244
Hoffman-La Roche & Co. *v.* Secretary of State for Trade and
    Industry [1975] A.C. 295 (H.L.) 126

Macarthys *v.* Smith [1979] 1 W.L.R. 1189; [1979] 3 All E.R. 325 295
Minister for Economic Affairs *v.* Fromagerie Franco-Fuisse "Le
    Ski" [1972] CMLR 330 81
Minister of the Interior *v.* Cohn-Bendit [1980] 1 CMLR 543 .... 4, 170,
    171, 293
Moorcock, The, (1889) 14 P.D. 64 258

R. *v.* Barnsley Metropolitan Borough Council, *ex p.*, Hook [1976] 1
    W.L.R. 1052 263
—— *v.* Henn and Darby [1982] A.C. 850 255
—— *v.* Marlborough Street Stipendary Magistrate, *ex p.*
    Bouchereau [1977] 1 W.L.R. 414 230
—— *v.* Secchi [1975] 1 CMLR 383 259
Re a Holiday in Italy [1975] 1 CMLR 184 169
Russell *v.* Duke of Norfolk [1949] 1 All E.R. 109 165

Schorsch Meier *v.* Hennin [1975] Q.B. 416 259
Steinike and Weinlig *v.* Bundesamt für Ernährung und Forstwirt-
    schaft [1980] 2 CMLR 531 272

Terrapin (Overseas) Ltd. *v.* Terranova Industrie [1978] 3 CMLR
    102 173

TABLE OF COMMUNITY TREATIES

ECSC Treaty
Art. 4 76
Art. 31 263
Art. 32 33
   (1) 25
   (2) 118
Art. 33.................. 84, 92, 93,
               102, 103, 105,
               108, 112, 114,
               115, 116, 153,
               243, 246, 252,
               263
Art. 34 ....109, 133, 134
Art. 35 ....92, 110, 112, 114, 134
Art. 36 ....104, 113
   (3) 114, 115, 116
Art. 38 95
Art. 40 ....119, 122, 125, 134
Art. 41 ....25, 151, 152, 154, 163
Art. 60 108
Art. 61 108
Art. 65 108
Art. 80 ....102, 134
Art. 88 ....76, 84, 85, 134
Art. 89 82
Art. 92 115
Art. 95 74

EEC Treaty
Art. 2 ....254, 256
Art. 3 256
Art. 4 144
   (1) 2
Art. 7 264
Art. 9 ....241, 249, 251
Art. 12 .... 77, 162, 173,
               176, 241, 243,
               249, 251
Art. 13 ....241, 251
Art. 16 .... 77, 241, 251
Arts. 19–29 242
Art. 30 ....77, 152, 264

EEC Treaty—*cont.*
Art. 31 ....78, 152, 264
Arts. 32–35 ....152, 264
Art. 26 ....152, 251, 264
Art. 37 256
   (1) 249
Art. 38(1) 260
Art. 40(3) 127, 264, 265
Art. 48 ....81, 82, 241, 257
   (3) 243
Arts. 49, 50 257
Art. 51 ....154, 252, 257
Arts. 52–58 223
Arts. 59–66 223
Art. 84(2) 81
Art. 85 ....9, 100, 109,
               161, 267
   (1) 242
   (2) 161
Art. 86 ....100, 241, 243,
               255, 256, 258,
               259
Art. 92 ....84, 86
Art. 93 .... 83, 84, 85,
               86, 87, 88, 116
   (2)(3) 84
Art. 111 66
Art. 113 .... 66, 179, 180, 181
   (3) 180
Art. 115 .... 47, 50, 67
Art. 117 257
Art. 119 ....257, 264, 265
Art. 144 3
Art. 148 6
Art. 149 7
Art. 164 .... 3, 55, 263, 268,
               270, 286
Art. 165(2) 25
Art. 166 ....54, 55
Art. 167 .... 3, 31
Art. 168 ....17, 54

EEC Treaty—*cont.*

Art. 169 ....26, 68, 75, 77, 78, 79, 80, 82, 83, 85, 86, 87, 88, 94, 162, 171, 210, 224

Art. 170 ....75, 82, 85–89, 162

   (3) 83

Art. 171 .... 76, 77, 87

Art. 172 118

Art. 173 ....41, 92–95, 99, 102–105, 107–109, 111–114, 116, 127, 129, 130, 142, 145, 148, 175, 180, 212, 241, 243, 262, 263

   (1).............. 93, 94, 96

   (2).......97, 99, 100, 211

   (3) 103

Art. 174(2) 175

Art. 175 ..92, 110, 111, 112, 129

   (1) 110

   (2) 111

   (3) 110

Art. 176 109

Art. 177 .... 25, 46, 47, 50, 57, 60, 90, 127, 130, 142, 151, 153–156, 158–168, 170, 171, 174–176, 178, 182, 215, 216, 282, 284, 285, 290, 293

   (2) 169

   (3).........168, 169, 172

Art. 178 ....119, 121, 122

Art. 179 .... 114, 119, 121, 135, 144, 150

Art. 180 74

Art. 181 .... 74, 119, 120

Art. 182 74

EEC Treaty—*cont.*

Art. 183 ....120, 121

Art. 184 .... 104, 112–114, 116, 130, 142, 146, 174, 265

Art. 186 .... 77, 85, 88

Art. 188 194

Art. 189 .... 4, 94, 241

Art. 190 ....105, 106, 247

Art. 192 207

Art. 193 8

Art. 215 ....107, 119, 121, 123, 127–130

   (1) 119

   (2).......... 41, 122–128, 130, 134, 140, 142, 242, 253, 254

Art. 216 10

Art. 219 74

Art. 220 156

Art. 223 83

Art. 224 83

Art. 225 83

Art. 226 ....78, 79

Art. 228 .... 74, 163, 179, 180, 182, 183

   (1) 181

Art. 229 180

Art. 236 179

Art. 238 ....163, 180, 181

Annex II 242

Euratom Treaty

Art. 103 ....179, 182

Art. 150 .... 25, 151, 163

Art. 188 254

   (2) 122

Merger Treaty

Art. 1(3) 163

Art. 2 6

Art. 4 7

Art. 10(2) 7

Art. 11 3

Art. 13 ....3, 74

Art. 30 163

Act of Accession
  Art. 102 182
Protocol on the Statute of the
  Court of Justice
  Art. 4 36
  Art. 18 225
  Art. 20........................46, 48
  Art. 43.....................128, 129
Rules of Procedure of the
  Court of Justice...... 183, 194,
                            201, 202
  Art. 37 220
  Art. 38(3) 226

Rules of Procedure of the
  Court of Justice—*cont.*
  Art. 70 149
  Art. 83 77
  Art. 95........................25, 26
      (2) 26
      (3) 26, 148
      (4) 279
  Art. 104 ....217, 224, 227
1972 European Communities
  Act 177
  s. 3 281
    (1).....................173, 238

TABLE OF COMMUNITY LEGISLATION

Regulations

Reg. 3, J.O. 1958, 561 252
Reg. 17, J.O. 1962, 204 100
   Art. 15 93
   Art. 17 188
Reg. 99/63, J.O. 1963,
   2268 268

Reg. 1612/68 J.O. 1968,
   L.257/2 272
Reg. 1408/71 J.O. 1971,
   L.149/2 252
Reg. 1111/77 O.J. 1977,
   L.134/4 265

Decisions and Directives

Dec. 22/54 J.O. 1954, 346 115
Dec. 14/55 115
Dir. 64/221 J.O. 1964,
   850 .... 242, 272

Dir. 77/249 O.J. 1977,
   L78/17 233

Chapter 1

GENERAL INTRODUCTION

When, on May 9, 1950, the French Foreign Minister, Robert Schuman, announced his proposal to place the whole of French and German coal and steel production under a common High Authority, in an organisation open to the participation of other European countries, he took care to include in the proposal the establishment of a court of justice which would subject the new Authority to judicial control.

Less than one year later, on April 18, 1951, the Treaty establishing the European Coal and Steel Community (the ECSC) was signed in Paris, creating, among other institutions, the Court of Justice. The elaborate institutional apparatus, including, as well as the High Authority and the Court, a Special Council of Ministers and a Common Assembly, was no doubt intended to ensure that the new Community should be based on democratic principles and the rule of law. The judicial structure was strongly influenced by ideas derived from continental, especially French, administrative law. But there was also a hint, in the Preamble to the Treaty, of a wider function for the institutions; the Preamble recalled that the six founding Member States—Belgium, France, Germany, Italy, Luxembourg and the Netherlands—were resolved "to lay the foundations for institutions which will give direction to a destiny henceforward shared."

When the same States signed the two Treaties of Rome, on March 25, 1957, establishing the European Economic Community (the EEC) and the European Atomic Energy Community (Euratom) respectively, the institutions were indeed given a wider task. Each of the new Communities was endowed with a Court of Justice, as well as a Commission (rather than a High Authority), a Council of

1

Ministers, and an Assembly. At the same time it was provided that there should be a single Court (and a single Assembly) to serve all three Communities; this was effected by the Convention on Certain Institutions Common to the European Communities. Thus the Court of the ECSC became the Court of Justice of the European Communities.

Later, the "Merger Treaty" of 1965 provided that there should be a single Council and a single Commission for all three Communities. But the functions and powers of all four institutions—Council, Commission, Court and Assembly—are separately assigned in the three founding Treaties. In practice the EEC Treaty is by far the most important, and it is with the working of the Court under the EEC Treaty that this book is primarily concerned. The provisions governing the Court are substantially identical in the EEC and Euratom Treaties; they differ in more or less important respects from those in the earlier ECSC Treaty. Frequently, where provisions of the EEC Treaty are cited in this book, there are corresponding provisions in the other founding Treaties. The composition of the institutions is the same under all three Treaties. When, on January 1, 1973, the three Communities were enlarged to include Denmark, Ireland and the United Kingdom, the institutions were correspondingly enlarged under the Treaty of Accession, but their jurisdiction was not affected except in its territorial extent. The same can be said of the further enlargement by the inclusion of Greece on January 1, 1981.

In addition to their specific functions, the four institutions are required, under Article 4(1) of the EEC Treaty, to carry out the tasks entrusted to the Community; each institution is to act within the limits of the powers conferred upon it by the Treaty. Both the Council, composed of government ministers from the Member States, and the Commission, an entirely independent body, are given legislative and decision-making powers. The part played by the Assembly in the legislative process (at present only consultative) is considered below. The role of the Court, in the pregnant formula of Article 164 EEC, is to ensure that, in the interpretation and application of the Treaty, the law is observed. It is thus required to ensure that the other bodies act within the limits of their respective powers. Subsequent Articles of the Treaty spell out the Court's wide-ranging and multifarious jurisdiction, the main aspects of which will be discussed in Part Two of this book.

All four institutions are in principle equal under the Treaties; but, inevitably in the real world of politics as in the world of George Orwell, some are more equal than others. The formal equality of the institutions is symbolised by the fact that the members of the Court and of the Commission are appointed not by the Council—for that might be taken to imply the superiority of the Council—but "by common accord of the Governments of the Member States" (Art. 167 EEC; Art. 11 of the Merger Treaty). On the other hand, the Commission may be collectively dismissed by the Assembly (Art. 144 EEC); and an individual member of the Commission may be compulsorily retired by the Court (Art. 13 of the Merger Treaty).

We shall see that the relationship between the Council and the Commission is by no means that between political superior and inferior, even though the Council is undoubtedly the supreme expression, subject only to summit meetings of heads of government (below, p. 6), of the political will (or absence of will) in the Community. The relationship between the Council and the Court is also very different from that between government (or legislature) and judiciary, at least as it is known in the United Kingdom. While a decision of even the highest court in the United Kingdom can be reversed by Act of Parliament, even with retroactive effect, the decisions of the Court of Justice cannot be reversed by an act of the Council; on the contrary, any measure of the Council having legal effect can be annulled by the Court if contrary to the Treaties or other provisions of Community law. Although not a frequent occurrence, this has occasionally happened; we shall see an example in Case 81/72, the first *Staff Salaries* case (below, p. 96). In fact a ruling of the Court could be reversed only by the Court itself in a subsequent case, or by an amendment of the Treaties which, since it requires the unanimous approval of the Member States, each acting through its own constitutional processes, is not normally a practical possibility. Conversely, the political obstacles to amending the Treaties lend added significance to the Court's rulings on their interpretation, especially as the Court (as we shall see in Chapter 13) has been ready to interpret boldly in the face of political deadlock between the Council and the Commission. This boldness has led in turn to a hostile reaction from at least two national supreme courts; thus, the French *Conseil d'Etat* has rebelled against the well-settled case-law of the Court of Justice on the direct effect of directives, partly on the ground that law-making by the Court is less to be tolerated now that there is a directly elected European Parliament to take political initiatives (*Cohn-Bendit* C.E. December 12, 1979, *conclusions* Genevois [1980] 1 CMLR 543; see also German Federal Finance Court, judgment of July 16, 1981 [1982] 1 CMLR 527).

We shall have occasion to revert to the novel character of Community law which it is the Court's business to interpret and apply; here we must say a word about the sources of that law. In addition to, and derived from, the founding Treaties which make up the constitution of the Communities, it includes the regulations, directives and decisions of the Council and of the Commission, made under Article 189 EEC. These instruments are officially styled "acts" of the institutions. The acts of general application—regulations and directives—are sometimes referred to as "secondary legislation," the implication presumably being that the Treaties are in some sense "primary legislation." This classification is misleading since, although the implementing regulations of the Commission are often akin to subordinate or delegated legislation, there is nothing secondary, in character or in scope, about the basic regulations of the Council in such fields as agriculture, the free movement of workers, social security, and competition. This legislation is both as fundamental in character and as broad in scope as any national legislation, and its relationship to the founding Treaties is comparable to that which national legislation has to a national constitution, with the Court of Justice fulfilling the role of a constitutional court. Consequently we shall refer to regulations and directives of the Council as Community legislation, and for convenience we shall include in that term all enactments of both the Council and the Commission.

The Assembly, which adopted in 1962 the title of European Parliament, has as yet no legislative powers. Its role is primarily consultative: under numerous provisions of the Treaties its opinion must be sought and given before legislation can be enacted, but this need not be followed. It also has the power, in certain circumstances, to initiate proceedings before the Court: we revert to this in Chapter 6 (p. 110). In other respects the European Parliament is more like a national parliament. It has been given gradually increasing control over the Community budget; historically, budgetary powers have been of much importance to national parliaments in their struggles with the executive. The European Parliament also exercises supervisory functions over the Community executive: its members can put questions to the Commission (and to the Council), and it can even dismiss the Commission. Until 1979, its effectiveness had been limited by many factors, not least by the fact that its members had to combine their duties with serving the national parliaments, from which they had been appointed. With direct elections, although such a "dual mandate" remains possible, most M.E.P.s are able to give more time to their duties, and their increased authority as a result of direct election has already led them to reject the Community budget in 1979. Clearly, the European Parliament is destined in future to play a greater role, and perhaps to arrogate to itself a more active part in the legislative process. Nevertheless, for the present, the supreme Community legislature remains the Council, representing the Governments of the Member States.

The founding Treaties conceived of the Council as a Community institution rather than as an intergovernmental body. Thus, although the Council consists of representatives of the Member States (Art. 2 of the Merger Treaty), each State being represented either by the foreign minister or by the minister responsible for the subject in question (agriculture, education, finance, transport, etc.), nevertheless the Treaties provide for majority voting on most matters, in contrast with the unanimity rule often found in intergovernmental organisations. Again, in contrast with the normal rule of one State, one vote, the Treaties provide for weighted voting (Art. 148 EEC) in certain important areas of Community activity. But in practice, under the so-called "Luxembourg Accords" of 1966, unanimity has become the rule in cases where vital national interests are claimed to be at stake, although this convention was not observed in May 1982 when the Council (of Agriculture Ministers) overrode a British veto concerning farm prices. The obstacles to legislative progress caused by disagreements at the political level have been partially overcome, as we shall see, by the creative use of its powers by the Court of Justice and by the development there of judicial law-making.

Apart from the four institutions set up under the Treaties, mention must be made of the "summit" meetings of heads of government, formerly arranged ad hoc when the occasion arose—a famous occasion being the Hague summit of November 1969 which opened the way to the enlargement of the Communities—but now institutionalised under the name of "European Council." This "European Council" must be distinguished from the

Council of the European Communities, one of the four Treaty bodies, which is a permanent institution based, like the Commission, in Brussels, although holding its meetings at any convenient venue.

The Council and the Commission are sometimes contrasted as the legislature and executive respectively of the Community. This contrast accords well with the traditional doctrine of the separation of powers, distinguishing legislature, executive and judiciary. But the analogy is somewhat misleading about the role of the Commission, which has many functions beyond those of a mere executive and has important political responsibilities which it exercises in its own right.

Of most importance in this respect is the crucial role of the Commission in the legislative process. In almost every area of major policy under the EEC Treaty, the Council can legislate only on a proposal of the Commission. This exclusive "right of initiative" is vested in the Commission to ensure that legislation respects the Community interest; for "The members of the Commission shall, in the general interest of the Communities, be completely independent in the performance of their duties . . . they shall neither seek nor take instructions from any Government or from any other body" (Art. 10(2) of the Merger Treaty). Moreover, under Article 149 EEC, a proposal of the Commission can be amended only by a unanimous vote of the Council; so that if there is disagreement among the ministers, no decision at all can be taken until the Commission puts forward a different proposal. This has important consequences: not only is the Council unable to legislate unilaterally; the Commission is also actively involved in the law-making process within the Council. In practice, the Commission will have discussed its proposals with the Committee of Permanent Representatives of the Member States, which prepares the work of the Council (Art. 4 of the Merger Treaty); the proposals will have been considered, in collaboration with the Commission, by the European Parliament, and by the Economic and

Social Committee (Art. 193 EEC) if the Treaty so
requires; the Commissioner most closely concerned with
the proposal will attend the meetings of the Council at
which the proposal is discussed, and will take part in the
discussion. The Community thus has, in a sense, its own
seat at the Council table, although the Commission has no
vote in the Council. To describe the Commission,
therefore, as the Community executive is misleading
unless the notion of executive is understood as including
responsibility for policy and for implementing the aims
and general programme of the Community.

The Court of Justice has normally no direct part to play
in this formal legislative process. No doubt it will be
consulted if the proposals affect its jurisdiction; but
normally its concern is only with the end-product, the law.
Here, as has been mentioned, the Court may have to
adjudicate on the limits of the powers of the other
institutions. In this way it has a constitutional role in
determining the balance of power between the Community on the one hand and the Member States on the other,
as well as the institutional balance between the Council
and the Commission. In exploring the jurisdiction of the
Court in Part Two we shall have frequent occasion to
illustrate this constitutional role of the Court.

The description of the Commission as the Community
executive is also misleading about the nature of the
Communities themselves. For it conceals the fact that,
except to some extent under the ECSC Treaty, and in the
field of competition under the EEC Treaty, the Community executive is not a Community body at all. Generally,
Community policies are carried out, and Community
legislation applied, by the national authorities of the
Member States. It is the national customs administrations
which are responsible for applying the common customs
tariff, *e.g.* Case 22/76 *Import Gadgets* (below, p. 46) and
Case 26/62 *Van Gend en Loos* v. *Nederlandse Administratie der Belastingen* (below, p. 162); it is the national intervention agencies which implement the common agricultural

policy, *e.g.* Case 146/77 *British Beef Co.* v. *Intervention Board for Agricultural Produce* [1978] ECR 1347; it is the national social security offices which apply the regulations on the social security of migrant workers, *e.g.* Case 17/76 *Brack* v. *Insurance Officer* (below, p. 252).

The Community is not, therefore, a State writ large; or at least not a centralised State, like France or the United Kingdom. Community policies are made in Brussels and the legislation enacted there, but the regulations, directives and decisions of the Council and Commission are implemented by the Member States themselves. In this sense the Community's administration is decentralised.

So too with the judicial organisation of the Community: litigation involving questions of Community law is normally for the national courts. A dispute between individuals, or between an individual and the national authorities, falls within the jurisdiction of the appropriate national court or tribunal. It may come before the Court of Justice on a reference from the national court, as will be seen in Chapter 9, but it cannot be brought directly before that Court.

Thus a person claiming the right to enter a Member State, under the Treaty provisions on the free movement of workers and the implementing Community legislation, must seek his remedy before the courts of that State against the immigration authorities who have refused the right he claims, as in the *Van Duyn* case (below, p. 241). Or if the defendant, in an action for breach of contract, alleges that the contract was void under Article 85 of the Treaty, that defence must be decided upon by the national court, subject again to the possibility of a reference to the Court of Justice on the interpretation, or validity, of Community law.

Only if the individual litigant seeks to challenge directly some Community measure affecting his interests may he go directly to the Court of Justice; and even then, his right to do so, as will be seen in Chapter 6, is limited. In most cases, his forum is his national court.

It follows that, although the Court in Luxembourg is often described as the Community Court, an essential role in the application of Community law is played by the whole range of national courts and tribunals. In civil and commercial matters, in administrative and industrial disputes, and even in criminal cases, all these courts may have to apply Community law, and they too are therefore, in a very real sense, Community courts. In this capacity they are to be guided and assisted by the Court of Justice, and to adopt the principles of interpretation developed by the Court—principles which, as we shall see, have had a far-reaching effect on the evolution of Community law.

This introduction would be incomplete without mention of a matter of geography. Article 216 EEC provides that the seat of the institutions of the Community shall be determined by common accord of the Governments of the Member States. No such accord has yet been reached upon permanent seats for the institutions, and even their provisional places of work have, for political reasons, not been gathered together in one place but are spread between the cities of Brussels, Luxembourg and Strasbourg, to the inconvenience of those who work in, or have business with, the institutions. Thus, the Council and Commission are based in Brussels, while the European Parliament sits at present in Strasbourg. Before 1981 the Parliament also sat occasionally in Luxembourg, where its officials had (and still have) their headquarters. The Court of Justice has its seat in Luxembourg, where it is in permanent session.

That Luxembourg, the mini-State among the Ten, should have become the judicial centre of the Communities, has consequences that may escape the notice of anyone unfamiliar with the Grand Duchy and its capital. The City of Luxembourg, where the Court has sat since its inception, numbers some 90,000 inhabitants and has very much the atmosphere of a pleasant provincial town. There is neither the bustle of Brussels nor the sophistication of Strasbourg. Letzebuergers (as the natives of Luxembourg call themselves) are sober and hardworking people. There are no frivolities and few distractions, apart from the quiet charm of the surrounding countryside. Expatriates who work at the Court tend to entertain each other in their homes and to restrict their social life to a small circle of colleagues. This helps produce a sense of camaraderie and of loyalty to the Court that transcends national differences. On the other hand, narrowness of outlook is avoided because of the great diversity of backgrounds from which the personnel of the Court are drawn: this aspect is returned to in Chapter 3.

PART ONE: ORGANISATION AND COMPOSITION

Introductory

This part will be devoted to what may be termed the judicial administration of the Court. Chapter 2 will examine the administrative organisation of the Court and of its non-judicial staff, of which the head is the Registrar. Chapters 3 and 4 concern the two categories of members of the Court, the judges and advocates general. Considerable descriptive and biographical information is included in this part, the better to convey to those who have not visited it the atmosphere of the Court and the character of the men and women who operate there the central machinery of Community justice. Included as appendices to Chapters 3 and 4 are a typical judgment of the Court and the opinion of the advocate general in the same case. Further reference to these examples of the Court's work will be made in later chapters of this book.

Chapter 2

COURT ORGANISATION

Introduction

The Court shares certain organisational features generally found in most courts. But it has also certain peculiar features of its own.

Among features generally present in any court, one may mention the Registry under its administrative head, the Registrar, which carries out the normal administrative functions associated with a court Registry. There is also at Luxembourg the dichotomy made in several continental legal systems between, on the one hand, those who sit in judgment—the Bench, as we would say in England, or *la magistrature assise* as the French jargon puts it, and, on the other, "the standing magistracy" (*la magistrature debout*), by which are meant the five advocates general. The latter do not themselves sit in judgment but rather stand to proffer advice to the Bench on how it should decide the cases before the Court: their distinctive function will be examined further in Chapter 4.

At Luxembourg both judges and advocates general together constitute the judicial personnel of the Court and as such are to be contrasted with the members of the Bar who represent the parties and plead before the Court. But "the Bar" entitled to practise in the Court of Justice is very different from any single national Bar: its potential membership includes every member of the national Bars of the ten Member States, and in the case of the United Kingdom this may include solicitors as well as members of the Bar in certain circumstances (below, p. 228).

Again, like any court, the Court of Justice has a certain defined jurisdiction. This jurisdiction however is not open-ended in character, in the way, for example, that the

English High Court has a certain *inherent* jurisdiction.
Rather, as the French would say, the Court has only a
compétence d'attribution, that is, only such jurisdiction as
is expressly conferred upon it by the Treaties or by a
convention. In Part Two we shall see how extensive that
attribution is; nevertheless its limits are precise.

Finally, the Court is sub-divided into Chambers. This
common device to enable a greater work-load to be
handled or a greater specialisation achieved is being
extensively resorted to at Luxembourg, there now being
three Chambers which, under the latest revision of the
rules, deal severally with the greater part of the cases
before the Court. The most important cases, however, are
still reserved to the full Court.

Features peculiar to the Court of Justice arise from its
multi-national and multi-lingual character.

Thus, its judges are of ten different nationalities—one
from each of the Member States, together with an
additional judge drawn in rotation from one of the "big
four," France, Germany, Italy and the United Kingdom.
This is nowhere prescribed by rule but is a necessary
consequence of the principle that membership of the
Court requires a unanimous decision of the ten governments. The judges do not of course in any sense represent
their governments or their countries but must (and do)
reach their decisions with complete independence and
impartiality. Nevertheless, the fact that each nationality of
the Ten has its place on the bench of the Court does bring
to its decisions a special authority transcending national
viewpoints. The authority of the Court is also enhanced by
the invariable practice of framing its decision as a single
collegiate judgment: the oracles of Community law thus
speak with one voice.

The Court functions in no fewer than eight languages,
Irish being accepted there in addition to the seven official
Community languages. Thus, a case may be conducted in
Danish, Dutch, English, French, German, Greek, Irish or
Italian. But, as we shall see (p. 21, below), Irish has not

yet been used in any case. Rules have been framed to determine the language of the particular case: these will be discussed later (p. 199, below). For practical convenience, however, as we shall see, French has been adopted as the working language of the Court—at least up to the present time. But the variety of languages available and the inevitable need for assistance from translators and interpreters have determined, to some extent, the procedures which the Court follows in handling its case-load. This will become apparent in the discussion of these procedures; but one general influence of the problem of language diversity has been to emphasise written procedure at the expense of orality and to diminish the impact of counsel when pleading in the less familiar of the seven languages.

The Registry

The duties of the Registrar are set out in the Protocol on the Statute of the Court and the Rules of Procedure. The Treaties merely require that "the Court shall appoint its Registrar and lay down the rules governing his service" (Art. 168 EEC). Like the Registrar of the International Court of Justice in The Hague or that of the European Court of Human Rights in Strasbourg, the Registrar in Luxembourg is dignified with an importance and status quite unlike that normally associated with the officer of the same name in the English court system or the French *greffier*. This difference is evident from his being seated at the bench of the Court, to one side of but at the same level as the judges; he wears the same formal robes, though of humbler fabric in place of silk, and will accompany the members of the Court upon ceremonial visits; his photograph and *curriculum vitae* are given equal prominence with those of the judges and advocates general in the official handbook of the Court; and like them he is mentioned in the founding Treaties.

According to the Protocol the Registrar must reside in

Luxembourg as the seat of the Court. The Rules of Procedure require that he be appointed by secret ballot by the judges and advocates general for a term of six years. He is eligible for re-appointment, and the first holder of the office, Mr. Albert Van Houtte, had the remarkable distinction of having served as Registrar for 29 years from 1953 when the Court began its existence as the Court of the Coal and Steel Community. Previously, Mr. Van Houtte, a doctor of laws and *avocat,* had held academic and governmental posts in his native Belgium; from 1945 to 1952 he was attached to the Food and Agriculture Organisation of the United Nations. Mr. Paul Heim, the present Registrar, who succeeded Mr. Van Houtte in February 1982, is British and a member of the English Bar; he had previously served as a senior official in the Council of Europe and the European Parliament.

Upon appointment (or re-appointment) the Registrar swears an oath to perform his duties impartially and conscientiously and to preserve the secrecy of the Court's deliberations although, in fact, he does not accompany the Court when it withdraws to deliberate. He performs all his duties under the authority of the President. These duties are two-fold.

In the first place, he is responsible, under the President of the Court, for the conduct, at all stages, of proceedings before the Court. The Registry serves all documents upon the parties, verifies that the documents comply with the Rules of Procedure, and gives the parties the notices and communications required under the Rules. It also distributes copies of the documents in all cases to each member of the Court. The emphasis on the written procedure, which will be considered in Part Three, results in a considerable volume of documents being distributed in the Court; in the corridors of the Court the visitor is most likely to be met by the sight of trolleys laden with piles of documents, being circulated by a small army of porters (or *huissiers*), sometimes with the help of miniature lift-cum-railways specially installed for the transport of documents and books within the building. The Registry is responsible also for publishing the Court's decisions.

Secondly, the Registrar is the head of the administration of the Court. When the Court is convened for an administrative meeting (as distinct from its judicial sittings) the Registrar is always present, although, unlike the judges and advocates general (all of whom attend) he has no vote. In general, he has a heavier responsibility than the Registrar of a national court whose administration and finances would be the ultimate responsibility of a Minister of Justice.

Reports of cases before the Court

The official series of reports of cases before the Courts is known (in English) as the European Court Reports, which are cited as "ECR" with the year of publication preceding in square brackets. As this series is published in all seven official languages (*i.e.* English, French, German, Italian, Dutch, Danish and Greek—but not Irish), the different versions are distinguished by the colour of their binding: the English series is bound in purple (like this book).

An alternative, but unofficial, series are the Common Market Law Reports (cited as "CMLR"). This series has the advantage not only of more speedy publication of cases before the Court, but it also includes reports of cases before national courts involving important points of Community law. By reporting foreign cases in English, the series provides a particularly valuable service.

Both the ECR and the CMLR include not only the judgment of the Court but also the opinion of the advocate general delivered in the case. In advance of publication of the printed reports in the ECR the Registry makes available photostat copies of both judgments and opinions as soon as they are delivered: a limited number of copies of these are made available free of charge at the door of the courtroom. Further copies may be obtained from the Internal Services Department of the Court, for

100 Luxembourg or Belgian Francs each or, provided the
subscriber already takes the ECR, by subscription.

The official series published by the Registry provides
the only authentic source for citation of judgments of the
Court. Authenticity, moreover, attaches only to the
judgment in the original procedural language of the case
(for the choice of this language, see below, p. 199), even
though the judgment may have been drafted in some
other language.

The Registry, through the Court's Information Office,
provides summaries of the more important decisions of
the Court to the national press in the Member States.
Thus, *The Times* of London occasionally publishes a
report of a case before the Court under the heading
"European Law Report": see *e.g. R.* v. *Bouchereau, The
Times*, October 31, 1977, at p. 10; also, Case 8/81 *Frau
Ursula Becker* v. *Finanzamt (Tax Office) Münster, The
Times*, January 25, 1982, at p. 6.

Library and documentation service

In addition to the Registry, of which the day-to-day
running is in the hands of the Assistant Registrar, there
are five other departments which make up the administration of the Court.

The first of these is "the Library and Documentation
Directorate." The library has a very extensive collection
of legal materials, especially those published in the ten
Member States. As well as a complete collection in the
field of Community law, it maintains comprehensive
collections of the laws of all the Member States. It is open
to any lawyer of a Member State. It is in the charge of the
Librarian, whose staff includes lawyers trained in each of
the principal legal systems (and languages) of the Ten.
The Librarian also organises a "Documentation Service":
his staff provides the judges and advocates general (and
their legal secretaries) with background papers on problems currently before the Court. These papers will set out
relevant Community law, in particular case law of the

Court, and may survey relevant provisions of the laws of the Member States.

Translation service

A vital branch of the Court's administration is the Translation Directorate. A team of some 80 legally qualified linguists have to cope with the heavy demand for translations which the multi-lingual character of the Court promotes. Pleadings may need to be translated into French as the working language as well as into whatever language is prescribed for the particular case; for publication the opinions of the advocates general and the Court's judgments have to be translated into all seven official languages. The two enlargements of the Community produced a need for the pre-1973 or pre-1981 decisions of the Court to be translated into English, Danish and Greek. All the Court's decisions between 1953 and 1972 are now available in English. Only the principal decisions prior to 1973 have been translated into Danish: they extend to six volumes as compared with the 20 volumes of the complete reports. A similar abridgement is in preparation in Greek of the principal decisions prior to 1981.

The Directorate is divided into seven language divisions, to correspond with the official languages, and a terminology branch.

Irish is a special case. Although it is accepted as a procedural language (below, p. 199), in practice, all cases emanating from Ireland have been conducted so far in English. There are no official versions in Irish of the Court's decisions. Indeed, the Translation Directorate have no translators for the Irish language, nor does the Interpretation Division (below) have interpreters competent in that language. If it should be necessary for a case to be conducted in Irish, linguists would need to be specially hired for the purpose. Hitherto, however, the Irish Government has adopted English when faced with the choice of the language of the case. If it should happen (as one day it may) that a reference is made for a preliminary ruling (see Chapter 9) from an Irish court or tribunal where the proceedings have been conducted in Irish, Irish would become the procedural language of the case, the judgment would be authentic only in that language, and presumably the Court would publish an official report in Irish of the opinion and the judgment. By way of analogy, there have been occasional publications of the Official Journal in Irish in order to provide official texts in Irish of certain Community acts or conventions.

Whether a court in Wales could rely upon the Welsh Courts Act in order to submit a preliminary reference in Welsh is a moot point: unlike Irish, Welsh is not accepted under the rules as a procedural language.

Interpretation service

Besides its team of translators, the Court has need of interpreters to provide simultaneous translations during the oral proceedings or at other meetings organised by the Court (such as judicial conferences). Before 1980 the Court did not have these scarce specialists in its exclusive employ but used to hire a number of free-lance interpreters who also served the European Parliament (which frequently met in Luxembourg where it has its administrative headquarters, although it now generally meets in Strasbourg). In recent years, the Court has recruited its own specialists in legal interpretation. This Interpretation Division, as it is termed, falls under the direct control of the Registrar. By 1982 it included nine interpreters but is being expanded so as to provide, eventually, interpretation from and into all the official languages (other than Greek, for the time being), that is 30 possible combinations. If Greek, Spanish and Portuguese are to be added, the possible combinations would amount to an horrendous total of 72.

Information Office

The Court maintains an information service which is also, in effect, a press office and public relations department. Like other Community institutions, the Court is inundated by requests from interested individuals and groups to visit the Court. National judges, professors and law students flock to Luxembourg to study its working. The Information Office is responsible for the organisation of such visits and for offering explanatory talks and conducted tours of the Court building.

This branch also issues press statements on new judgments. It publishes weekly summaries of hearings and a quarterly bulletin. The latter gives valuable information on recent cases before the Court (or before national courts if involving Community law) and is very widely distributed.

Administration and personnel

The staff of the Court numbered some 440 established posts in mid-1982, and because the Court has to be administered as a self-contained institution, it requires the services of a personnel department. This department, together with a Finance Department and a Department of "Internal Services," constitutes the Directorate of Administration. Internal Services is the "house-keeping" branch, responsible for the Court building, furnishings, equipment, security and such like.

Legal secretaries

Key figures in the work of the Court are the "legal secretaries"; two are attached to each judge and advocate general as personal assistants. They do not fall under the day-to-day control of the Registrar, although they are ultimately responsible to him as head of the administration of the Court. They work in the closest association with the judge or advocate general to whom they are attached. This personal relationship is reinforced by physical proximity: the legal secretary occupies the adjoining office in the judge's or advocate general's "chambers." Each judge and advocate general has a suite of offices, designated as his or her chambers, on the third floor of the Court building.

Legal secretary is the term in English which has come to be preferred since British members joined the Court. The previous term employed was either, in French, *Attaché* or the more imposing title *Référendaire*. *Conseiller-referendaire* is used in the French *Cour de Cassation* to describe a class of career judges who are attached to that Court to assist its senior members. In Germany, *Referendar* is used to denote a legal apprentice, and to avoid this confusion the word *Referent* has been adopted to designate the German legal secretaries. The closest analogy in the common law world is the law clerk of the American judicial system. In the United States, an outstanding law graduate may be invited upon graduation to serve for a year or two as personal assistant to a senior judge. The analogy breaks down in that at Luxembourg a legal secretary usually has had other legal experience after qualifying, commonly serves a longer term, and some have served in that rank for a considerable period of years. Nevertheless, "law clerk" is the term officially used for legal secretary in the Staff Regulations. Usually but not invariably the legal secretary is of the same nationality as the judge or advocate general to whom he (or she) is attached.

The exact function of the legal secretary will become clearer in Chapter 11 which deals with the procedure and practice of the Court. No account however of the Court's organisation would be complete without some reference to them.

Assistant rapporteurs

The Statute provides for the appointment of assistant rapporteurs to co-operate with the judge-rapporteur (whose function is described in Chap. 11): no such appointments have yet been made.

Chambers

To facilitate its work the Court has been divided into three Chambers, each consisting of three judges, one of whom is designated as President of that Chamber.

Power to set up Chambers was included in the Treaties (see, *e.g.* Art. 32(1) ECSC, Art. 165(2) EEC), and the Rules of the Court now provide that "The Court shall set up Chambers" in accordance with the Treaty provisions "and shall decide which judges shall be attached to them" (Art. 9, r. 1). The Rules further provide that "The Court shall lay down general principles governing the assignment of cases to Chambers."

On a point of nomenclature, the term "Chamber" is used in the texts to translate the French "Chambre" as indicating a division or section of the court. It does not, of course, carry the connotation of the English term "Chambers" as suggesting a hearing *in camera* or in the private room of the judge or judges.

The evolution of the use of Chambers is of some importance. Originally, a Chamber was used in lieu of the full Court only for the hearing of "staff cases," that is, cases where Community civil servants or officials are in dispute with the Community institution which employs them: here the Court sits in effect as an industrial tribunal of first and last resort. Staff cases are more fully considered in Chapter 8; they form a significant part of the business of the Court.

A modest extension of the use of Chambers took place by an amendment of the Rules in 1974 so as to provide that a reference for a preliminary ruling under Article 177 EEC (or Art. 41 ECSC, Art. 150 Euratom) could be assigned to a Chamber if it was "of an essentially technical nature" or concerned "matters for which there was already an established body of case-law." The first such assignment took place in 1976.

Following a substantial increase in the Court's workload, a more drastic amendment of the Rules was made in 1979. The new text of Article 95 of the Rules extends not only to references for preliminary rulings but also to direct actions other than those instituted by a Member State or a Community institution. Under the new provisions, the Court may assign to a Chamber any reference for a preliminary ruling or any direct action instituted by a natural or legal person, in so far (in either case) "as the difficulty or importance of the case or particular circumstances are not such as to require that the Court decide it in plenary session."

The decision whether to assign to a Chamber is taken by the Court at the end of the written procedure upon consideration of the preliminary report of the judge-rapporteur and after the advocate general has been heard (Art. 95(2)). A case may not, however, be assigned to a Chamber if trial by the full Court is requested by a Member State or a Community institution taking part in the proceeding whether as a party, or as intervenor in a direct action, or by submitting written observations on a reference for a preliminary ruling (Art. 95(3)). These detailed matters of procedure are more fully explained in Chapter 11, as is the function of a Chamber in undertaking the *instruction*, or preparatory inquiry, which may be an important phase of the procedure in some cases brought before the Court (below, p. 200).

The formulation of the new rule in Article 95 and the use made of it by the Court in practice has meant that from October 1979 cases are commonly heard by a Chamber rather than by the full Court. But cases brought by a Member State or by a Community institution must still be heard by the full Court; of these the only numerically significant group are actions brought by the Commission against a Member State under Article 169 EEC (below, p. 75). Nor may cases be assigned to a Chamber if trial by the full Court is requested by a State or institution taking part in the proceedings (see above).

The device of subdividing a court to enable it to handle a heavier case-load is a familiar one in the Member States. Thus the French *Conseil d'Etat* now has 10 *sous-sections* of its *Section du Contentieux*. Subdivision of a court may also be a means for ensuring specialisation, as with the Divisions of the English High Court, but there has not yet developed any such specialisation at Luxembourg.

The Court building

Pericles expressed the view that it was not walls that made a city great but the men within them. Physical environment however does have important influences, both practical and psychological, upon human activity. Some description therefore is appropriate here of the actual premises and location in which the Court operates.

In January 1973 the enlargement of the Community was the occasion of the addition to the Court of three new judges and an advocate general. On the same day as they swore their judicial oaths, the Luxembourg Government handed over to the President of the Court the new Courthouse (if we may so translate Palais de Justice). Previously the Court had enjoyed no permanent home. From 1953, as the Court of the Coal and Steel Community, it had occupied the Villa Vauban, a large mansion in a suburb of Luxembourg, now used as an art gallery; in 1959 it became the Court of Justice of the European Communities and moved to a more modern building in the city centre.

The new building is situated on the Kirchberg Plateau, a magnificent, elevated site on the further bank of one of the deep ravines which encircle the ancient fortified City of Luxembourg. The Plateau was mostly woodland and fields until acquired in 1961 by the Luxembourg Government to provide a special precinct for the various European institutions based in the Grand Duchy. As well as the Court, the Plateau contains the Parliament Building (the administrative headquarters of the European Parliament), a newly built "Hemi-cycle" where the Parliament occasionally sat before 1981 (see p. 10, above), the Council Building and the Commission Building (where some staff of the Council and the Commission work on detachment from Brussels), the Computer Centre for the Communities, and the European Investment Bank. The complex of buildings also includes the large European School to provide schooling in English and other languages for the children of the international community, and, inevitably, that commercial enterprise found at every international crossroads—a Holiday Inn.

The Courthouse is a remarkable building on many counts. Despite its five storeys it appears squat because of its large dimensions. Its exterior structure is predominantly of glass and rustproof steel, left unpainted and now acquiring a natural brown hue. The interior is functional but elegant with much use of granite, marble and plain carpeting. The library has extensive stack-space and staff offices but a relatively small reading-room.

Already the Courthouse has proved too small for the needs of the enlarged Community. The large Translation Directorate has had to move out into the Commission Building, and the third floor is no longer adequate to provide separate "chambers" for the increased number of judges and advocates general. To help relieve the congestion, the construction of an extensive annexe adjoining the Courthouse is being considered. The main feature of the present Courthouse, indeed its *raison d'être,* is the set of three courtrooms, a main courtroom for plenary sittings of the Court and two for use by the Chambers. Each courtroom has striking and distinctive colour schemes and they are decorated with modern tapestries or mural paintings; the public accommodation is spacious and consists of luxurious tip-up seats, each fitted with earphones for simultaneous translation.

Across the head of each courtroom is the raised bench for the judges and at each end of the bench a separate seat for the advocate general (on the left) and the Registrar (on the right).

The judges, advocates general and Registrar wear dignified robes of deep crimson; their French-style caps of the same colour have been discarded (alas) even for ceremonial occasions. Lawyers appearing before them wear the gowns of their own national profession: the wig made its appearance with British entry.

The judicial sittings are held on Tuesdays, Wednesdays and Thursdays. The overall impression upon most visitors is one of a dignified and orderly procedure. No time is wasted but there is no feeling of haste: the mills of Community justice grind smoothly. There is none of the drama, the cut and thrust and impromptu repartee of an English trial. The advocates deliver their set speeches: the rhetoric is subdued and often misunderstood, and humour intervenes rarely, and then lightly.

Chapter 3

JUDGES

Introduction

The reputation of a court depends upon the quality of its judges. Judicial quality is itself dependent upon the ability of an institution to attract outstanding lawyers into its service. Long-established institutions like the English High Court or the French *Conseil d'Etat* exert this attraction by the prestige accumulated over generations or even centuries. A new institution such as the Court of Justice lacks this power in its formative years: those called to serve it have been attracted rather by a sense of mission or vocation. But within the 30 years of its existence the Court has built up, by bold and imaginative judgments, its own tradition that should ensure the highest level of recruits to its ranks.

In this chapter, we will examine the Treaty provisions governing the appointment of members of the Court and their conditions of service. Much of what is said will apply both to the judges and the advocates general, although the distinctive function of the latter warrants their being made the subject of a separate chapter. Some account will be given of the backgrounds from which the past and present judges of the Court have been drawn. In order to show the end-product of their labours, the judgments of the Court will be considered, especially from the point of view of their form and style: a recent judgment is appended as a specimen. Judgments are further considered in later parts, but it is thought desirable to provide this early introduction to their form and to the way in which they should be read.

Appointment

Number

The Court now consists of 11 judges, assisted by five advocates general. This makes it possible for the Court to sit in two Chambers of five (without the President) or in three Chambers of three: the three-fold division is that presently adopted, as we have seen (above, p. 25).

The number of judges is mainly a reflection of the number of the Member States. The principle, however, of collegiality, whereby the Court, when sitting *in pleno*, must reach a single judgment, if necessary by a majority, means that an uneven number of judges is required. Thus, in the original Community of the Six the Court was composed of seven judges; at one time, two of these were Dutch, and at the moment of the Six becoming the Nine, two were Italian. For the same reason, the Accession Treaty of 1972, in anticipation of Norway's entry, raised the required number of judges to 11 and so had to be amended later to nine when the Norwegian people decided, by referendum, against entry. The accession of Greece in 1981 has now led to the appointment, in addition to the Greek judge, of an eleventh judge. He will serve a single term and be drawn in rotation from each of the four large Member States, France, Germany, Italy and the United Kingdom.

In contrast with membership of the Commission, it is nowhere stipulated that each Member State shall provide a judge for the Court. Inevitably, in practice, this happens. For every appointment of a judge (or advocate general) requires the common accord of the Governments of the Member States (Art. 167 EEC): no State is likely to forego its representation on the Court, nor has this happened. Again, whereas the Treaties expressly restrict membership of the Commission to citizens of the Member States, there is no such restriction in regard to the Court. But political considerations make it almost inconceivable that someone who is not a national of a Member State would be appointed. The general acceptability of each State's candidate is a matter of prior informal consultations between the 10 Governments.

Qualifications

The Treaties require that judges and advocates general "shall be chosen from persons whose independence is beyond doubt and who possess the qualifications required for appointment to the highest judicial offices in their respective countries or who are jurisconsults of recognised competence." This formulation follows closely that for appointment to the International Court of Justice at The Hague which also provided the model for judicial appointment to the European Court of Human Rights.

It is significant that the independence of candidates is made a first and paramount consideration. This moral requirement counters any notion that a judge is representing his Member State or the Government which has nominated him. Nevertheless, the criticism has been made that political considerations have entered into the selection of judges from some Member States where party affiliation is an important consideration in domestic judicial appointments. Once so appointed, a judge who failed "to please" his Government might then be in danger of not being re-appointed; but the principle of collegiality and the secrecy of the Court's deliberations would appear adequate safeguards against this risk.

The professional qualifications for appointment are expressed in the alternative. In some countries of the common law tradition, such as England or Ireland, the alternative is a real one, inasmuch as legal scholarship as such is not in itself a qualification for appointment to the highest judicial office. In most civil law countries, on the other hand, the second alternative is subsumed in the first. Thus, in all the original six Member States the holder of a University chair of law may be translated to the bench, sometimes at the highest levels.

So far as the United Kingdom is concerned, only the

first alternative has been used, up to the present, although there are not lacking precedents for academic appointments by the British Government to international courts and tribunals. The first two British appointments to the Court in 1972 involved, respectively, a judge of the Scottish Court of Session and a leading English barrister who held the post of Junior Counsel to the Treasury, the third most senior government lawyer. The eligibility of a Treasury Junior to be appointed to the English High Court was properly regarded as fulfilling the first alternative. The third British appointment, in 1981, was that of an English High Court judge, at the time of his translation President of the Employment Appeal Tribunal.

Under the ECSC Treaty a prior legal qualification was not necessary: Article 32 ECSC, as originally drafted, merely stipulated that candidates should be "persons of recognised independence and competence." Two of the original judges of the Coal and Steel Court were not possessed of formal professional qualifications in law. The Dutchman Joseph Serrarens was a parliamentarian and a leading figure in the international labour movement, and the Frenchman Jacques Rueff was an expert in finance and banking who had distinguished himself in administrative and ministerial posts in France. The former was replaced in 1958 when the Court became the Court of the three Communities but the latter continued as a judge until 1962 when he was succeeded by Robert Lecourt.

Oath

On taking up their appointment, the judges take an oath in the following terms: "I swear that I will perform my duties impartially and conscientiously; I swear that I will preserve the secrecy of the deliberations of the Court."

Term of appointment

Appointment is for a term of six years, but a judge (or advocate general) is eligible for re-appointment for a further term or terms. Appointments are "staggered" in such a way that five or six of the 11 judges (and two or three of the five advocates general) come up for renewal at triennial intervals. This guarantees a measure of continuity of membership even if new appointments were always made. In practice, most of the members of the Court have had their terms of office renewed at least once, and some twice or thrice. There is no prescribed age for retirement. Indeed, at least one judge was a septuagenarian when appointed.

Nevertheless, despite the practice of renewal, the term of six years can be objected to as too short and in conflict with that security of tenure which is the hallmark of judicial independence in all the legal systems of the Member States. Such relatively short terms of appointments are commonly adopted for international courts or tribunals (for example, nine years in the case of a judge of the International Court of Justice), but they seem undesirable in what is held out to be, and is, a distinct legal order of a novel kind, neither international nor national but more akin to an embryonic federation. Even with a quasi-federal judiciary the impression should not be created that those appointed may be looking over their shoulders every six years towards their political masters, the Governments of the Member States.

Dismissal

As we have seen, the opportunity to discard a judge occurs every six years. During the term of appointment dismissal can only take place by the unanimous decision of the other judges and advocates general that their colleague no longer fulfils the requisite conditions or no longer meets the obligations arising from his office. This procedure of trial by one's peers (copied from the International Court of Justice) provides a very effective safeguard against dismissal. The procedure has never yet been invoked. A judge may, however, submit his resignation at any time, and this has happened on several occasions. Thus, Judge O'Dalaigh resigned in 1975 in order to become the President of the Republic of Ireland.

President of the Court and Presidents of Chambers

The judges (but not the advocates general) choose one of their number to serve as President of the Court for a term of three years. This appointment is renewable. Thus, President Robert Lecourt, who retired in October 1976, served three terms as President (1967–1976); his immediate predecessor was Charles Hammes of Luxembourg. The President from 1958 to 1964 was a Dutchman, Professor A.M. Donner, who remained a judge of the Court until his retirement in 1979. The German judge, Hans Kutscher, succeeded Robert Lecourt as President in October 1976, and upon his resignation in October 1980 was in turn succeeded as President by the Belgian judge, J. Mertens de Wilmars.

The President's functions, in the words of the Rules of the Court, are to direct the judicial business and the administration of the Court and to preside at hearings and deliberations.

The choice of President is made by secret ballot, being determined by a simple majority. The same process is used to elect annually a President for each of the three Chambers of the Court, the composition of which is also determined annually. In practice the composition of each Chamber remains constant, but its presidency rotates annually.

After the President, the Presidents of the Chambers and the First Advocate General, the members of the Court (both judges and advocates general) rank equally in precedence according to their seniority in office. Where there is equal seniority in office, by reason of appointments having been made on the same date, precedence is determined by age. When the Court sits *in pleno* the President will be flanked to right and left by his fellow judges seated in order of seniority, a right-hand seat being superior to the equivalent position on the left.

Immunities, privileges and salary

The judges (and advocates general) enjoy, as might be expected, immunity from suit or legal process. This immunity is retained after they vacate office in respect of acts performed by them in their official capacity. This is provided by the respective Protocols on the Statute of the Court of Justice annexed to the three founding Treaties.

Under the Protocol on the privileges and immunities of the Communities annexed to the Merger Treaty, the judges have the benefit of certain privileges relating to taxation, customs duties and currency or exchange regulations. In particular, they are exempt from national taxes on their Community salaries. Although such salaries are subject to a Community income tax, the level of the latter is lower (in comparison with British income tax, very much lower) than national tax levels. Accordingly, the privileges enjoyed by the judges represent a very considerable fringe benefit over and above the rates of salaries which they receive. In addition, they are supplied with a car and chauffeur.

Judicial salaries (and those of the advocates general, which are identical) are fixed according to scales determined by the Council. A judge's salary is the same as that of a member of the Commission and is very substantial. It would however be very misleading to compare it with the salary of an English High Court judge, for, with the exception of the Luxembourg judge, the members of the Court of Justice naturally have to maintain two homes; they also find themselves called upon to fulfil a semi-diplomatic function and to foster links with judges and lawyers in their own countries.

Incompatibilities

It is incompatible with his appointment for a judge to hold any political or "administrative" (that is, governmental) office (Art. 4 of the Statute of the Court). Nor may he be engaged in any occupation, whether gainful or not, unless exemption is exceptionally granted by the Council (*ibid.*). In practice, several members of the Court have been permitted to undertake teaching engagements in University faculties and institutes.

In addition, when taking up their duties, the judges undertake that they will behave with integrity and discretion as regards the acceptance, after they have ceased to hold office, of certain appointments or benefits. Not to canvas more extravagant possibilities, this would, it was thought, prevent a former judge from appearing as counsel at the bar of the Court: this has, however, occurred.

Composition of the Court

When the Court sits as a full court, a quorum of seven judges is required. A relatively low quorum is felt desirable to allow for illness or other unavoidable absences. But normally all eleven judges attend when the Court sits *in pleno*. For instance, the full court of (then) all nine members sat in the relatively trivial Case 22/76 *Import Gadgets,* of which the judgment is appended to this chapter. Today, however, since the enlargement of the jurisdiction of the Chambers, such a case would be heard by a Chamber, for which the quorum is three.

As the President has no casting vote, an uneven number must sit for decisions to be valid. If a judge is prevented from attending the hearing (*e.g.* through illness), the most junior judge drops out to maintain an uneven number.

The Statute of the Court provides specifically that a party may not apply for a change in the composition of the Court (or of a Chamber) on the grounds of either the nationality of a judge or the absence from the Court (or Chamber) of a judge of the nationality of that party. This is in contrast with the Statute of the International Court of Justice which allows an ad hoc judge in certain circumstances; similar provision exists for the European Court of Human Rights at Strasbourg.

Form of Judgment

The Court follows the general continental practice in delivering judgment as a collegiate body. In contrast to the International Court of Justice, and the European Court of Human Rights, no separate or dissenting judgments are permitted. The strict secrecy which surrounds the Court's deliberations means that only the judges themselves know whether their decision was reached unanimously or by a majority. The natural desire to achieve unanimity will lead to compromises which are then reflected in the somewhat equivocal language of the judgments, criticised by one English practitioner as "simply oracular and almost apocryphal" (L. Melville in (1978) 75 L.S.Gaz. 567).

Help in understanding a judgment can be derived from the opinion of the advocate general in the case. Usually, it is better to start by reading this opinion and then to turn to the judgment. Often, the Court follows the path urged upon it by the advocate general, but as mentioned in the next chapter (p. 60, below) there have been notable instances where the Court has gone its own way.

An example of a judgment (in the *Import Gadgets* case) is included below in the appendix to this chapter. It will be seen that the form of the judgment is very different from that of an English or Scottish judgment. In the formative years of the Court's history, after essaying other styles, it decided to adopt the practice of the higher French courts in framing the whole judgment as, grammatically, a single Ciceronian sentence, with the facts of the case, the steps in the procedure and the legal reasons all recited in a long series of subordinate clauses leading eventually to the main sentence: "the Court hereby rules." Thus, in the *Import Gadgets* case, the preliminary recitals extend over some nine pages, culminating in 15 numbered paragraphs of reasoning, before we arrive at the very short ruling: "Laughing devices suitable for use principally in dolls that are representations of human beings come within heading 97.02 B of the Common Customs Tariff."

As is apparent, the English version of the judgment has departed from the French model by the conversion of the subordinate clauses from ablative absolutes into separate sentences. Nevertheless, as judgments are normally drafted first in French, even the English version retains the succinct, even sybilline, quality of the original; notionally, it remains if not a single sentence, at least a single coherent whole. The influence which this style of drafting judgments has upon the law which they contain is not to be underestimated, even though it be intangible.

In 1979 the Court decided, even for its judgments in French, to move away from the original model and no longer to confine its reasoning within the grammatical strait-jacket of a single sentence. The increased linguistic diversity of the Court has also led, on rare occasions (but these may now increase) to a judgment being drafted first in English and then translated into French, especially where English has been the language of the case.

If we return to the judgment in *Import Gadgets*, it starts "In Case 22/76" (each case being referred to by the docket number and the year) and after mentioning the parties, the subject-matter of the case, and the composition of the Court, the main body of the judgment is in two parts, facts and law, ending with the ruling of the Court.

The first part is entitled "Facts" in *Import Gadgets* (but, since 1977, the title "Facts and Issues" has been adopted for this part). Originally, in the French text (before the relaxation introduced in 1979) this part was introduced by the conjunction "attendu que" which might be rendered in English "whereas," although the conjunction was omitted in the English text. This part summarises, first, the facts of the case and the procedure before the Court, secondly the submissions made to the Court. As the case was a reference from a national court for a preliminary ruling, observations in writing were invited from the parties, the Member States and the Commission. In the present case the defendant in the main action (*i.e.* the action before the national court) and the Commission put in observations which are summarised in this part. This part of the judgment is based on the "report for the hearing" which is described in Chapter 11. Then the oral hearing and the delivery of the advocate-general's opinion (reproduced in the appendix to Chapter 4) are mentioned.

The second part of the judgment contains the law and is so entitled in *Import Gadgets* (below, p. 50); but since 1978 the title "Decision" is preferred. After an introduction explaining how the question or questions for decision have arisen, this part sets out the *motifs* or reasons for the Court's ruling, followed by the ruling itself. This part is set out in a series of propositions, again linked in the French version by the conjunction "Attendu que," omitted in the English text. The paragraphs are numbered for ease of reference. The ruling, introduced by the phrase "On those grounds" (*pour ces motifs*), is usually quite short, as in the example chosen. The original copy of the judgment bears the signatures of all the participating judges and is authenticated by the President and the Registrar.

Judicial Style

The collegiate nature of the Court's judgments lends them a certain flatness such as we associate with the language of a governmental report. The tone is measured; there is neither excitement nor humour. One must not expect the often elegant, sometimes idiosyncratic, prose of an English judgment, upon which the individual judge will have imprinted his own personality and particular style. At Luxembourg the individual voices are muted; they blend in unison; there is a single refrain. The only solo will have been that of the advocate general.

On the other hand, collegiality has in no way inhibited the development of Community law through judicial decisions. The Court's judgments have become an important, if secondary source of that law, as this book will demonstrate. Here mention may be made of one particular technique which law-making in committee, Luxembourg-style, appears to encourage.

Study of the case-law of the Court reveals certain *leitmotifs* that recur through whole sequences of its decisions. Phrases or passages will be repeated in case after case, sometimes in identical terms, sometimes with subtle variations. By constant rehearsal the Court, like a Welsh choir, finds the exact note it wants to sound. Examples abound of this technique whereby phrase-building becomes law-making: elsewhere in these pages we refer to the Court's classic definition of the nature of the Community legal order (p. 176 below, Case 6/64 *Costa* v. *ENEL* [1964] ECR 585 at 593, which refined the definition in Case 26/62 *Van Gend en Loos* [1963] ECR 1 at 12); to the *Zuckerfabrik Schöppenstedt* formula as a yardstick for certain actions for damages under Article 215(2) EEC (p. 126, below, Case 5/71 [1971] ECR 975 at 984); and to the *Plaumann* text for locus standi of "non-privileged" applicants under Article 173 EEC (p. 98, below, Case 25/62 [1963] ECR 95 at 107). The same technique has defined, and is still refining, the key concept of the direct effect of Community law, in a sequence of cases extending from Case 26/62 *Van Gend en Loos* to Case 148/78 *Ratti* [1979] ECR 1629 and Case 8/81 *Becker* v. *Finanzamt Münster* [1982] ECR 53.

Biographical Background of the Judges

During the 30 years of its existence the Court has had almost 40 members, if we include for this purpose both judges and advocates general. Some account is given in the next chapter of the background of the past and present advocates general. Here it is proposed to give brief biographical details of the men (31 in all) who have served, or are serving, as judges of the Court: a woman has still to be appointed to this office, although (as we shall see in the next chapter) the French, with true republican 'égalité' chose a woman for appointment as advocate general in 1981. Our attention will be directed mainly to the present membership, but some knowledge of the previous careers of the past as well as present judges will be helpful to a proper understanding of the Court's philosophy and approach to its daily tasks.

Of the past judges of the Court (20 in number), mention has already been made of Serrarens and Rueff as exemplifying appointees to the Coal and Steel Court without formal legal qualifications. The other 18 had a variety of legal backgrounds. Only six, Hammes, Grévisse, Kutscher, Riese, Rossi and Touffait had extensive judicial experience in their own countries; Pilotti, van Kleffens and Strauss also began their careers as judges, but Pilotti turned to international law (he was Assistant Secretary General of the League of Nations from 1932 until 1937), van Kleffens moved into legal practice and then held important posts in the Dutch Ministry of Economics, and Strauss served in high administrative and governmental posts in post-war Germany as well as being politically active in the Christian Democratic Party.

Several judges had held ministerial posts in their own countries. Delvaux was Belgian Minister of Agriculture in 1945–6. Lecourt had been French Minister of Justice for several periods between 1948 and 1958 and was Minister for Overseas Departments shortly before his appointment to the Court in 1962. Strauss was Secretary of State in the Federal Ministry of Justice from 1949 up to his appointment to the Court in 1963. Rueff had been French Minister of Finance in Poincaré's Government as long ago as 1926. Catalano held senior governmental posts in Italy. O'Dalaigh was the Irish Attorney-General before being appointed to the Supreme Court: he resigned from the Court in Luxembourg in order to become President of the Irish Republic. At some stages of their earlier careers, Catalano, Delvaux, Lecourt and van Kleffens all practised law or acted as legal counsel to commercial or public

institutions. Also significant as a group are those who had
an academic career: Monaco and Trabucchi occupied
Chairs of Law in the Universities of Rome and Padua,
Sørensen a Chair of Law in the University of Aarhus, and
Donner a Chair of Constitutional and Administrative Law
in the Free University of Amsterdam; Riese taught in the
University of Lausanne from 1932 to 1951 before return-
ing to Germany as judge of the Federal Supreme Court;
and Catalano and Hammes combined professorial
appointments with their other functions.

Several past judges had been active in politics. As
already mentioned, Strauss was a prominent Christian
Democrat and ran (unsuccessfully) for election to the
Bundestag. Lecourt was Deputé for Paris 1945–1958 and
was a leading member of the MRP. Delvaux and
Serrarens were both elected to their respective parlia-
ments. O'Dalaigh was a prominent lawyer in the Irish
Fianna Fail party, before accepting judicial office.

This varied background, ranging far beyond the narrowly legal, is well designed to serve the needs of the
Court, whose jurisdiction, as we shall see, touches
economic, social, fiscal, administrative and even political
issues lying beneath the surface of Community law. The
American commentator, Werner Feld, has perceptively
remarked:

> "The broad knowledge possessed by some of the
> justices in the field of economics, finance, and
> administration may be a significant factor in arriving
> at decisions which transcend narrow judicial consid-
> erations and which reflect an application of the
> Treaties with a keen eye on the purpose of the
> Communities and with an appreciation for the future.
> The assumption is justified that the diversity of
> interests, experiences, and values represented in the
> deliberating sessions of the Court may have stimu-
> lated a fertile interchange of concepts and ideas and
> thus broadened the views of the participants."

When we turn to the present judges, a similar diversity is evident. *Chloros* came to the Court directly from an academic career, having received his early legal education at Athens and Oxford before being elevated to the Chair of Comparative Law at King's College in the University of London. *Koopmans* also had pursued an academic career as Professor and Dean in the University of Leyden before becoming in 1978 a Judge of the Netherlands Supreme Court. *Bosco* combined a long career in Italian Universities with political service in various ministerial appointments and as head of the Italian delegation to the General Assembly of the United Nations. *Everling* held various governmental posts in the Federal Ministry of Economics in Bonn as well as acting as Honorary Professor at Münster University where he taught and wrote extensively on Community law. *Bahlmann,* the other German judge (appointed in 1982), held important posts in the Federal Ministry of Justice after serving as a judge in Cologne. The French judge is *Galmot* (also appointed in 1982). He had been adviser to his Government on legal aspects of mining, chemical and oil development and was a *Conseiller* in the *Conseil d'Etat* at the time of his appointment. This, France's supreme administrative court, has supplied several French members of the Court, whether as judges or advocates general. Galmot's French colleague at Luxembourg, Advocate General Simone Rozès, was previously President of the Paris *Tribunal de grande instance*; thus, between them, they appear in French eyes to continue to provide a balanced representation from the "administrative" and "judicial" hierarchies of the French courts, as did the two outgoing French judges, Grévisse (*Conseiller d'Etat*) and Touffait (*Procureur Général près la Cour de Cassation*). *Pescatore,* who shares with President Mertens de Wilmars the distinction of being one of the two longest serving members of the Court, held high office in the Luxembourg Ministry of Foreign Affairs and helped to found the Institute of European Legal Studies at the University of Liège. *Due*, who is currently the Benjamin of the Court, held various posts in the Danish Ministry of Justice; he also directed courses in Community law for practitioners and civil servants.

The President of the Court, J. Mertens de Wilmars, a judge of the Court since 1967 and President since 1979, had practised in Antwerp as an advocate since 1935, specialising in administrative law and later in European law, and had appeared as an advocate before the Court of Justice. He had also been active in political life in Belgium, having been a member of the Chamber of Representatives from 1952 to 1962, and a member of Parliamentary committees on foreign affairs, justice and reform of the constitution.

The British judge, Lord Mackenzie Stuart, became the youngest member of the Court when appointed in 1973 at the age of 48. After war service he graduated in law from Cambridge and Edinburgh and practised as an Advocate at the Scots Bar in a wide variety of fields, becoming Queen's Counsel in 1963. His first judicial (part-time) appointment was as Sheriff Principal of Aberdeen, Kincardine and Banff in 1971, and in the following year he was elevated to the Court of Session.

Andreas O'Keeffe, the Irish judge, qualified as a Barrister in Dublin in 1935 and became Senior Counsel in 1951. Subsequently he was Attorney General of Ireland. Judge of the Supreme Court, and President of the High Court; he represented the Government of Ireland before the European Commission and Court of Human Rights in Strasbourg and before the International Court of Justice at The Hague.

Postscript

We note with great sadness that Aleck Chloros, the Greek judge at the Court and our former colleague in England, died whilst these pages were in the press.

APPENDIX

Translation   Case 22/76

JUDGMENT OF THE COURT

In case 22/76

REFERENCE to the Court under Article 177 of the EEC
Treaty by the Tribunale di Pavia for a preliminary ruling
in the action pending before that court between

Import Gadgets, S.à.r.l., Paris

and

L.A.M.P., S.p.A., Pavia

on the interpretation of headings 97.02 and 97.03 of the
Common Customs Tariff,

The Court

composed of: R. Lecourt, President, H.Kutscher and A.
O'Keeffe, Presidents of Chambers, A.M. Donner, J.
Mertens de Wilmars, P. Pescatore, M. Sørensen, Lord
Mackenzie Stuart and F. Capotorti, Judges. Advocate
General: J.-P. Warner. Registrar: A. Van Houtte, gives
the following

Judgment

Facts
   The order making the reference and the written
observations submitted under Article 20 of the Protocol

on the Statute of the Court of Justice of the EEC may be summarized as follows:

I *Facts and procedure.* In February 1970 and February 1971 respectively, Import Gadgets, whose registered office is in Paris, bought from L.A.M.P., whose registered office is in Pavia, 2,000 and 1,600 "laughing devices" for use in the manufacture of talking dolls.

The first consignment, which was accompanied by a certificate of Italian origin issued by the Pavia Chamber of Commerce and declaring that they came under tariff subheading 97.02 B (parts and accessories of dolls), was, on arrival in Paris, declared under the same subheading.

The second consignment, which left Italy under the same conditions as the first, was, however, on arrival in Paris declared under subheading 97.03 B (other toys; working models of a kind used for recreational purposes).

On the latter occasion, the French Customs found that the devices in question bore the inscription, partly deleted, "made in Japan," refused them Community treatment, ordered them to be confiscated and imposed a fine of 10,000 FF. Subsequently, the Customs declared that the first consignment also was of Japanese origin and, holding that the appropriate tariff heading was heading 97.03 B and not 97.02, imposed a further fine of 5,000 FF on Import Gadgets.

Import Gadgets brought an action for dissolution of the contract for sale of 1,600 devices before the Tribunale di Pavia, and for damages.

That court took the view that, before the case could be decided, it was necessary to obtain a preliminary ruling on the interpretation of customs headings 97.02 and 97.03 since at the material time the French Republic had taken protective measures within the meaning of Article 115 of the EEC Treaty only in respect of the second heading. It therefore stayed the proceedings and, by order of January 22, 1976, referred to the Court of Justice under Article 177 of the EEC Treaty the question: "Do laughing devices constitute mechanisms capable of being used by themselves as toys (97.03) or, on the other hand, do they merely constitute parts of dolls (97.02 B)?"

The order of the Tribunale di Pavia was entered at the Court Registry on March 5, 1976.

Observations were submitted by the defendant in the main action and by the Commission of the European Communities in accordance with Article 20 of the Protocol on the Statute of the Court of Justice of the EEC.

On hearing the report of the Judge-Rapporteur and the views of the Advocate General, the Court decided to open the oral procedure without any preparatory inquiry.

II *Summary of the observations.* The *defendant in the main action* points out that it manufactures only dolls' parts and accessories which cannot be used for any purpose other than the construction of dolls. As these component parts cannot be submitted as or in the form of separate toys, they must be classified under tariff subheading 97.02 B.

The first point made by the *Commission* with regard to the facts is that the dispute with the French Customs was, in the case of the second consignment imported, concerned solely with the origin of the imported products but, in the case of the first consignment imported, also with the tariff classification which was unsupported by any statement of reason or assessment.

Note No. 4 of Chapter 97 of the Common Customs Tariff (1972 numbering) concerning subheading 97.02 B of heading 97.02 (dolls) which reads " . . . parts and accessories which are suitable for use solely or principally with articles falling within any heading of this Chapter are to be classified with those articles," lays emphasis on the "normal" or "natural" use of the parts and accessories, which must not necessarily be the exclusive but may be merely the principal use. The actual use to which the importer or trader puts the product is not a decisive factor.

Under the description "Other toys, working models of a

kind used for recreational purposes," heading 97.03 embraces a large number of different toys because it covers items not included under the two headings which precede it: 97.01 (dolls' prams and dolls' push-chairs) and 97.02 (dolls).

Though submitted as parts or accessories of toys, the devices cannot work on their own and do not constitute toys within the meaning of heading 97.03 but must be classified under subheading 97.02 B. If submitted as finished products, namely as incorporated in a toy, the appropriate heading would be that applicable to the toy: 97.02 A if the toy is a laughing doll, 97.03 B if the toy is a laughing teddy bear and 97.05 if the toy is a "novelty" such as a jack-in-the-box used for practical jokes or amusement (which would mean that the classification problem in the present case is largely one of the relation between headings 97.02 and 97.05).

The reply must therefore be that, when submitted as parts and accessories recognisable as being exclusively or mainly for use for dolls under tariff heading 97.02, the products in dispute are classified under subheading 97.02 B of the Common Customs Tariff.

Although the court making the reference has not in so many words submitted questions involving the intra-Community system of trade in force at the material time, the Commission points out that the liberalisation of imports into the Community from third countries in respect of products coming under heading 97.02 came into force on January 1, 1969 and that no derogation has been allowed from the principle of free circulation.

If a Member State to which products in free circulation are in transit were to demand a certificate of origin this would breach the principle prohibiting measures having an effect equivalent to quantitative restrictions.

Only products coming under tariff heading 97.03 have not been liberalised for importation from third world countries. Under the commercial agreement of May 14, 1963, which continues in force, France limits the importation of toys from Japan; it is therefore possible to have recourse to protective measures under Article 115 of the EEC Treaty only for toys of Japanese origin coming under heading 97.03. But France received authorisation only for the period from July 17 to December 31, 1970 (Decision of July 17, 1970, Journal Officiel No. L 171, p. 23) and for the period from September 30, 1971—March 31, 1972 (Decision of September 30, 1971, Journal Officiel No. L 232, p. 40), that is to say, outside the period when the disputed imports occurred. Moreover, contrary to the provisions of Articles 30 *et seq.* of the EEC Treaty, France subjected the imports of the products in question, admitted to free circulation in Italy, to the compulsory advance licence system.

The foregoing considerations should be sufficient to clarify, for the court making the reference, the question whether " . . . there were measures in force in France restricting free circulation."

The plaintiff in the main action, represented by Mr. Camerini, of the Milan Bar, and the Commission of the European Communities, represented by its Legal Adviser, Mr. Abate, acting as Agent, submitted oral observations at the hearing on June 29, 1976.
The Advocate General delivered his opinion on July 14, 1976.

Law

1 By order of January 22, 1976, which reached the Court on March 5, 1976, the Tribunale di Pavia referred under Article 177 of the EEC Treaty for a preliminary ruling on the interpretation of headings 97.02 and 97.03 of the Common Customs Tariff.

2 This question was raised in connection with a dispute concerning the importation into France by the plaintiff in the main action of "laughing devices" which it had purchased in Italy from the defendant in the main action for use in the manufacture of talking dolls.

3 2,000 of these devices, dispatched in February 1970,

accompanied by a certificate of Italian origin declaring that they came under tariff subheading 97.02 B (parts and accessories of dolls), were, on arrival in Paris, declared under the same subheading.

4 1,600 of these devices, dispatched in February 1971 under the same conditions as the previous ones, were on arrival in Paris declared under subheading 97.03 B (other toys; working models of a kind used for recreational purposes).

5 The French Customs found that the devices in question bore the inscription, partly deleted, "made in Japan," refused them Community treatment, ordered them to be confiscated and imposed a fine on the plaintiff in the main action.

6 In consequence, Import Gadgets, the plaintiff in the main action, brought an action for dissolution of the contract of sale before the Tribunale di Pavia and for damages.

7 The question is asked whether the laughing devices constitute mechanisms capable of being used by themselves as toys (97.03) or, on the other hand, whether they merely constitute parts of dolls (97.02 B).

8 Note 3 to Chapter 97 of the Common Customs Tariff (1972 numbering) reads: "In heading 97.02 the term 'dolls' is to be taken to apply to such articles as are representations of human beings."

9 Note 4 provides that "parts and accessories which are suitable for use solely or principally with articles falling within any heading of this Chapter are to be classified with those articles."

10 The Explanatory Notes to the Brussels Nomenclature which, in the absence of specific provisions of Community law, are an authoritative and valid aid to the interpretation of the Common Customs Tariff headings, contain the following clarification of heading 97.02:

"The term 'dolls' is to be taken to apply *only* to such articles as are representations of human beings (including those of a caricature type) . . . *"Parts and accessories* of dolls falling within this heading include: heads, bodies, limbs; wigs; voice and other mechanisms; dolls' clothing, shoes and hats; dolls' eyes whether or not mounted on moving mechanisms, but unmounted dolls' eyes of glass are *excluded* (*heading 70.19*)."

11 On the other hand, the long list of examples of toys falling within heading 97.03 given by the Notes does not include anything resembling laughing devices, nor are the latter included in the list of examples of novelty jokes falling within heading 97.05.

12 This justifies the conclusion that "voice and other mechanisms" are suitable for use, if not solely, at least principally, in dolls which are representations of human beings, notwithstanding that they may be suitable also for other uses.

13 In consequence, the reply to the question submitted by the Tribunale di Pavia must be that laughing devices suitable principally for use in dolls that are representations of human beings come within heading 97.02 B of the Common Customs Tariff.

Costs
14 The costs incurred by the Commission of the European Communities, which has submitted observations to the Court, are not recoverable.

15 As these proceedings are, in so far as the parties to the main action are concerned, a step in the action pending before the Tribunale di Pavia, costs are a matter for that court.

On those grounds,

The Court
in answer to the question referred to it by the Tribunale di Pavia by order of January 22, 1976 hereby rules:

> Laughing devices suitable for use principally in dolls that are representations of human beings come within heading 97.02 B of the Common Customs Tariff.

Lecourt	Kutscher	O'Keeffe
Donner		Mertens de Wilmars
Pescatore		Sørensen
Mackenzie Stuart		Capotorti

Delivered in open court in Luxembourg on September 22, 1976.

A. Van Houtte   R. Lecourt
Registrar   President

Chapter 4

ADVOCATES GENERAL

While the functions of a judge are universally understood, the role of the advocate general in the Court is less easily grasped, especially in countries where the legal system has no precise equivalent. His title, too, is something of a misnomer, since he is really no more an advocate than he is a general. On the contrary, he is a member of the Court. But that term is itself ambiguous, being sometimes restricted to the judges alone, as in the first paragraph of Article 166 EEC, which provides (as amended) that "The Court of Justice shall be assisted by five Advocates General." This ambiguity may reflect a certain ambivalence, in the minds of the authors of the Treaties, about the role of the advocate general: although a member of the Court, he acts as its independent adviser. Unlike however his counterpart in the French *Conseil d'Etat*, the *commissaire du gouvernement,* he is not permitted to attend the judges' deliberations (see p. 205, below), even in a consultative capacity. On the other hand, the advocates general do join the judges and vote in parity with them on matters of administration of the Court, *e.g.* to appoint a new Registrar (Art. 168 EEC).

In 1982 the Court assumed the practice (despite the spelling adopted in the Treaties) of omitting the hyphen in written references to the advocate general, thus complying with the English usage commended by the great Fowler, although a hyphen should still be used in the possessive case.

The advocates general serve in turn for one year as "First Advocate General." As each case arrives at the Court, it is assigned to one of the advocates general. While the President of the Court designates the "judge-rapporteur" (below, p. 200), it is the First Advocate General who allocates the cases among the corps of advocates general (including himself). Judge-rapporteur and advocate general are designated on similar principles, the aim being to achieve a balanced work-load but not to produce any particular specialisation by way of subject-matter. There is however one difference in the designation of the advocate general: the unwritten rule that the judge-rapporteur should not be a judge from a Member State concerned in the case does not apply to the advocate general, no doubt because the latter performs his function in public so that there can be no suspicion of his opinion being influenced by political considerations.

It is the main task of the advocate general, again according to Article 166, "acting with complete impartiality and independence, to make, in open court, reasoned submissions on cases brought before the Court of Justice, in order to assist the Court in the performance of the task assigned to it in Article 164." This he does by delivering what is termed an "opinion," (in French, "conclusions"), after the case has been heard and normally at a later hearing, in which he gives the judges his view of the case and seeks to help them to reach their judgment. Usually in his opinion he will review the facts of the case, deal with the submissions of the parties and of any others who have taken part in the proceedings, review the law, and finally express his own opinion on how the judges should decide the case. He takes no further part in the case and does not attend the private meetings at which the judges deliberate. He also advises the Court, in private, on questions of procedure before the case comes up for hearing; more will be said of this in Chapter 11.

The position of the advocate general is symbolized by his physical position at Court hearings: he sits on the Bench, together with the judges, but apart from them, to the side of the Court, and opposite the Registrar. After the case has been argued by the parties, and usually after an adjournment to enable him to prepare his opinion, he delivers it from the Bench, but standing, and addresses it to the judges.

To the English lawyer the closest analogy to the advocate general might be an institutionalised *amicus curiae* or a Queen's Proctor, who intervened in every case, but as will be apparent neither analogy is at all exact. The advocate general may also see himself as in effect delivering a reserved first instance judgment in a case taken on appeal, but his opinion, while it may have authority in future cases, does not of course decide the instant case, even provisionally. The parties may not comment on his opinion, which closes the oral procedure. In continental legal systems, such as the French, the institution of a legal representative for the public interest is well established before the higher courts. Thus, in France the *ministère public* may interpose its view ("conclusions"), distinct from that of the parties, in civil cases before the *Cour de Cassation, Cours d'appel* and *Tribunaux de grande instance;* and in the *Conseil d'Etat,* the *commissaire du gouvernement* is often regarded as having provided the model for the advocate general, although the former (unlike the latter) retires with the judges and may participate in their deliberations, whilst having no vote in the ultimate decision.

The status of the advocate general as a member of the Court is illustrated by the fact that his appointment, and the terms and conditions of his office, are governed (as we saw in the previous chapter) by the same provisions as those of the judges, and that according to the Rules of Procedure judges and advocates general rank equally in precedence according to their seniority in office. On two occasions, a judge has changed roles to become advocate general, Mr Trabucchi taking this step in 1973 and Mr Capotorti, another Italian judge, in 1976; the reverse has not yet occurred. The First Advocate General ranks equally with the three Presidents of Chambers, the other four taking precedence between themselves according to their respective personal seniorities.

An advocate general enjoys, in a sense, a greater independence than a judge, since he is free to speak his mind in public, and is not bound by the collegiate character of the Court's judgments. He can also range beyond the questions for immediate decision. In addition to presenting his own view on those questions, he can also comment on the circumstances in which the case has arisen, on the way in which it has been presented, on any irregularities or special features of the procedure, and can deal generally with other matters beyond the purview of the Court's judgment with its more formal style (see Dashwood (1982) *Legal Studies* 202, at 208).

As an illustration of the role of the advocate general, the opinion in the *Import Gadgets* case is reproduced at the end of this chapter and may be compared with the judgment in that case set out at the end of the previous chapter. The Court is confronted here with a reference for a preliminary ruling, under Article 177 EEC, on the interpretation of certain provisions of the Common Customs Tariff—an area which, although of no special legal significance, is of great importance to trade and a fruitful source of litigation.

It will be seen that the advocate general, as well as setting out the facts, expounding the law, and proposing the reply which the Court in his view should give to the question referred, also comments on other matters, such as the compatibility with Community law of the actions of the French customs authorities, which are outside the scope of the Court's judgment.

Similarly, the opinion often ranges more widely in setting out the sources of law, referring for example in some detail to relevant previous decisions of the Court, to decisions under national law from the courts of the Member States where national law is relevant, and also occasionally to the opinions of legal writers ("doctrine"). The Court's judgment, by contrast, is less free and less full, usually setting out only those propositions which are necessary to its decision, and often not seeking to justify or substantiate them.

The advocate-general's opinion is normally written in advance of delivery and translated as necessary, by the Court's translation department, into the language of the case and into the working language of the Court, but he is free to deliver it in his own language and commonly does: the version in his own language should be looked to in case of doubt on any point. Subsequently it will be translated into the other official languages for publication in the European Court Reports (see p. 19, above), where it invariably appears immediately after the judgment to which it relates, thereby facilitating citation from it as persuasive authority (see Chapter 15). In the Common Market Law Reports it is printed *before* the judgment, according thus with the actual sequence of events.

Although the advocate general may have started work in preparing a case before the oral hearing of the parties, he will normally write it in the week or fortnight following that hearing. He will work closely with his legal secretaries, whose role has been mentioned in Chapter 2; in some respects, his relationship with his legal secretaries may be closer than that of the judges with theirs, since the judges will be able to discuss the case among themselves, while the advocate general is on his own. Usually he will not want to know too much of the minds of the judges, so that he can preserve his independent viewpoint.

About three weeks after the oral hearing, when the opinion has been prepared and translated as necessary, it will be delivered in open court. This is something of a formality, since the judges will often have the written text, and the parties, as has been mentioned, have no right to comment on the opinion, so that there is no need for them to attend. The reading by the advocate general of his opinion closes the oral procedure, although there is a rarely used provision, in the Rules of Procedure, for the oral procedure to be re-opened before the Court gives judgment (see p. 205, below). Judgment itself is always reserved, so that there is a full opportunity for the judges to consider the advocate-general's opinion.

The judges are of course in no way bound to follow the opinion and indeed they not infrequently depart from it. It is not now customary for the judgment to refer directly to the opinion at all. It has often been asked why there is any need for the advocate-general's opinion. Yet even when the judges disagree with him, they may derive much assistance from his opinion, if only because it provides a single coherent picture of the complexities of the whole case and a starting-point for their own deliberations. Its value may be greater the larger the Court, and especially with one whose judges come from different legal systems and speak, at least metaphorically, no common language.

In some respects, the assistance which the Court is given by the advocate general may be compared with that which an English or Scottish court obtains from the Bar. The standard of counsel appearing before the Court of Justice is extremely varied, the right of audience being very wide, as will be seen in Chapter 12, and forensic traditions varying considerably among the Member States. To take one illustration only, there is no convention, as in Britain, requiring counsel before the Court to cite authorities which are against him. Thus the advocate general may fill a considerable gap.

Apart from the immediate practical utility of their opinions, the advocates general have contributed over the years to the development of Community law, and are frequently cited on questions which the judges have not found it necessary to decide. The authority of such pronouncements is a question to which we shall return when we come to the subject of precedent in the Court. But in developing the law, and in guiding the Court in its early years over the uncharted terrain of the Community Treaties, the first advocates general, Maurice Lagrange of France and Karl Roemer of Germany, made a remarkable impact which can still be seen in the reports of the latest cases. For illustrations of their respective contributions one need look only at the opinion of Maurice Lagrange in the first reference to the Court under Article 177 EEC (Case 13/61 *Bosch* [1962] ECR 45), or his dicta on the subject of interpretation of Community law (see for example Case 8/55 *Fédéchar* v. *High Authority* [1954–1956] ECR 245); or, in the case of Karl Roemer, at many of the early cases on judicial review under the ECSC Treaty (see for example Cases 7 and 9/54 *Groupement des Industries Sidérurgiques Luxembourgeoises* v. *High Authority* [1954–1956] ECR 175).

An incidental advantage of the institution of advocate general, as was pointed out in the previous chapter, is that the opinion, which is printed in full as part of the report of the case, often provides a clearer introduction to a case than the judgment itself, and so is best read first.

Comments are sometimes made on the proportion of cases in which an advocate general is or is not followed by the Court. But it seems doubtful whether any reliable statistics could be assembled on this question. Frequently the Court will agree with the advocate general on some aspects of the case but disagree on others; or it may arrive at the same result but on grounds which diverge to a greater or lesser extent from his reasoning. Some suggestions of the advocate general may be passed over in silence, so that it is not possible to state with certainty whether the Court accepts them or not. It is true, however, that in some of the cases which represent the most striking advances in its jurisprudence, the Court has gone against the views of the advocate general. Examples of such landmarks can be found in cases like *Van Gend en Loos* (p. 162), *Continental Can* (p. 255), and the *ERTA* case (p. 94), of which more will be said in later chapters. The explanation of this phenomenon may lie partly in the fact that the advocate general often regards it as one of his principal functions to remind the Court of its previous case-law and to emphasise the virtue of a consistent and harmonious development of the law; it may also be simply easier for the judges collectively to advance further than an individual advocate general. Although it may only be a matter of impression, it does not seem that an advocate general, despite his more exposed position, is more influenced by his national background or is any less "Community-minded" than the judges.

The number and national origins of the advocates general have been determined by somewhat arbitrary factors. In the original Community of the Six there had to be seven judges in order to ensure that there was an uneven number of judges and not less than one from each Member State. As the larger Member States were considered entitled to a second member of the Court, there were from 1952 to 1972 a French and a German advocate general, with Italy, towards the end of that period, having two judges.(Earlier, there had been two Dutch judges.) After the first enlargement of the Communities to nine, there was one judge from each Member State and an advocate general from each of the "big four," France, Germany, Italy and the United Kingdom. Following the second enlargement, a Greek judge was added, as well as a second French judge in order to preserve an uneven number; by way of concession to the smaller Member States, a fifth advocate general was added, drawn initially from the Netherlands.

Following Maurice Lagrange, advocate general from 1952 to 1964, a succession of French advocates general was drawn from the *Conseil d'Etat,* appropriately enough since the *commissaire du gouvernement* in that institution is probably the closest model for the Court's advocate general. Indeed one has the impression, in reading the opinions of a French advocate general, that he sees his function in Luxembourg as the same as that of his counterpart in Paris. Maurice Lagrange was succeeded in turn by Joseph Gand, Alain Dutheillet de Lamothe, and Henri Mayras. However, with the appointment of Simone Rozès, this pattern has been broken, although, as we have seen, the second French judge was drawn from the *Conseil d'Etat.* For, before being appointed to the Court,

Mme Rozès had risen through the career judiciary to the presidency of the *Tribunal de grande instance de Paris,* the busiest and most important court of first instance in all France. Karl Roemer, who served from 1952 to 1973, was succeeded by Gerhard Reischl, who had combined judi- cial and political experience in Germany and had been a member of the European Parliament. The previous Italian advocate general, Francesco Capotorti, achieved emi- nence in his own country as a professor of international law; both he and his immediate predecessor as advocate general had previously been judges of the Court, a change of role to which we have already made allusion. Capotor- ti's successor as advocate general, Federico Mancini, had spent most of his previous career as an academic lawyer in Bologna and Rome. The new fifth post as advocate general is occupied by a Dutchman, VerLoren van Themaat, who had held a chair of law at the University of Utrecht and co-authored a widely used treatise (in both Dutch and English) on Community law.

The first British advocate general, Jean-Pierre Warner, had been Junior Counsel to the Treasury in Chancery matters from 1964 to 1972. After distinguished service in Luxembourg from 1973 to 1981, he became a Judge in the Chancery Division of the High Court. He was succeeded as advocate general by Sir Gordon Slynn, who had previously been Junior Counsel to the Treasury in common law, Senior Counsel to the Crown, High Court Judge, and President of the Employment Appeal Tribunal.

But the diverse backgrounds of the advocates general seem to have influenced the style rather than the substance of their opinions. One may read more like the reserved judgment of an English court; one may read more like the *conclusions* of a *commissaire du gouverne- ment;* one may be more clearly marked by a particular national legal system; but taken as a whole the opinions are as much the product of a Community view, and of the *esprit de corps* which characterises the Court as a whole, as are the judgments themselves.

For ease of expression, the advocate general has been referred to in this chapter in the masculine gender; the authors intend no disrespect to the first woman advocate general, Mme Simone Rozès, or the other Portias who will follow her on the Kirchberg.

APPENDIX

OPINION OF THE ADVOCATE GENERAL
In Case 22/76 *Import Gadgets s.à.r.l., Paris*
v. L.A.M.P., S.p.A. Pavia

Reference for a preliminary ruling by the Tribunale of
Pavia

Opinion
of Mr. Advocate-General
J.P. Warner
delivered on 14th July 1976

My Lords,

This case comes to the Court by way of a reference for a
preliminary ruling by the Tribunale of Pavia, before which
there is pending an action for breach of a contract for the
sale of goods. The Plaintiff in that action is "Import
Gadgets" s.à.r.l., of Paris. The Defendant is L.A.M.P.
S.p.A., of Pavia.

The question referred to the Court by the Tribunale
concerns the interpretation of Chapter 97 of the Common
Customs Tariff. This is entitled "Toys, Games and Sports
Requisites; Parts thereof." More precisely the question is
as to the correct classification within that Chapter of
certain "laughing devices" bought by the Plaintiff from
the Defendant and intended to be incorporated into dolls.
Your Lordships saw (and heard) a specimen of those
devices, which was supplied to the Court, at its request, by
the Plaintiff. It is a small battery-powered gadget, in a
pink plastic casing, which, when a button on it is pressed,
makes a noise like human laughter. In the case of this
particular specimen the laughter was masculine and
somewhat sardonic. The question that the Tribunale
wishes to have the assistance of the Court in deciding is

whether that gadget is within Heading 97.02 or Heading 97.03 of the Common Customs Tariff. So far as material, Heading 97.02 covers, under A, "Dolls" and under B, "Parts and accessories" thereof, whilst Heading 97.03 covers "Other toys."

The way in which the question arises is this.

In February 1970 the Plaintiff bought 2,000 of the devices in question from the Defendant, taking delivery of them at Pavia, and, through forwarding agents, imported them into France. The date of importation was April 24, 1970. For the purposes of clearing them through French Customs the goods were entered by the forwarding agents under Heading 97.02, which was the Heading shown in the Defendant's invoice. The French Customs asked for a certificate of origin and this was obtained by the Defendant from the Chamber of Commerce of Pavia on May 5, 1970. It certified the goods to be of Italian origin. They were cleared through customs on May 12, 1970.

In February 1971 the Plaintiff bought a second batch of 1,600 of the devices from the Defendant. Again the Plaintiff took delivery of them at Pavia and again it imported them into France, through the same forwarding agents. The importation took place on February 15, 1971. On this occasion, however, although the Defendant's invoice showed the goods as falling under Heading 97.02, the forwarding agents entered them under Heading 97.03. The French Customs having again asked for a certificate of origin, such a certificate, stating that the goods were of Italian origin, was obtained by the Defendant from the Chamber of Commerce of Pavia on February 18, 1971. When, however, the French Customs came to inspect the goods (which they had not done on the previous occasion) they found that some were marked "Made in Japan" whilst others bore traces of such a mark having been erased.

The importance of this discovery for the French Customs lay in the fact that France had a Commercial Agreement with Japan, under which it imposed a quota

on imports from Japan of goods falling under Heading
97.03. By successive Decisions of the Council, adopted
under Articles 111 and 113 of the EEC Treaty, France had
been authorised to maintain that Agreement in force,
pending the adoption by the Member States of a common
policy as to imports of such goods from Japan. (The
relevant Decisions are cited in the Observations of the
Commission).

The position was quite different in the case of goods
falling under Heading 97.02. Imports of these from Japan
have, ever since 1968 been on the common liberalisation
list maintained by the Council, originally under Articles
111 and 113 of the Treaty, and now under Article 113
alone. They are not therefore subject to any quantitative
restrictions in any Member State. (There again the
relevant Regulations are cited in the Observations of the
Commission).

The immediate outcome of the discovery by the French
Customs of the falsity of the declaration of origin of the
goods comprised in the Plaintiff's second importation was
that those goods were forfeited and that the Plaintiff was
required to pay a penalty of 10,000 FF. A further outcome
was that the French Customs re-opened the matter of the
earlier importation. They held that the goods involved in
that should have been entered under Heading 97.03 and
they imposed a penalty of 5,000 FF on the Plaintiff in
respect of the false declaration of the origin of those
goods. To make matters worse, it seems that, in order to
avoid anyone's prosecution, the forwarding agents signed
a document renouncing the Plaintiff's rights of recourse to
the French Courts.

Although no question as to the compatibility with
Community law of the action of the French Customs
authorities is referred to this Court by the Tribunale of
Pavia, the Commission drew attention to the fact that such
a question does arise.

The Commission points out that, whichever was the
correct Tariff classification of the goods in question, no

certificate as to their origin was called for if they had been in free circulation in Italy. By the combined effect of Articles 9, 10 and 30 of the Treaty they could then be freely imported into France. The only exception to that would have been if, assuming them to fall within Heading 97.03, and therefore subject, if imported direct from Japan into France, to the quota provided for by the Franco-Japanese Commercial Agreement, there had been in force a Decision of the Commission under Article 115 of the Treaty authorising France to treat them as subject to that quota even though they were in free circulation in another Member State. There was however no such Decision in force at the time of the importations here in question. Decisions to that effect covered only the periods July 17, to December 31, 1970 and September 30, 1971 to March 31, 1972. (See, for particulars of those Decisions, the Observations of the Commission).

Thus the question whether the action of the French authorities was compatible with Community law depends upon whether in fact the goods in question were in free circulation in Italy before being brought into France. On behalf of the Plaintiff it was vigorously asserted at the hearing that they were not. It appears from the Order for Reference that the Defendant (which was not represented at the hearing) asserts that they were. The Commission agrees with the Defendant. The French Republic has not thought fit to intervene, even though the attention of its Government was expressly drawn to the question by the Court.

In the circumstances Your Lordships cannot, in my view, do other than leave the matter open. It may have to be determined by the Tribunale of Pavia. As to that we know too little about the issues that are relevant in the action before that Court for me to be able to say. But in any case the matter must be pursued by the Commission. Indeed Counsel for the Commission told us at the hearing that a letter had already been sent by the Commission to the French Government about it. Quite properly he added that the contents of that letter were confidential, since they might lead to the Commission invoking its powers under Article 169 of the Treaty.

So I revert to the actual question referred to the Court by the Tribunale. In its Order for Reference the Tribunale expresses the view that "it is possible to maintain that the laughing devices constitute mechanisms capable of being used by themselves as toys (97.03) or, on the contrary, that they merely constitute parts of dolls (97.02 B)." In effect the Tribunale asks the Court to choose between those two possibilities.

As was pointed out at the hearing, both on behalf of the Plaintiff and on behalf of the Commission, the problem is unfortunately not quite as simple as that.

There are two Notes to Chapter 97 that have to be taken into account. The first is Note 3, which reads: "In heading No. 97.02 the term 'dolls' is to be taken to apply to such articles as are representations of human beings."

The second is Note 4, which provides that "parts and accessories which are suitable for use solely or principally with articles falling within any heading of this Chapter are to be classified with those articles."

From those provisions it can be deduced that laughing devices are within Heading 97.02 only if they are "suitable for use solely or principally" in dolls that are "representations of human beings."

For the Plaintiff it was submitted that the laughing devices here in question could as readily be used in dolls which were representations of animals, *e.g.* teddy bears or Mickey Mouses, which are within Heading 97.03. The Commission added that they could also be used in articles falling within the description "novelty jokes" in Heading 97.05. As an example of such an article Counsel for the Commission showed us at the hearing a "laughing sack." Nor do I doubt that the Tribunale of Pavia is right in suggesting that laughing devices can be used as toys on their own.

If the matter rested there one might be driven to the

highly unsatisfactory conclusion that each time a Customs officer or a Judge in any Member State was confronted with a batch of laughing devices he must decide, on such evidence as might be available, whether those particular devices were most suitable for use in human dolls, in toy animals, in novelty jokes or as toys in themselves.

Happily the matter does not rest there. The Explanatory Notes to the Brussels nomenclature, which the Court has many times held to constitute an authoritative guide to the interpretation of the Common Customs Tariff, state, under Heading 97.02: "Parts and accessories of dolls falling within this heading include . . . voice and other mechanisms . . . " (In the French text the reference is to "les voix et cris").

On the other hand the long list of examples of toys falling within Heading 97.03 given by the Notes does not include anything resembling laughing devices. Nor, for that matter, does the list of examples of novelty jokes falling within Heading 97.05.

I conclude that the compilers of those Notes have taken the view that "voice and other mechanisms" are suitable for use, if not solely, at least principally, in human dolls. That indeed was the view urged upon us by the Commission. I see no reason to differ from it.

I am therefore of the opinion that, in answer to the question referred to the Court by the Tribunale of Pavia, Your Lordships should declare that laughing devices suitable for use in dolls that are representations of human beings are within Heading 97.02 B of the Common Customs Tariff notwithstanding that they may be suitable also for other uses.

PART TWO: FUNCTIONS AND JURISDICTION

Introductory

In the Community legal order the Court of Justice has a crucial role. It has to see that the Council and the Commission, as the decision-taking and policy-making organs of the Community, keep within their powers under the Treaties. It has to restrain Member States who act in breach of the Treaties. It has also a legislative function, inasmuch as it often falls to the Court to fill gaps in the legal system arising from the political impotence of the Council.

For those important and varied tasks the Court is armed by the Treaties with an extremely wide jurisdiction. Indeed, the Court is vested with powers which in most continental countries lawyers would expect to find shared between a number of specialist courts. But in the Community legal order the Court of Justice has to serve as a judicial maid of all work.

Thus, the Court acts as an administrative court to impose judicial control on the other institutions of the Community. It also acts as would a continental administrative court by providing a tribunal to which the public servants of the Communities may appeal in disputes relating to their terms of service. Such staff disputes constitute numerically an important slice of the Court's business—about one third of the total case-load up to the present. Again, in certain circumstances, an individual may bring before the Court a suit for damages against an institution of the Communities.

The Court exercises powers of judicial review not only over administrative acts but also over Community legislation, such as regulations or directives of the Council or Commission. The Court may also rule upon the conformity with the Treaties of any international agreement entered into by the Communities. In this respect, the

Court resembles a constitutional court such as that of the German Federal Republic or the Supreme Court of the United States.

If the Court in these respects resembles the administrative or constitutional courts familiar to continental lawyers, it also serves, in a sense, as an international court by hearing suits brought against a Member State for an alleged violation of the Treaties. Such suits may be brought by another Member State but are usually instituted by the Commission in the exercise of its watchdog function.

Among the Court's functions, mention must be made of its jurisdiction to give preliminary rulings when requested to do so by a court of a Member State. Preliminary rulings may be given upon a question of the interpretation of Community law or of the validity of Community legislation. This head of the Court's jurisdiction has proved in the event to be much the most influential for the development of Community law and will be fully discussed in Chapter 9. From a procedural point of view preliminary rulings may be contrasted with the other heads of the Court's jurisdiction. For, whereas a reference for a preliminary ruling can only be made by the national court and not by the parties themselves, all other cases are brought directly before the Court by the party initiating the proceedings, whether this be a Member State, a Community institution, a legal person such as a firm or company, or a private individual.

In an Appendix to this part (below, p. 185) are included various Judicial Statistics concerning the work of the Court from its inception up to January 1, 1982. There (Table 1, p. 186) the term "Direct actions" is used in contrast with "Staff cases," on the one hand, and "Preliminary Rulings" on the other. Direct actions may conveniently be divided into (A) actions against Member States (which will be the subject of Chapter 5) and (B) actions against Community institutions (which will be the subject of Chapters 6 and 7). Category (B) corresponds to what we have termed above the administrative and constitutional jurisdiction of the Court; category (A) to its international jurisdiction.

This last expression must be treated with caution. To receive and decide suits against States is the characteristic function of an international tribunal; contemporary examples are the International Court of Justice at The Hague or the European Court of Human Rights at Strasbourg. In this sense one may speak of the Luxembourg Court's international jurisdiction, for under various provisions of the Treaties the Court may be seised of complaints that a Member State is failing to fulfil its treaty obligations, including the failure to implement obligations arising under regulations or directives.

Nevertheless, this jurisdiction of the Court differs in significant respects from that of a traditional international tribunal. Thus, it differs from the Hague Court in that the breaches by Member States with which it is concerned are breaches primarily of Community law, not of international law (except in so far as they stem from a treaty infringement). The concern here of the Luxembourg Court is with upholding and enforcing the Community legal order, whereas that of the Hague Court is the settlement of international disputes. Again, suits against Member States are usually brought to Luxembourg not by another State but by the Community's own policeman or watchdog, the Commission. A somewhat similar relationship exists at Strasbourg between the European Court and the European Commission of Human Rights, but such a filtering device is not characteristic of international tribunals. Furthermore, preliminary references to Luxembourg from courts in Member States have, as we shall see later, the same effect as certain direct actions in putting a particular Member State in the dock there for a treaty infringement with the watchdog role of the Commission being played by the individual plaintiff; but such references are not normally thought of as falling within the international jurisdiction of the Court.

The last head of jurisdiction to be considered in this part does have an international aspect. Under Article 228 EEC the Court may be asked its opinion on whether an international agreement which the Community is contemplating entering into is compatible with the provisions of the Treaty. This jurisdiction was exercised for the first time in 1975 and, although exercised infrequently, has recently acquired enough significance to warrant a separate chapter (Chapter 10).

The six chapters which form this part will cover then the main categories of cases falling within the Court's jurisdiction. But this manifold jurisdiction also extends to a few exceptional types of case not dealt with below, such as the power of the Court under Article 13 of the Merger Treaty compulsorily to retire a member of the Commission who no longer fulfils the conditions required for the performance of his duties or if he has been guilty of serious misconduct: this power has been used only once, in 1976, when a Commissioner was permanently incapacitated by a stroke.

Potentially more significant, but rarely exercised, is the jurisdiction of the Court under Article 95 ECSC to give an opinion if it is found necessary to amend, subject to certain limitations, the provisions of the ECSC Treaty. Other heads of jurisdiction can be found in Articles 180 to 182 EEC. Frequently contracts concluded by the Community with outside bodies include an arbitration clause conferring jurisdiction on the Court pursuant to Article 181 EEC (or Article 153 Euratom: an instance of this jurisdiction is mentioned below, p. 120).

Article 182 EEC confers upon the Court jurisdiction in any dispute between Member States which relates to the subject matter of the Treaty, if the parties agree to submit their dispute to the Court. Moreover, Member States whose disputes concern the interpretation or application of the Treaty are bound by Article 219 not to submit their dispute to any other method of settlement than those provided by the Treaty.

Chapter 5

ACTIONS AGAINST MEMBER STATES

Introduction

Proceedings may be brought in the Court of Justice against Member States to establish that they have infringed their Community obligations. Under the EEC Treaty such direct actions against Member States arise, principally, under Articles 169 and 170. They may also be brought under Article 93 in the special context of "State aids." In the ECSC Treaty, as we shall see, it is the Commission which acts, in effect, as a jurisdiction of first instance to determine the infringement and issue a decision addressed to the Member State in breach of the Treaty.

Articles 169 and 170 EEC provide two distinct but inter-related procedures. Under the former Article it is the Commission which brings the action against the Member State, whereas under the latter the action is brought by another Member State.

Procedure under Article 169

An action by the Commission under Article 169 involves three phases. The formal procedure however is invariably preceded in practice by the Commission writing a letter to the Member State warning it of its breach and inviting its comments. If this does not settle the matter, and in two cases out of three it does so, then the first formal step is for the Commission to invite the State formally to submit its observations on the alleged breach, after which the Commission will deliver a reasoned opinion. This pre-contentious phase may well result in a settlement of the matter by the State recognising its breach and correcting it. In practice, a high percentage of the cases terminate at this stage.

If the State is recalcitrant, the second phase in the procedure is for the Commission to bring the matter before the Court. Settlements are also sometimes reached at this stage. The third and final phase is for the Court to give judgment. Under Article 171 this judgment is only declaratory: there are no sanctions for non-compliance. Article 171 simply declares that the State shall be required to take the necessary measures to comply with the judgment. Yet the violation of a treaty obligation by a Member State is a serious matter which must carry political consequences in its relations with other Member States. The Commission has also indirect means of bringing pressure upon the defaulting State through its powers to grant (or withhold) various authorisations which the State may seek from it under numerous Articles of the Treaty. Again, in some Member States it has been accepted that it may be possible for an individual citizen, with a sufficient interest, to sue his government for damages in respect of its breach of Community law. The question has not yet been settled in the English or Scottish courts. To date, almost every judgment against a Member State has been complied with, although in a few instances only after considerable delay.

Under Article 88 ECSC the procedure is different. Thus, under the first phase the Commission reaches a *decision* whether the State is in breach: it does not merely deliver an *opinion*. In the second phase it is therefore the State which must bring the matter before the Court by way of a challenge to the Commission's decision. Finally, in the third phase, if the State does not challenge the decision or if the Court upholds it, then the Commission is empowered to impose certain sanctions, provided the Council supports this by a two-thirds majority. The sanctions include the suspension of payments otherwise due to be paid by the Commission to the State in default or the taking of discriminatory measures which would normally be proscribed under Article 4 ECSC (*e.g.* a ban on imports from the State in question).

In practice, Member States have generally come to heel. The two most notorious instances to date of reluctance to conform concern, respectively, Italy and France. The Italian Government imposed a tax, pursuant to a Law of 1939, on the export of art treasures, which it was only prevailed upon to repeal as a tax on exports contrary to Article 16 EEC, after having been declared in breach in three different proceedings before the Court (Case 7/68 *Commission* v. *Italy* [1968] ECR 423; Case 18/71 *Eunomia* v. *Italian Ministry of Education* [1971] ECR 811, Case 48/71 *Commission* v. *Italy* [1972] ECR 527).

In the so-called Lamb War between France and the United Kingdom (1978–80), a French ban on the import of mutton and lamb from the United Kingdom was declared by the Court, in proceedings under Article 169 EEC, to be an infringement of Articles 12 and 30 EEC (Case 232/78 *Commission* v. *France* [1979] ECR 2729). When France did not comply with this judgment, the Commission began a second action under Article 169 (Case 24/80, lodged in January 1980), based upon France's infringement of Article 171, which (as we have seen) requires a State to take the necessary measures to comply with any judgment of the Court. Before this case was heard, the Commission, in March 1980, lodged a further action (Case 97/80) against France under Article 169 in respect of an illegal charge upon mutton and lamb imports and of the continuing defiance of the first judgment. Cases 24/80 and 97/80 then proceeded as joined cases, in the course of which the Commission, pursuant to Article 186 EEC and Article 83 of the Rules of Procedure, made an application for the adoption of "interim measures" in which it invited the Court "to order the French Republic to desist forthwith from applying any restriction and/or levying any charge on imports of mutton and lamb from the United Kingdom." For reasons which will be discussed below (p. 209) when interim measures are explained, the Court refused the order requested. Nevertheless, in September 1980 a compromise was reached in the Council of Agricultural Ministers by the adoption of a sheepmeat regime (long demanded by France) which induced the latter to remove the charge on imports, thus ending this twentieth century "War of Jenkins' ear."

By contrast with the earlier dispute with Italy over the art treasures tax (above) or the later dispute with the United Kingdom over an import ban on potatoes (Case 231/78 *Commission* v. *United Kingdom* [1979] ECR 1447 and Case 118/78 *Meijer* v. *Department of Trade* [1979] ECR 1387), in the Lamb War no challenge to the French action was brought in the French courts, though this might have proved more effective.

An illustration of Article 169 procedure is provided by the *Pigmeat* case (Case 7/61 *Commission* v. *Italy* [1961] ECR 317). By a Decree of June 1960 the Italian Government decided to suspend the import of certain pigmeats from all countries until August 31, 1960. This suspension was subsequently extended a number of times. In October 1960 the Commission told the Italian Government that in its opinion the suspension was contrary to Article 31 EEC whereby Member States should refrain from introducing between themselves any new quantitative restrictions upon imports. After giving the Italian Government an opportunity to present its observations, the Commission wrote a letter on December 21, 1960 requesting the Italian Government to put an end to the alleged infringement within one month and repeating its view that the Italian measures stopping import of pigmeat were contrary to Article 31 EEC. This letter did not contain a full review of the economic situation on the Italian market for pigmeat nor a discussion whether this situation might justify the Italian measures.

In a letter of January 1961 the Italian Government informed the Commission that it had decided to extend the measures once more until March 31, 1961 and requested the Commission to authorise them under Article 226 EEC. This Article provides that if serious economic difficulties arise, Member States may apply to the Commission for authorisation to take protective measures in order to rectify the situation. The Commission replied that, while prepared to consider the request for special authorisation, this could not affect the continuation of the Article 169 proceedings. In fact, the Commission proceeded to bring a suit against Italy in the Court on March 20, 1961. Before the Court gave judgment on December 19, 1961, the Italian Government had, as from July 1, 1961, repealed the import measures and substituted a system of minimum prices, which system had been recommended by the Commission.

Before the Court the Italian Government raised three preliminary objections to the admissibility of the action (for admissibility, see p. 199). First, it argued that the letter from the Commission of December 21, 1960 was not a 'reasoned opinion" within the terms of Article 169 so as to satisfy the first phase of procedure under that Article. In particular, it claimed that the letter did not examine the relevance of the Government's arguments regarding the grave crisis in the pigmeat market and the need for temporary measures to deal with that crisis. Secondly, it argued that the Commission should have postponed action under Article 169 until it had decided whether the Italian measures could be authorised under Article 226. Thirdly, it argued that the suit should have been discontinued after July 1, 1961, from which date the Italian Government had repealed the disputed measures: in effect, the suit had then lost its object and become merely academic.

All three arguments were rejected by the Court. The Commission's letter was sufficiently reasoned because it had presented a coherent statement of the reasons that had led the Commission to believe that Italy had failed in one of its obligations under the Treaty. The fact that the Commission was considering a special authorisation under Article 226 did not prevent it believing, rightly or wrongly, that Italy was in breach of its obligations so as to justify proceedings under Article 169. And it was still proper for the Court to declare whether or not a Member State had failed in its obligations, even though, subsequently to the bringing of the action, the State may have put an end to its infringement of the Treaty.

On this last point, the Court appears to have changed its position in the later decision of Case 26/69 *Commission* v. *French Republic* [1970] ECR 565, and will now examine whether a sufficient interest can be shown by the Commission for seeking a judgment on a matter which has become moot. In the later case, the Commission succeeded in showing a sufficient interest by reason of the fact that the Court's decision would govern a number of similar cases then pending.

In Cases 2 and 3/62 *Commission* v. *Luxembourg and Belgium* [1962] ECR 425, the Court re-affirmed its view that a subsequent request for special authorisation does not operate to suspend Article 169 proceedings; to decide otherwise would deprive the Article of its effectiveness.

A different line of defence to Article 169 proceedings was attempted in Cases 90 and 91/63 *Commission* v. *Luxembourg and Belgium* [1964] ECR 625 (the *Dairy Products* case). Here the two Governments argued that the action against them was inadmissible because the Council was itself in default in having delayed the setting up of a common organisation for dairy products, although it had resolved that it would do so by regulation before July 31, 1962. The Governments therefore argued that their own protective import duties would have been unnecessary if the Council had done its job by the date it had itself proposed and made a regulation governing dairy products generally. They argued that under the theory of interdependence of obligations in international law a party which is affected by the failure of another party to fulfil its obligations has the right not to fulfil its own obligations. The Court roundly rejected this plea as having no place in Community law: the Treaty created a new legal order whose structure, except for cases expressly covered by the Treaty, involved the prohibition of Member States taking justice into their own hands. Hence, the Council's failure to fulfil its obligations could not excuse the defendant Governments from carrying out their own obligations. Furthermore, self-help was not an appropriate remedy where an agency (namely, the Commission) existed for law enforcement. Accordingly, the import duties were declared contrary to Community law.

Although the Belgian Government then abolished the duties, the recovery of duties already paid was prohibited by statute. This led to further proceedings in the Belgian courts, culminating in the landmark decision of the Court of Cassation upholding in Belgium the supremacy of Community law over conflicting national law: *Minister for Economic Affairs* v. *Fromagerie Franco-Suisse "Le Ski"* [1972] CMLR 330.

It is well established that a Member State may not rely upon provisions, practices or situations in its internal legal system in order to justify a failure to fulfil obligations arising under Community law. Thus, in Case 58/81 *Commission* v. *Luxembourg* [1982] 3 CMLR 482, the Grand Duchy was held in breach of a directive on equal pay despite its plea that it needed time to enact implementing legislation and to study the budgetary consequences of the directive.

In Case 167/73 *Commission* v. *French Republic* [1974] ECR 359 the long-standing rule of French law was challenged under which a certain proportion of the crew of French merchant ships had to consist of French nationals. The Commission argued that this was contrary to Community law, in particular Article 48 EEC enshrining the principle of movement of workers. The French Government did not agree that this principle automatically applied to transport, especially transport by sea in view of the terms of Article 84(2) EEC; but it did indicate its intention to amend the offending provision of the *Code du Travail Maritime,* although not accepting that it was under any treaty obligation to do so. The Court held that the basic principle of free movement of workers was not subject to any qualifications in relation to sea transport and that consequently France was in breach of Article 48, nor had France in any way atoned for this breach by its declared intention to amend its ways. Moreover, the principle of legal certainty required the removal from the French statute book of a provision contrary to Community law.

Procedure under Article 170

The alternative procedure to Article 169 is that under Article 170 which permits any Member State to bring another Member State before the Court if it considers the latter has failed to fulfil an obligation under the Treaty. This form of action has rarely been used. Like the procedure under Article 169, Article 170 procedure is in successive phases. The first phase requires the complaining State to bring the alleged infringement before the Commission. The Commission must then deliver a reasoned opinion, as under Article 169, after allowing the States concerned to submit their observations. Only then (or if the Commission has not delivered an opinion after three months) may the complaining State bring the defaulting State before the Court.

That procedure under Article 169 is preferred to that under Article 170 is readily understandable. Direct confrontation between Member States as litigants at Luxembourg is better avoided by leaving it to the Commission to initiate any suit. In any event, the Commission has still to be involved whichever alternative procedure is used, although under Article 170 a Member State could commence an action in the Court even if the Commission's opinion was that no treaty infringement had occurred. Under the corresponding Article of the ECSC Treaty (Article 89) only one action was begun, by Belgium against France, but it was not pursued. Under the EEC Treaty actions have occasionally been threatened but only rarely pursued. Thus, Italy threatened to proceed against France during the "Wine War" of 1975–76. Only one case to date has proceeded to judgment: Case 141/78 *France* v. *United Kingdom* [1979] ECR 2923, where the United Kingdom was adjudged in breach of its obligations under the EEC Treaty by adopting a national measure governing the minimum size of mesh for fishing nets used in British territorial waters. As required by Article 170(3), the Commission gave a reasoned opinion, which was in support of the French application; it also intervened in the proceedings (for such interventions, see p. 211 below).

Procedure under Article 93

In addition to the general enforcement procedure available to the Commission under Article 169 EEC, certain categories of infringements by Member States may be the subject of a more expeditious procedure which dispenses with the requirement of the Commission delivering a reasoned opinion. Instead, the Commission may proceed directly to the taking of a binding decision. Such derogation from the general procedure under Article 169 EEC is permitted by Articles 93 and 225: the latter Article concerns improper use by a Member State of the powers given it by Articles 223 and 224 to disregard the provisions of the EEC Treaty in the essential interests of its security, where these involve arms production or the withholding of information; the former Article concerns State aids to industry and has proved the more important in practice.

Under Article 93, where a State aid distorts or threatens to distort competition within the common market, the Commission, after giving notice to the parties concerned to submit their comments, may proceed to decide that the State concerned shall abolish (or alter) such aid within a prescribed time. if the State does not comply with this decision within the time prescribed the Commission (or any other interested State) may refer the matter to the Court of Justice direct.

The special procedure under Article 93 resembles therefore the enforcement procedure under Article 88 ECSC in that the Commission (erstwhile, the High Authority) takes a decision that the State is in breach of the ECSC Treaty; as we have seen (p. 76 above), it does not merely deliver an opinion. It differs, however, from Article 88 in that under Article 93 it is the Commission which must seise the Court of the fact that the offending State has not complied with the decision, whereas Article 33 leaves it to the State to challenge the decision before the Court. For, if not challenged, or if challenged but upheld, the decision under Article 88 ECSC carries with it certain sanctions for non-compliance, though none have ever in fact been imposed. No such (theoretical) sanctions attach to a decision under Article 93, although, as we shall see, when brought before the Court, it may be the subject of interim measures, and although not enforceable in the national courts, it will render Article 93 directly effective.

An example of the special procedure under Article 93 is provided by the *Pig Producers* case (Cases 31/77 and 53/77R *Commission* v. *United Kingdom* [1977] ECR 921). The British Government introduced a subsidy for United Kingdom pig producers to help them compete with Dutch and Danish imports subsidised by the Community. The Government had informed the Commission of its intention to introduce the subsidy, but before the Commission had decided whether the subsidy was compatible with the common market within the terms of Articles 92 and 93, it brought the subsidy into operation, thereby infringing the clear prohibition in Article 93(3).

The Commission thereupon took a decision on February 17, 1977 which required the United Kingdom to terminate the pig subsidy "forthwith." As the British Government did not comply, the Commission began an enforcement action under Article 93(2) on March 11, 1977. And it went further, for on May 12, 1977 it asked the Court to make an interim order requiring the United Kingdom to stop paying the subsidy. As we will see later, the power for the Court to grant what are, in effect, interlocutory injunctions is contained in Article 186 EEC, which states:

> "The Court of Justice may in any cases before it prescribe any necessary interim measures."

Despite advice to the contrary by the advocate general in his opinion, the Court in a laconic order on May 21 directed the United Kingdom to end the subsidy, again "forthwith." In fact, payment of the subsidy did cease towards the end of June, so that the enforcement action was not pressed to judgment.

What sanctions, other than political, could have been applied if the Member State had remained recalcitrant is a question discussed in the next section.

Effect of Judgments against Member States

It may be helpful to summarise the effects of a judgment delivered in proceedings brought under Articles 169, 170 and 93. Such judgments, unlike those to be discussed in the next chapter, are not made against a Community institution, but against a Member State. They touch, therefore, the tender nerve of national sovereignty.

In contrast with Article 88 ECSC, a judgment under any of these three Articles is only declaratory: it has no executory force, no sanctions are provided, nor are any national measures thereby annulled. Essentially, it is left to the defaulting Member State to recognise the error of its ways and to comply with its treaty obligations.

Nevertheless, it is in the nature of the proceedings under these Articles that the Commission will have specified the acts which have given rise to the breach. If the Court finds the charges made by the Commission proved, then the Member State is left in no doubt as to what it must do. Thus, in Case 70/72 *Commission* v. *Germany* [1973] ECR 813 Germany had provided State aids for certain mining regions which the Commission

alleged was an infringement of Article 92. In an enforcement action under Article 93 the Commission invited the
Court to declare not only that Germany had infringed the
Treaty but also that it should be required to obtain
repayment of the aids from the recipients. For the
German Government it was submitted that such a ruling
for repayment could be neither requested by the Commission nor made by the Court. The Court did not accept this
submission, although, on the merits of the case, it
dismissed the action: had it found against Germany, it
could not formally have ordered the repayment of the
aids, but it could have achieved the same result, in
substance, by an appropriate wording of its declaratory
judgment. Moreover, the Court made clear that its
approach would be no different in proceedings brought
under Articles 169 and 170: under these Articles as under
Article 93, the Commission may specify what measures
must be taken by the Member State concerned to meet its
treaty obligations, and, in the event of non-compliance,
the Court may grant a declaration in no less specific terms.

Likewise, where the breach consists in the enactment
(or retention) of legislation contrary to Community law,
the Court has no power to annul the offending national
measure. It will confine itself to condemning such measure
as conflicting with Community law. The Member State
concerned should then be in no doubt how it must amend
its own law. Thus, in Case 167/73 *Commission* v. *France*
[1974] ECR 359, as we have seen (p. 81 above) the
successful action under Article 169 induced the French
Government, albeit reluctantly, to amend its *Code du
Travail Maritime*. The Court brushed aside the Government's plea that, even if its own law did conflict with
Community law, it would therefore be inapplicable and so
not require to be repealed: the Court made clear that the
unamended Code would leave Community seamen uncer-
tain of their rights to seek employment on French ships;
nor was it a sufficient answer that the French Government
no longer applied the offending provision of the Code.

In enforcement actions under Articles 169, 170 and 93 the Court of Justice has no power to award damages against a Member State in favour of those who may have been prejudiced by the infringement: this follows from the declaratory nature of the judgment. Moreover, such actions are normally brought, not by the parties prejudiced, but by the Commission acting in the Community interest. Nevertheless, an ingenious attempt may have been made in the *Lamb War* cases (Cases 24/80 and 97/80 R [1980] ECR 1319) to achieve indirectly what could not be done directly. Thus, the British Government is reported to have proposed to the Commission that it should invite the Court to make a declaration that France was in further breach of the Treaty by reason of its failure to pay compensation to British meat exporters prejudiced by the import ban which the Court had already declared illegal in the previous proceedings (Case 232/78 [1979] ECR 2729). The British Government considered, presumably, that the language of Article 171 was wide enough to permit the Court to do this. The Commission, however, did not adopt the British proposal, and the claim for compensation was dropped once the dispute over lamb was settled. Accordingly, it remains a moot question whether an appropriately worded declaration could be issued by the Court if the Commission (or another Member State) proved that the particular breach consisted in the State's failure to pay compensation or damages to an injured party.

As we have seen above (*e.g.* in the *Lamb War* cases) proceedings under Article 169, 170 or 93 culminate in a judgment given under Article 171. Under this Article the State is required to take the necessary measures to comply with the judgment: it is required to do so by the Treaty, it is not *ordered* to do so by the Court. We have also seen that the failure to comply with the judgment may constitute a further treaty infringement by the Member State, this time of Article 171, for which a new enforcement action may be brought under Articles 169 or 170.

We shall see later how to such proceedings under Articles 169 and 170 may be attached a request for interim measures to be prescribed by the Court under Article 186; we shall see too that an interim measure may be couched as an actual *order* by the Court to the offending State that it shall desist from certain conduct on its part, pending judgment in the principal action (see *Pig Producers* case, Case 31, 53/77R [1977] ECR 921).

We have already noted in the previous section how the general enforcement procedure available to the Commission under Article 169 EEC is replaced, for certain categories of treaty infringement by a Member State, by a more expeditious procedure, notably under Article 93 EEC relating to impermissible State aids. Where the offending State fails to comply with the Commission's decision requiring the abolition or alteration of the aid, the Commission may refer the matter to the Court, which may then prescribe any necessary interim measures pursuant to Article 186.

It will now be appreciated that the Court enjoys wider powers in interim proceedings under Article 186 than it has when giving final judgment in enforcement actions (an anomaly justifiable by the interim or interlocutory nature of the relief), although it may be most reluctant to use these powers, where it has already given judgment against a Member State, to seek to compel the State to comply. The Court dislikes merely beating the air, so that when it has a discretion (as it has under Article 186), it may well refuse the interim measures sought for fear of further undermining respect for the authority of the Court by provoking disobedience of its specific order: a recalcitrant child who disobeys its parent's first request is just as likely to disobey the second or third.

In the last resort, a Member State complies only when it has the political will to do so. Defiance, however, puts in jeopardy the whole future of the Community.

Even if there is no completely effective remedy in the Court of Justice, a remedy may lie in the national courts of the Member State in breach. For, as the Court ruled in its landmark decision in Case 26/62 *Van Gend en Loos* [1963] ECR 1 at 13 (see p. 162), "The vigilance of individuals concerned to protect their rights amounts to an effective supervision in addition to the supervision entrusted by Articles 169 and 170 to the diligence of the Commission and of the Member States." And furthermore, as the Court has constantly held, the individual will have such a right of action in the national court whenever the Community provision in question is categorised by the Court of Justice as having direct effect. However, the remedies available to the individual will vary according to the way in which the issue comes before the national court. Thus, in Case 88/77 *Minister for Fisheries* v. *Schoenenberg* [1978] ECR 473 a Dutch fisherman was acquitted by the Irish court on a charge of illegal fishing in Irish waters because he established, as his defence, that the Irish Government had imposed restrictions which were contrary to Community law. Community law may afford not only, as here, a shield, but also a sword. Thus, a Dutch potato exporter successfully sought a declaration in the English High Court that the United Kingdom's ban on potato imports infringed Community law and was, therefore, invalid (Case 118/78 *Meijer* v. *Department of Trade* [1979] ECR 1387). In both these cases Community law was effectively upheld in the national courts of the Member State concerned in its breach. Both cases involved preliminary references to the Court of Justice for rulings that Community law was being infringed. Parallel actions under Article 169 were brought by the Commission against the infringing State in both cases (Case 61/77 [1978] ECR 417; Case 231/78 [1979] ECR 1447); but such enforcement at Community level should not conceal the important function of the national judiciary in sanctioning breaches of Community law by their own governments. While the Article 169 procedure is an effective method of bringing Member States into line for the future, an action in the national courts coupled with a reference for a preliminary ruling under Article 177 may provide, as we shall see in Chapter 9, an immediate remedy for the individual in the instant case.

Chapter 6

JUDICIAL REVIEW OF COMMUNITY ACTS

Introduction

In national constitutions, limits are normally set to the powers exercisable by the agencies of government. Thus, in the United Kingdom there are legal limits upon the powers of the central government and local authorities; these limits are one of the main topics falling within the subject of English administrative law and are found under such headings as "the doctrine of ultra vires" or "the judicial control of administrative authorities." In all the Member States of the European Communities the powers of governmental bodies are confined within prescribed limits and so, in Dicey's sense, subject to the rule of law. In some, the policing of these limits is the task of a separate system of administrative courts. This is the case, for instance, in France where the *Conseil d'Etat* acts as the supreme administrative court and hears appeals from the score or more of regional *Tribunaux administratifs*.

Again, in most countries the constitution sets limits upon the permissible extent of legislation, and the legislature may then be subject to control by a constitutional court exercising judicial review of the constitutionality of its enactments. The United States and the Federal German Republic provide examples of such courts. In the United Kingdom, on the other hand, the doctrine of Parliamentary sovereignty prevails absolutely, at least south of the Scottish border.

In the Community legal order, the administrative (or executive) agencies are the Commission and, to some extent, the Council, although the function of the latter is, first and foremost, that of the legislature. As in the Member States, so in the Communities the administrative agencies have only limited powers of rule-making and individual decision. The Treaties serve as constitutional documents to define those powers, including those of the Council when acting as a legislature. The Treaties also vest in the Court the necessary jurisdiction to control the lawful exercise of such power. Hence, Valentine refers to the Court, neatly, as a Conseil d'Etats (Valentine, *The Court of Justice of the European Communities* Vol. 1, 1965). Hence also we might adopt the heading "administrative jurisdiction" under which to describe this part of the Court's jurisdiction. Nevertheless, the jurisdiction may also be regarded as "constitutional" in so far as the Court reviews the legality of legislation by the Council or Commission. For, as we have seen in Chapter 1, many regulations and directives of these institutions are better regarded as Community legislation than likened to delegated or subordinate legislation as that term is used in English law.

In the EEC Treaty the relevant Articles to be considered first are 173 and 175; these are the counterpart of Articles 33 and 35 of the ECSC Treaty and deal respectively with actions to annul an act of the Council or Commission and actions for inactivity, or the failure to act, on the part of those institutions.

But it must be borne in mind that, in addition to the action for annulment, there are various ways in which the legality of Community measures may be the subject of indirect challenge. Firstly, there is the "plea of illegality," considered later in this chapter (p. 112). Second, an action for damages (Chapter 7) may put in issue the legality of a measure alleged to have injured the applicant; and in practice actions for damages have frequently led the Court to examine the legality of Community legislation. Third, a reference from a national court to the Court of Justice for a preliminary ruling (Chapter 9) may be directed to the validity of any measure adopted by a Community institution; so that an aggrieved person may be able to obtain, not by a direct action in the Court of Justice but by proceedings in a national court, a ruling by the Court of Justice that a Community measure is invalid.

A. *Actions to Annul* (*Article 173*)

Our discussion will consider in sequence the following questions:

(1) What acts can be attacked?
(2) Who can attack?
(3) Within what time limit?
(4) On what grounds?
(5) What effect has annulment?

1. *What acts can be attacked?*

Article 173(1) states: "the Court of Justice shall review the legality of acts of the Council and the Commission other than recommendations or opinions."

Having regard to the terms of Article 189, which lists the acts of the Council and the Commission as "regulations, directives, decisions, recommendations or opinions" one might expect that only the first three were subject to review under Article 173(1). The Court however has adopted a more liberal interpretation. What is required is an act binding in law, and the Court has always been prepared to look behind the label of an act to its substance. Thus, under the ECSC Treaty, in Cases 1 and and 14/57 *Saar Tubes* [1957 and 1958] ECR 105 it was argued by the applicants that what was in form an opinion did in fact impose binding obligations, and the Court accepted that it had a duty to consider whether the act complained of, though in form and name an opinion, did constitute a disguised decision. In the event, it held that it was only an opinion and that consequently the action to annul was inadmissible (under Article 33 ECSC).

Again, in Cases 8 to 11/66 *Cement-Convention* [1967] ECR 75 a "communication" issued by the Commission under Regulation 17, Article 15, to remove protection

from certain cartels was held by the Court to constitute
not a mere opinion but a decision (and consequently to be
binding in law); the plea of inadmissibility under Article
173(1) raised by the Commission was accordingly rejected, and the Court proceeded to review the legality of
the communication in issue.

On the other hand, the Court has not accepted as a
reviewable act the "statement of objections" which, under
the regulation governing competition proceedings, the
Commission is required to send to a firm whose marketing
practices are under investigation: Case 60/81 *IBM* v.
Commission [1981] ECR 2639. Similarly, in Case 7/61
Pigmeat [1961] ECR 317, the Court made clear that the
reasoned opinion which is required under Article 169
proceedings (discussed at p. 79, above) cannot be the
subject of review for illegality under Article 173.

The *ERTA* case (Case 22/70 *Commission* v. *Council*
[1971] ECR 263) well illustrates the bold approach of the
Court to the interpretation of the term "acts" in Article
173(1). In this case the Commission challenged the action
of the Council in laying down guidelines for Member
States to follow in the negotiations to revise the European
Road Transport Agreement, such action being allegedly a
usurpation by the Council of a function reserved to the
Commission by the EEC Treaty. The Court, although
deciding against the Commission on the merits, held the
action to be admissible: the Commission had *locus standi*
(see below), and the Council's action in laying down
guidelines did amount to an act having legally binding
consequences for the Member States and one therefore
reviewable under Article 173. On this last point the Court
disagreed with the advocate general in whose view the
Council's discussion of the guidelines could not constitute
an act of the Council open to review under Article 173(1).
The Court did not accept that the Article was confined to
the category of acts (regulations, directives and decisions)
enumerated as legally binding in Article 189.

Although Article 173 refers only to "acts of the Council

and the Commission," the question was raised in two cases recently brought before the Court whether acts of the European Parliament can be challenged under that Article. In Case 230/81 *Luxembourg* v. *European Parliament* the Government of Luxembourg challenged a resolution of the European Parliament purporting to decide that future sessions of the Parliament should be held in Strasbourg (and not, as previously, in either Strasbourg or Luxembourg). The Government argued that, under the Treaties, it was for the Member States to fix the seat of the Community institutions. The action was based in part on Article 38 ECSC which does provide for annulment of a measure adopted by the Parliament, but there is no corresponding provision in the EEC and Euratom Treaties and it is open to question whether a provision of the ECSC Treaty can confer jurisdiction in respect of acts common to the three Communities. It is easier to contend that the EEC Treaty governs such common acts. The difficulty then is that Article 173 does not refer to the Parliament. The action was also based on Article 173: it was argued that, by analogy with the *ERTA* decision, that Article provides a remedy against any measure of any institution having legal effects. The Court was content to allow the action under Article 38 ECSC.

The example set by Luxembourg was followed by the Council itself, which in 1982 brought proceedings under Article 173 against the Parliament (Case 72/82) for annulment of the act of the President of the European Parliament declaring that the general budget of the European Communities for the financial year 1982 had been finally adopted. Here it could be argued that, although the gap in Article 173 can be explained historically by the fact that the Parliament had no legally binding powers when the EEC Treaty was drawn up, nevertheless with the development of the Parliament's budgetary powers the Treaty should be interpreted dynamically to avoid the development of a hiatus in the system of judicial protection. However the budgetary dispute was settled on the political level and the Council's action withdrawn.

2. *Who can attack?*

In the first place Article 173(1) enumerates a Member State, the Council or the Commission as competent to bring an action to annul: they are accepted as having a sufficient legal interest to give them *locus standi* for such an action, and for this reason they are sometimes referred to as "privileged applicants." It does not matter that the Member State is attacking some act of a Community institution which relates to another Member State. Thus, in Case 6/54 *Netherlands* v. *High Authority* [1954 to 1956] ECR 103, the Court permitted the Netherlands to seek annulment of a decision of the High Authority relating to German coal companies: not only Germany but the other Member States had a sufficient interest in the legality (or otherwise) of that decision. Again, the Council has *locus standi* in relation to the acts of the Commission, and *vice versa*. Suits of this kind are very rare: one example is the *ERTA* case (22/70, discussed above). Another is the pair of *Staff Salaries* cases (Case 81/72 *Commission* v. *Council* [1973] ECR 575; Case 70/74 *Commission* v. *Council* [1975] ECR 795).

These cases concerned the Staff Regulations governing Community civil servants, which provide for an annual review of salaries by the Council after a report by the Commission. The Council is required to take into account various factors, including inflation, the rise in salaries of civil servants in the Member States, etc. How to quantify these factors had led to disagreement with the staff associations, to resolve which a scheme was eventually negotiated and embodied in a Council decision. The decision was expressed to be applicable for three years, but at the next annual review the Council made a salaries regulation which the Commission alleged to be in breach of the scheme. Accordingly, it sought to annul the regulation. The main issue before the Court was whether the decision of the Council was legally binding or a mere statement of policy, a "policy decision." The Court, declining to follow the view of Advocate General Warner, held the policy decision to be binding on the ground, first, that it laid down basic principles for reviewing salaries, and, secondly, that it was announced as applicable for three years and consequently the Community staff were entitled to rely upon it. It followed that the salaries regulation was invalid in that it conflicted with the policy decision; the Council had therefore to devise new arrangements. These were in turn the subject of proceedings to annul brought by the Commission (Case 70/74, above): this failed for reasons which need not concern us here.

More troublesome has been the defining of the sufficiency of interest requisite for natural and legal persons under Article 173(2). The Court has not pursued a consistent policy, being anxious, on the one hand, to allow individuals or companies an opportunity to seek annulment of acts of the Council or the Commission, yet on the other hand fearful of finding itself overwhelmed by a flood of such suits. Accordingly, it is difficult to reconcile the conflicting cases. One conclusion is clear: it is now exceedingly difficult for an individual or company to satisfy the test of "direct and individual concern" as prescribed under the second limb of Article 173(2).

That limb allows only a decision to be attacked, not a (true) regulation: Case 789/79 *Calpak* [1980] ECR 1949. If the decision is addressed to the applicant, no problem arises. A common instance is where the Commission has issued a decision declaring the applicant to be infringing the competition law of the Community: landmark cases in which the applicants have then challenged such decisions include Cases 56 and 58/64 *Consten and Grundig* v. *Commission* [1966] ECR 299; Case 6/72 *Continental Can* [1973] ECR 215; Case 17/74 *Transocean Marine Paint Association* v. *Commission* [1974] ECR 1063. If however the decision is in the *form* of a regulation or is addressed to some other person, the applicant has then to establish that it is of direct and individual concern to him.

In relatively few cases have applicants succeeded in satisfying the Court of their direct and individual concern. In Cases 106 and 107/63 *Toepfer* v. *Commission* [1965] ECR 405, the Commission addressed to the German Government a decision authorising it to impose a levy on the import of maize. The applicants were two of the largest maize importers and sought to have the decision annulled. On the question of admissibility the Court held that the applicants were *directly* affected by the decision addressed to their Government, since a decision authorising protective measures of this kind was to be regarded as directly applicable. The applicants were also individually concerned because at the time of the decision the Commission knew that there were only 27 importers (of which the applicants were two) whose import applications could be affected by the decision in issue.

The Court here applied a formula which it had first propounded in the *Clementines* case (Case 25/62 *Plaumann* [1963] ECR at 107) where it stated:

> "Persons other than those to whom a decision is addressed may only claim to be individually concerned if that decision affects them by reason of certain attributes which are peculiar to them or by reason of circumstances in which they are differentiated from all other persons and by virtue of these factors distinguishes them individually just as in the case of the person addressed."

Plaumann, an importer of clementines, was held not to satisfy this test.

The *Plaumann* formula was again applied by the Court in Case 62/70 *Bock* v. *Commission* [1971] ECR 897, where the applicant was one of a limited category of importers of Chinese mushrooms who would be affected by a decision of the Commission addressed to the German Government authorising it to prohibit some mushroom imports, a prohibition which that Government had already made clear it wished to impose. At the date of the decision the

number and identity of the importers concerned was
already fixed and ascertainable, and this factor differentiated them from all other persons in accordance with the
Plaumann formula, distinguishing Bock and his fellow
importers individually just as in the case of the person
addressed. Accordingly, the application was held
admissible.

The *Apples* case (Cases 41 to 44/70 *International Fruit
Company* v. *Commission* [1971] ECR 411) concerned not
a decision but a regulation. The Commission had introduced a system whereby it issued licences for import of
dessert apples into the EEC, on the basis of weekly data
which Member States supplied setting out the licences
applied for in each State; the Commission gave its
decision by means of regulations. At the moment when
the regulation was adopted, the number of applications
was fixed and no new applications could be added. It was
on the basis of the global amount applied for that the
Commission decided what percentage of each individual
application should be allowed. A Dutch apple importer
objected to the reduction of its application and challenged
the relevant regulation under Article 173. The Court held
that the regulation had to be regarded as a bundle of
individual decisions taken by the Commission, each of
which, although in the form of a regulation, affected the
legal position of one of the applicants. Thus, the decision
was of individual concern to the Dutch importer within
the terms of Article 173(2). As the decision directly
affected the applicant, it was also of "direct concern" to
him.

The Court did not attempt to reconcile this decision
with the earlier case of *Compagnie Française Commerciale
et Financière* v. *Commission* (Case 64/69 [1970] ECR 221)
where it refused to accept Advocate General Roemer's
view that the regulation in question was really a decision
since the persons affected by it were a closed category
whose identity was ascertainable. But in the more recent
case of *C.A.M., SA* v. *Council and Commission* (Case 100/74

[1975] ECR 1393) the Court disregarded (*sub silentio*) the *Compagnie Française* case and followed its approach in the *Apples* case: since the applicant was one of a fixed and identifiable category he was individually concerned; and the Court also found that he was also directly concerned. It followed that the application was admissible.

As we have seen, Article 173(2) refers to "a decision addressed to another person" being open to challenge if the claimant can show the necessary direct and individual concern. In most of the cases the decision has been addressed to a Member State government, but the Court from the first saw no difficulty in interpreting "person" to include a government (*e.g. Toepfer*, above). A further and novel point of interpretation arose in Case 26/76 *Metro* v. *Commission* [1977] ECR 1875.

Here the Commission had addressed a decision to SABA, a German producer of electronic equipment. The decision followed a complaint lodged with the Commission by Metro, who operated as self-service wholesalers of such goods. SABA had refused to recognise Metro as distributors of their products because Metro was unable (or unwilling) to comply with their usual conditions of sale. Metro then asked the Commission to strike down these conditions as in restraint of competition and so contrary to Article 85 EEC; they invoked the procedure under Council Regulation 17 under which anyone with a "legitimate interest" may complain to the Commission of infringements of Articles 85 and 86.

The Commission, after an investigation, concluded that, subject to some minor modifications, the SABA conditions did not infringe Article 85 and it addressed to SABA a decision to this effect. It also informed Metro of its decision.

Metro challenged the decision addressed to SABA. The Court upheld the action as admissible under Article 173(2). In a somewhat cryptic judgment, illuminated by the opinion of Advocate General Reischl, who invoked the *Plaumann* formula (p. 98 above), the Court simply ruled that it was in the interests of a satisfactory administration of justice that Metro should be considered to be directly and individually concerned by the Commission's decision. Certainly, by complaining the applicants had "distinguished themselves individually" and "differentiated themselves" from self-service wholesalers generally (all of whom were affected by the conditions of sale in issue). As for directness, the judgment appears to endorse *sub silentio* the argument of the advocate general that, although the decision merely *empowered* SABA to maintain their sale conditions, it was a commercial certainty that they would embrace the decision in order to keep the system complained of by Metro.

As the above cases demonstrate the Court has laid more emphasis on the requirement of individual concern than that of direct concern: if the more difficult obstacle of the former can be overcome, the latter seems almost at times to be assumed. Nevertheless, the Court has sought to define direct concern and has done so by analogy to the doctrine of direct effect. Thus, if the addressee of the decision is left no margin of discretion as to how the decision is to be applied, then that decision will be of direct concern to the applicant. As we saw above, in *Toepfer,* the Commission's decision addressed to the German Government was one falling within the doctrine of direct effect: since the applicant could have invoked that doctrine in relation to the decision, the latter was also of direct concern to him. Likewise, in the *Japanese Ball-Bearings* cases direct concern was accepted because the national measures implementing the Community provisions in question were purely automatic. On the other hand, in Case 69/69 *Alcan* [1970] ECR 385, the applicant was not directly concerned because the two Member States to whom the decision (refusing them a certain import quota) was addressed retained a complete discretion how (if at all) to allocate any quota granted to them. Moreover, quite apart from the question of direct effect, direct concern is established if it can be shown (as

in *Bock* above) that the addressee has already tied his own
hands in advance of the decision; for there is then a close
causal connection between the eventual decision and the
application of that decision by the addressee with regard
to the applicant. The same reasoning was extended, as we
have just seen, in the *Metro* case.

On *locus standi* Article 33 ECSC differs in several
respects from Article 173 EEC. In the first place, only
undertakings (*entreprises,* in the French text) can sue and
not individuals: and the right of action is further limited to
undertakings engaged in production in the coal and steel
industries (Art. 80 ECSC). Secondly, the undertaking
must show *either* that the challenged decision or recommendation (the term used in the earlier Treaty for a
directive) is "individual in character" *or* that the decision
or recommendation, although general in character, involves a misuse of power affecting that undertaking.
Thirdly, there is no requirement under Article 33 ECSC
of *direct* concern: no doubt because, under the scheme of
the ECSC Treaty, the High Authority is the hub of the
Community, decisions radiating directly from the High
Authority to the undertakings without the mediation of
the national authorities.

In the early decisions on this Article the Court adopted
a liberal interpretation: the floodgate which the Court has
hesitated to open too wide under Article 173 EEC could
at most under Article 33 ECSC only admit the limited
number of coal and steel undertakings. Thus, in Cases 7
and 9/54 *Groupement des Industries Sidérurgiques Luxembourgeoises* v. *High Authority* [1954–1956] ECR 175 the
applicants brought proceedings under Article 33 ECSC
against the implied refusal of the High Authority to
declare illegal a Luxembourg levy on coal imports. The
Luxembourg Government intervened in the proceedings
to argue that the applicants had no *locus standi* as they
were a steel-producing, not coal-producing firm. The
Court had little difficulty in rejecting this plea. The Court
agreed with the advocate general that there was no

provision in the Treaty which required that the particular
product made by the producer should be connected with
the subject-matter of the dispute and that the silence of
the Treaty on this point could not be interpreted in any
manner which would be detrimental to companies. The
Court also appeared to accept that the act being challenged (namely, the implied refusal of the High Authority
to declare the levy illegal) was a decision "individual in
character," that is, that it did apply to the applicants
individually. This was hardly surprising as the Group
represented the main consumers of coal in the Grand
Duchy.

The absence of any reference to direct, as distinct from
individual, concern in Article 33 ECSC reflects the quite
different system of the earlier Treaty, in which the High
Authority, true to its name, was to be the real source of
power rather than the Member States. Hence, its relationship with the coal and steel enterprises was necessarily
assumed to be direct, being almost that of overlord to
vassals.

Under the EEC Treaty, covering as it does the entire
economy, the Community's functions are normally exercised through the Member States; and it was therefore
considered appropriate that anyone seeking to challenge a
Community measure directly before the Court should
have to show both individual and direct concern. In its
earlier decisions on Article 173 EEC, however, the Court
of Justice, perhaps conditioned by its experience under
the ECSC Treaty, laid more emphasis on the first of these
two requirements, as we have seen.

3. *Within what time limits?*

Article 173(3) EEC lays down a time limit of two
months for bringing proceedings to annul. This period is
calculated from the publication of the measure in issue, or
from its notification to the applicant, or, in the absence of
publication or notification, from the date when it came to
his knowledge. Under Article 33 ECSC the corresponding
time limit is one month.

So short a time limit as one or two months, while desirable in the interests of legal certainty, can give rise to problems. As we shall see below (p. 112) Article 184 (Art. 36 ECSC) may provide a partial solution, and, as we have already noted (p. 92), other forms of challenge to validity escape such stringent time limits. Moreover, in Cases 6 and 11/69 *Commission* v. *French Republic* [1969] ECR 523 the Court was prepared to entertain a plea by the French Government that the Commission had reached a decision in a field reserved by the EEC Treaty to the Member States, even though the time limits to challenge under Article 173 had expired, for in the Court's words, "if this allegation were valid, the above-mentioned decision would lack all legal basis in the Community legal system." It seems possible that the Court was here adopting from French administrative law the notion, well developed there, of the *inexistence* of an administrative act taken wholly without legal authority: such an act may be declared non-existent even outside the normal French time limit (of two months) for annulment proceedings.

4. *On what grounds?*

Article 173 EEC sets out four grounds for annulment. These are:

    (a) lack of competence (or authority)
    (b) infringement of an essential procedural requirement
    (c) infringement of the EEC Treaty or of any rule of law relating to its application
    (d) misuse of powers

All four grounds appear to raise only questions of law, not of fact nor of the merits of the challenged act. But the Court may be led inevitably into a review of the facts as found by the Council or Commission if, for example, the issue is whether there is such a manifest error of fact as to constitute a violation of law. The lines between the four grounds are fluid and one or more may be pleaded in the alternative or in combination. The Court is always at pains to avoid undue formalism in proceedings brought before it.

Historically, the grounds are derived from French administrative law where the *Conseil d'Etat* has elaborated in its case law the precise meaning of the corresponding French terms: *incompétence, vice de forme, violation de la loi, détournement de pouvoir.* Community law, however, has a life of its own, and reference to French decisions would, at best, be only persuasive authority in the Court of Justice. Moreover, German and, latterly, English administrative law have influenced the development of the grounds of review at Luxembourg.

The grounds in Article 173 EEC, with certain limited exceptions, correspond to those in Article 33 ECSC. Some of the illustrative cases now to be discussed derive from the ECSC Treaty.

Thus, Case 9/56 *Meroni* v. *High Authority* [1958] ECR 133 is a useful example of both lack of competence and an infringement of the ECSC Treaty. The High Authority imposed certain levies on scrap iron on the basis of decisions taken by a subordinate body (the Scrap Bureau) to which the Authority had purported to delegate its powers. The Court quashed the levies on the grounds, first, that the Treaty had been infringed inasmuch as it did not permit the Authority to delegate its decision-making powers (*delegatus non potest delegare*), and secondly, that there was a lack of competence on the part of the Authority to proceed as it had.

Procedural infringements are commonly invoked, and it is then for the Court to assess whether the infringement is of an *essential* requirement. Thus, in Cases 8 to 11/66 *Cement-Convention* case [1967] ECR 75, it was pleaded that the failure to give sufficient reasons for the decisions in question constituted the infringement of an essential procedural requirement, namely, the general rule in Article 190 that decisions of the Commission shall state the reasons on which they are based. The same Article was successfully invoked in Case 24/62 *Germany* v. *Commission* [1963] ECR 63, when the Commission partially rejected Germany's application to import a large quantity of wine from outside the Community for blending into "Brennwein" for domestic consumption. By way of reasons the Commission simply stated that its decision was based on "information that has been gathered indicating that the production of wines of this nature within the Community is amply sufficient."

The Court explained the purposes of the requirement of reasoning as follows:

> "In imposing upon the Commission the obligation to state reasons for its decisions, Article 190 is not taking mere formal considerations into account but seeks to give an opportunity to the parties of defending their rights, to the Court of exercising its supervisory functions and to Member States and to all interested nationals of ascertaining the circumstances in which the Commission has applied the Treaty."

To attain these objectives a decision must set out, in a concise but clear and relevant manner, the principal issues of law and of fact upon which it is based.

Another instance of an "essential procedural requirement" is the requirement that the Council should consult the European Parliament on proposals for legislation when the Treaty so prescribes. Thus in Cases 138 and 139/79 *Roquette* and *Maizena* v. *Council* [1980] ECR 3333 and 3393 producers of isoglucose sought the annulment of a Council regulation imposing a levy on isoglucose, contending that the requirement of consultation of the European Parliament had not been observed as the Parliament, although asked for its opinion, had not given its opinion when the regulation was adopted by the Council. The Parliament intervened to support the applicants (see p. 212) and the Court annulled the regulation.

The third ground of annulment includes, as we have seen, both treaty infringements and an infringement of any rule of law relating to the application of the relevant Treaty. This last expression has been liberally construed by the Court. Thus, it includes all legislation made pursuant to the Treaties (*e.g.* regulations or directives) and such general principles as are recognised in international law, or such "general principles common to the laws of the Member States" as the Court deems to be applicable in the particular case.

The expression "general principles common to the laws of the Member States" is only expressly referred to in Article 215 EEC where these principles are declared the basis of the non-contractual (below, p. 121) liability of the Community. The principles, however, have been extended beyond this narrow but important context and may be invoked under other Articles, such as Article 173. Moreover, despite the absence of any reference to such general principles in the ECSC Treaty, the Court has in several ECSC cases (some prior to the EEC Treaty) invoked these principles. Examples include the principle of proportionality of administrative acts (in Case 8/55 *Fédéchar* v. *High Authority* [1954–1956] ECR 245), and the principles of legal certainty and of due process (in Cases 42 and 49/59 *SNUPAT* v. *High Authority* [1961] ECR 53. More recently, there has been an important extension of this doctrine of general principles to embody fundamental rights, as in Case 29/69 *Stauder* v. *Ulm* [1969] ECR 419, the *Internationale Handelsgesellschaft* case (Case 11/70 [1970] ECR 1125), and the Second *Nold* case (Case 4/73 [1974] ECR 491) in which the Court roundly declared that "fundamental rights form an integral part of the general principles of law, the observance of which it ensures" (below, p. 272). But whereas, in the cases mentioned, the Court finally concluded that there had been no breach of the principles invoked, more than lip service was paid to the principles in the *Transocean Marine Paint Association* case, in which the Court decided, at the prompting of Advocate General Warner, that the Commission had acted in breach of the principle of natural justice as embodied in the maxim *audi alteram partem* (Case 17/74 [1974] ECR 1063).

The remaining ground for review under Article 173 EEC is misuse of powers. This is a well developed notion in some continental systems of administrative law: the French text speaks of *détournement de pouvoir*, a notion familiar in French administrative law. English law variously acknowledges the same notion under such labels as abuse of power, misuse of power or bad faith. As interpreted by the Court, the term includes not only the use of a power for an unlawful purpose but also its use for a purpose, itself lawful, but not the one contemplated in conferring the power in question. An early decision to explore this ground under Article 33 ECSC was Case 1/54 *French Republic* v. *High Authority* [1954–1956] ECR 1.

In this case the High Authority had taken three decisions purportedly on the basis of Article 60 ECSC so as to prevent discrimination in prices. The French Government argued that the real object of the Authority had been to secure a general reduction in prices and the prevention of price agreements: for these objects the Authority should have exercised the powers conferred upon it by Articles 61 and 65. Accordingly, it was argued, there had been a misuse of powers. The Court held that there was no misuse of powers where (as in the case) the act complained of has as its dominant or primary object the purpose for which that power is conferred, even though the act achieves incidentally some other object which is not properly the object of the power in question.

By contrast with the EEC Treaty, under Article 33 ECSC misuse of powers may be invoked by undertakings to challenge general, as distinct from individual, decisions or recommendations. This point arose in Case 8/55 *Fédéchar* v. *High Authority* [1954–1956] ECR 245. The applicants were an association of Belgian collieries. They challenged the validity of a decision of the Authority fixing lower prices for coal as a result of which three collieries within the Association would receive lower compensation payments. The Authority contested the argument of the Association that the decision was on that account individual in character and so open to review on any of the four grounds. The Authority maintained that the fact that a decision might have different effects for different collieries was not relevant in determining the nature of the decision: a decision was general or individual according to the scope of its application, and the decision in question had a general character as it was intended to be general in effect and to apply to all the firms falling within its scope. The Court accepted this argument, with the consequence that the applicants were limited to establishing a misuse of powers as the only ground for annulling the decision, and this they failed to show on the facts.

5. *What effect has annulment?*

Article 176 states that the institution whose act has been declared void shall be required to take the necessary measures to comply with the Court's judgment. Article 34 ECSC is in similar terms.

The Court has accepted the principle that a challenged act, like the curate's egg, may be bad in part only. Thus, in Cases 56 and 58/64 *Consten and Grundig* v. *Commission* [1966] ECR 299, C and G had entered into an agreement whereby C was to be sole agent for G in France. Competitors wishing to sell G's products in France complained to the Commission that the agreement infringed Article 85 EEC. The Commission agreed with the complainants and issued a decision declaring an infringement of Article 85. This decision was challenged by C and G under Article 173. The Court held that the decision was partly valid and partly invalid inasmuch as the agreement in part infringed Article 85 but in part did not. The Court followed in this respect its earlier decision in Case 6/54 *Netherlands* v. *High Authority* [1954–1956] ECR 103, under the ECSC Treaty, where part only of a decision was annulled for lack of adequate reasons. Not all the national laws of the Member States permit such severability of the good from the bad: the late Professor de Smith could discern no clear principle in English administrative law. (S.A. de Smith, *Judicial Review of Administrative Action* (3rd ed., 1973), pp. 91–92).

Where a regulation is annulled, Article 174(2) expressly provides that the Court may, if it considers this necessary, state which of the effects of the void regulation shall be considered as definitive. Thus, as we have seen above in Case 81/72 *Commission* v. *Council* [1973] ECR 575, a Council regulation laying down a scale for staff salaries within the Community institutions was declared void, but in order that salaries could continue to be paid the Court ordered that the regulation should continue in operation until the Council could pass a new (and valid) regulation.

B. *Actions for Inactivity (Article 175)*

The authors of both the ECSC and the EEC Treaties recognised that a remedy should be available not only where an institution had acted illegally but also where it had failed to act. Article 175 EEC and Article 35 ECSC seek to fill this gap.

Article 175(1) states: "Should the Council or the Commission, in infringement of this Treaty, fail to act, the Member States and the other institutions of the Community may bring an action before the Court of Justice to have the infringement established." And Article 175(3) confers upon individuals and companies the right to complain to the Court that an institution has failed to address to the complainant any act other than a recommendation or an opinion.

It should be noted that Article 175 permits the European Parliament, as one of "the other institutions of the Community," to bring the Council or Commission before the Court for a failure to act. This would enable the Parliament, as well as intervening before the Court as in *Roquette* and *Maizena* (above, p. 106), to sue in its own name, to enforce its right to be consulted in the many cases where this is required by the Treaties. But the Article would also permit the Parliament to bring an action in other cases of inactivity by the Council or Commission, for example, (prior to 1976) the failure to agree on direct elections to the Parliament itself. On at least two occasions the Parliament went so far as to threaten such proceedings.

An action under Article 175 is only admissible if the institution in default has first been called upon to act. If then, within two months of being so called upon, the institution has not defined its position, the action may be brought within a further period of two months. This procedure is prescribed by Article 175(2).

There are two further obstacles to success in proceedings under Article 175 which are more difficult to overcome. The first arises from the requirement that the applicant (if not a Member State or a Community institution) must apparently show that the desired act would have been addressed to him, when it will often be the case that he wanted the defendant (normally the Commission) to take a decision in respect of someone else: for example against another undertaking which he alleges is infringing the EEC competition rules. It would be more consistent with the purpose of Article 175 if the same test of *locus standi* were applied as under Article 173, namely that the desired act would have been of direct and individual concern to him: see the advocate-general's opinion in Case 15/71 *Mackprang* v. *Commission* [1971] ECR 797 at 807–808.

Secondly, the defendant will be able to meet the complaint of failure to act if it has "defined its position." As the cases show (see for example Case 48/65 *Lütticke* v. *Commission* [1966] ECR 19 and Case 125/78 *GEMA* v. *Commission* [1979] ECR 3173), the Commission may be able to "define its position" without adopting a measure which can be challenged under Article 173. In contrast, under the ECSC Treaty, the decisions of the Court establish that a complaint of inactivity (under Article 35) can be met only by a binding act, which will itself be liable to challenge under Article 33. There is therefore an apparent gap in the protection afforded under the EEC Treaty, although the existence of such a gap has been ingeniously disputed (see Hartley, *The Foundations of European Community Law*, pp. 406–409). The fact remains that no action brought under Article 175 EEC has to date succeeded.

C. *Plea of Illegality (Article 184)*

This (to English ears) curiously named remedy is derived from French administrative law where it is known as *l'exception d'illégalité*. A close parallel in English procedure is where a challenge is raised collaterally to the validity of a statutory instrument or byelaw in a prosecution for its infringement. In Community law it is a means of challenging an illegal act, even after the lapse of the time limit imposed by Article 173. The plea, if successful, renders the act, not void, but "inapplicable." This is made clear by the language of Article 184: "Notwithstanding the expiry of the period laid down in the third paragraph of Article 173, any party may, in proceedings in which a regulation of the Council or of the Commission is in issue, plead the grounds specified in the first paragraph of Article 173, in order to invoke before the Court of Justice the inapplicability of that regulation."

The remedy under Article 184 is an important supplement to that given under Article 173. In the first place it mitigates the effect of the very short time limit under the latter Article. For, although the regulation in issue may now have become immune from annulment by lapse of time, a decision based upon that regulation may be challenged by the person affected through the plea of illegality. This will permit a party to have the decision set aside upon satisfying the Court that the "parent" regulation is tainted with illegality on one or more of the grounds set out in Article 173. The Court will then hold the regulation "inapplicable" in the particular case, so that the decision becomes without legal foundation.

Whereas Article 173 may be invoked, as we have seen, against a wide category of acts, the plea of illegality only lies, on a strict reading of Article 184, against a regulation. But in Case 92/78 *Simmenthal* v. *Commission* [1979] ECR 777, the Court of Justice interpreted Article 184 as giving expression to a general principle conferring upon any party to proceedings the right to challenge, for the purpose of obtaining the annulment of a decision of direct and individual concern to that party, the validity of previous acts of the institutions which form the legal basis of the decision that is being attacked, but which that party lacked *locus standi* to challenge under Article 173.

Thus, in *Simmenthal,* the applicant was allowed to bring the plea against a general notice of tender issued by the Commission for the purchase, by importers such as Simmenthal, of meat held by an intervention agency. The general notice, though not in form a regulation, was held to be analogous in effect and normative in character: it could therefore be challenged by way of Article 184, although the applicant was directly and individually affected only by the consequent decision of the Commission which fixed the price for tenders from Italian importers at a price above that offered by Simmenthal, thereby leading to the rejection of the tender.

The plea of illegality reconciles two otherwise conflicting policies of Community law. On the one hand, there is the policy, in the interest of legal certainty (*sécurité juridique*), of making the acts of Community institutions unimpeachable after short time limits; on the other, there is the countervailing policy, exemplified in Article 184 (Article 36 ECSC), of not allowing an illegal act, although perfected by lapse of time, to "father" further illegal acts: a party affected thereby may challenge the offspring as illegal because of the original illegality of the parent regulation. If the challenge succeeds, the regulation is rendered inapplicable in the particular case. To that extent, one may speak of the "relative nullity" of the regulation, that is, relative to the particular party who has invoked the plea. But the regulation is not thereby rendered absolutely null and void: in the unlikely event of it being invoked again to found a further decision, a party affected by that decision will be obliged, in turn, to invoke the plea: otherwise the decision will be valid.

The plea is also important in another respect. We have seen that the rules of *locus standi* under Article 173 are very restrictive so far as actions by individuals or companies are concerned. In particular, a private party cannot challenge a regulation, unless it is in substance a decision of direct and individual concern to him. The plea, however, permits the private party to plead the illegality of any regulation (or a general decision or recommendation under the ECSC Treaty) which is now being applied in a specific decision affecting him.

It should be emphasised that the plea does not provide an independent cause of action but can only be invoked where proceedings are already properly before the Court under some other Article of the Treaties. The Court has made this clear in the *Wöhrmann* and *Dalmas* cases relating to Article 184 EEC and Article 36(3) ECSC respectively (Cases 31 and 33/62 [1962] ECR 501 and Case 21/64 [1965] ECR 175). Commonly, the plea is made in conjunction with an action to annul under Article 173 (or Art. 33 ECSC). But in Cases 42 and 49/59 *SNUPAT* v. *High Authority* [1961] ECR 53, it was invoked in an action for inactivity under Article 35 ECSC. It could also arise in a staff case under Article 179 EEC (see Case 20/71 *Sabbatini* v. *European Parliament*, p. 146, below).

An illustration of the plea is provided by Case 9/56 *Meroni* v. *High Authority* [1958] ECR 133, a case arising under the ECSC Treaty and involving, *inter alia,* Article 36(3) which states: "In support of its appeal, a party may, under the same conditions as in the first paragraph of Article 33 of this Treaty, contest the legality of the decision or recommendation which that party is alleged not to have observed."

M was appealing against a decision of the High Authority of October 24, 1956 which imposed a pecuniary obligation and was accordingly enforceable pursuant to Art. 92 ECSC. By the decision the Authority requested M to pay a levy on scrap bought by M for its steel production. This decision was based upon two general decisions (No. 22 of 1954 and No. 14 of 1955) which founded the general system of levies on scrap imports, a system administered by a special "Scrap Bureau." To support its action (under Art. 33 ECSC) challenging the decision of October 24, 1956, M alleged (under Art. 36(3) ECSC) the illegality of decisions Nos. 22/54 and 14/55 on grounds which we have previously discussed. The Authority argued that M's case should be dismissed as the time limit of one month under Article 33 had long expired so that the question of the illegality of decisions Nos. 22/54 and 14/55 was out of time and statute-barred.

The Court held that the plea of illegality could be raised by M under Article 36(3). For, although the language of Article 36 is limited to appeals against pecuniary penalties, the Article is the application of a general principle, namely, the plea of illegality, and this can be raised at any time to challenge the irregularity of general decisions or recommendations upon which the individual decision is based. The plea, however, cannot lead to the annulment of the general decision but only to the annulment of the individual decision based upon it.

The Court went still further in its bold interpretation of Article 36(3). For it proceeded to hold that, notwithstanding the words "under the same conditions as in the first paragraph of Article 33," the scope of the plea was not limited to misuse of powers, despite this being the sole ground upon which a private party could challenge a general decision under Article 33: rather, all the four grounds could be invoked in support of the plea. As we saw in the previous discussion of this case, M successfully pleaded the grounds of both lack of competence and infringement of the Treaty.

Having considered the nature of the plea, we must now examine by whom it may be made. The plea may not be invoked by a Community institution, for the apparent purpose of this remedy is to protect the interests of a private party against the threatened application of an illegal general act, such as a regulation. Moreover, Community institutions are not subject to the restrictive rules of *locus standi* applicable to private parties in annulment proceedings: the Council or Commission have an unrestricted opportunity to challenge general acts under Article 173, subject only to the two months time limit.

So far as concerns private parties, an individual or a company can rely upon Article 184, but under Article 36(3) ECSC the plea of illegality may be invoked only by the limited class of undertakings having *locus standi* under Article 33 ECSC (above, p. 102).

Under Article 184 EEC the extent to which a Member State may invoke the plea is not entirely settled. In Case 32/65 *Italy* v. *Council and Commission* [1966] ECR 389 the Court impliedly accepted that a Member State could do so when challenging a regulation under Article 173: Italy there invoked Article 184 to extend its challenge to earlier (and related) regulations. The justification for this is questioned by some authors on the ground that a Member State has the same opportunity as the Council or Commission to challenge any act, including regulations, directly under Article 173. The Court went some way to recognise the point in Case 156/77 *Commission* v. *Belgium* [1978] ECR 1881 where, in the course of enforcement proceedings brought against Belgium by the Commission under Article 93 in respect of a prohibited State aid (above, p. 83), the Belgian Government sought to invoke the plea against a specific decision addressed to it which it had failed to challenge directly and timeously by an action under Article 173. The Court ruled that the plea "can in no case be invoked by a Member State to whom an individual decision has been addressed." If, then, a Member State may invoke the plea against a regulation, but not against an individual decision addressed to it, the question remains open whether it may do so against a directive, which may not be individual in character but may be addressed to it.

For the comparative lawyer the plea is a particular illustration of the insertion into the Treaties by the founding Member States of a concept well known in civil law systems but one which the common lawyer of the United Kingdom or the Irish Republic hardly recognises as a form of judicial review, although, as Professor Garner observes (*Administrative Law* (5th ed.), p. 217), in practice it is common enough for the substantive or procedural validity of byelaws, regulations or executive action to be raised as a defence in criminal proceedings taken to enforce administrative decisions.

Chapter 7

PLENARY JURISDICTION

Introduction

The title of this chapter calls for explanation, especially for common lawyers. In French administrative law a broad division is made, in suits brought to the administrative courts, between actions to annul and *recours de pleine juridiction,* that is, actions where the court is asked to exercise its fullest powers, for example by awarding damages against the administration or by itself revising (as distinct from merely quashing) the administrative act submitted to it. This notion of plenary jurisdiction was carried over into the EEC Treaty as one familiar to French and other continental systems of administrative law. It appears, for instance, in Article 172 EEC where, in the English text, the Court is given "unlimited jurisdiction" in regard to penalties provided for in the regulations made by the Council pursuant to the Treaty. This means that the Court can not only cancel such a penalty but also alter its amount. This is made explicit in Article 17 of Regulation 17/62 of the Council (relating to competition) which states:

> "The Court shall have unlimited jurisdiction within the meaning of Article 172 of the Treaty to review decisions whereby the Commission has fixed a fine or periodic penalty payment; it may cancel, reduce or increase the fine or periodic penalty payment imposed."

The Court's plenary jurisdiction in the above sense includes the following categories of actions:

    (a) Actions to review penalties (Art. 172 EEC, Art. 36(2) ECSC);

- (b) So-called "staff cases" involving disputes between the Communities and their staff in relation to their terms of service (Article 179 EEC);
- (c) Actions for damages based upon the non-contractual liability of the Communities (Art. 178 EEC, Art. 40 ECSC).

Category (a) has already been briefly referred to above, category (b) is the subject of a separate chapter below. The present chapter will be concerned with category (c). But first reference must be made to the contractual liability of the Communities.

Contractual liability of the Communities

Liability on the part of the Communities may obviously arise in contract as well as in tort: such is the wide range of their activities and functions. In the EEC Treaty, Article 215 draws a distinction, in the terminology more familiar to continental lawyers, between contractual and non-contractual liability, although the latter term, because of its residuary character, could extend beyond tort into the field, for example, of restitution. Under Article 215(1) contractual liability is governed by the law applicable to the contract in question. The law referred to will be whatever national law governs that contract as its proper law, and any litigation arising on the contract will come before the relevant national court.

The jurisdiction of the national courts is exclusive; for the jurisdiction of the Court of Justice arises only where it is expressly conferred by the Treaties, and there is no provision conferring jurisdiction on the Court in these cases, as there is (under Art. 178 EEC) in cases of non-contractual liability. Only where the contract contains an arbitration clause conferring jurisdiction in any dispute upon the Court of Justice (as Art. 181 EEC and Art. 153 Euratom permit) will a question of contractual liability come before the Communities' own Court: *e.g.* Euratom research contracts usually contain such clauses.

Articles 181 EEC and 153 Euratom are applicable whether the contract in question be categorised as "public" or "private"—a distinction derived from French administrative law and embodied in the terms of the Articles.

For a case involving such a contract with Euratom, see Case 23/76 *Pellegrini* [1976] ECR 1807, where the contract included an arbitration clause conferring jurisdiction upon the Court; it also provided that the contract was to be governed by Italian law: the Court accepted jurisdiction and resolved the dispute in accordance with Italian law. Similarly, contracts made between the Commission and universities in the Member States for the provision of various technical services usually embody an arbitration clause and provide for the contract to be governed by the national law of the university in question or of the seat of the Community institution concerned (in the case of the Commission, Belgium). In such cases the Court may find itself determining substantive questions of national law and treating such questions as ones of law (of which it has judicial notice) and not of fact (for which it would require expert evidence). Moreover, such cases in contract are the only instances in which a private individual may find himself the defendant before the Court in a direct action brought by the Community.

For avoidance of doubt, Article 183 EEC makes explicit that the Communities may be a party to a dispute brought before a court or tribunal of a Member State. Thus, "should the Court of Justice purchase some stationery in Luxembourg from a Luxembourg supplier and then, to imagine the unimaginable, default on the purchase price, the supplier would have his remedy in the Luxembourg courts according to Luxembourg law" (Lord Mackenzie Stuart, "The Non-Contractual Liability of the European Economic Community," Maccabaean Lecture in Jurisprudence 1975, 4).

Special considerations apply to contracts of employment entered into by Community institutions with their officials and other servants. As we shall see in the next chapter, such staff disputes are a separate head of the Court's jurisdiction under Article 179 EEC and so fall outside the sphere of application of Articles 178 and 215 EEC: Case 9/75 *Meyer-Burckhardt* [1975] ECR 1171. The law applicable to these contracts will be that laid down in the official Staff Regulations or Conditions of Employment or, in default, "the general rules of administrative law": see, for this phrase, Cases 43, 45, 48/59 *Von Lachmüller* v. *Commission* [1960] ECR 463; also Case 1/55 *Kergall* v. *Common Assembly* [1954–1956] ECR 151.

Non-contractual (including tortious) actions against the Community

This clear-cut pattern in contract contrasts with the Communities' non-contractual liability. Here Article 178 EEC confers exclusive jurisdiction on the Court, by virtue of Article 183.

Why there should be this fundamental divergence in the treatment of contractual and non-contractual liability of the Communities is an interesting question. M. Lagrange, a former advocate general of the Court, suggests an historical explanation (M. Lagrange in [1965–66] 3 C.M.L.Rev. 32). The framers of the ECSC Treaty saw that an independent legal order required special provision to be made for the legal liabilities of the Community arising from contract or of a non-contractual character. Contractual liability could be left to be governed by the more or less uniform principles found in the national laws of the original Member States. But non-contractual liability raised questions of delicacy and importance involving the activities of the Community as a "public authority": the rules governing the liability of public authorities differed considerably in the national laws of the various Member States, nor might they have been wholly appropriate to apply unchanged to the liability of the Community. Accordingly, a conscious choice was made to vest in the Court of Justice exclusive jurisdiction over the non-contractual liability of the Community and to entrust the Court with the fashioning of an independent Community law to govern such liability, guided only by the broad terms of Article 40 ECSC (and later Art. 215(2) EEC, Art. 188(2) Euratom).

M. Lagrange points out that the terms of Article 40 ECSC were borrowed directly from French administrative law. For that system was felt the most appropriate, since, unlike the systems prevailing in the other five Member States, France had entrusted jurisdiction over the tortious liability of public authorities exclusively to its administrative courts (in particular the *Conseil d'Etat*); moreover, that liability was governed by its own public law principles, elaborated in praetorian fashion by the *Conseil d'Etat* in complete independence of the private law principles enshrined in the Civil Code.

The ECSC Treaty therefore adopted the French solution of vesting in one and the same jurisdiction actions for the annulment of official acts and suits for damages arising from the tortious liability of public authorities. In this way, the Court of Justice would be fully equipped to exercise the most effective judicial control over Community institutions. This solution had the added advantage of excluding the national courts from sitting in judgment upon the administrative activities of Community institutions. To have permitted this would have threatened, it was thought, the Community's independence.

Subsequently, the principles in this respect embodied in the ECSC Treaty were carried over without substantial modification into the EEC and Euratom Treaties.

In the result, Articles 178 and 215(2) EEC, read together, render unnecessary any recourse to the principles of private international law so far as the Communities' non-contractual liability is concerned. For Article 178 settles categorically the question of which court shall have jurisdiction, and Article 215(2) determines what principles of substantive law shall govern that liability. In effect, for such liability the *lex causae* is to be the *lex fori:* the Community Court is to apply Community law. What, however, Article 215(2) offers as the Community law governing non-contractual liability is a mere reference to "the general principles common to the laws of the Member States." This vague formula has been left for the Court itself to elaborate in a series of cases. Dependent on the accidents of litigation, the working out of a consistent body of principles is still far from complete. Moreover, the Court has shown itself properly cautious in not wishing to expose the Communities to a flood of speculative claims in damages. The account which follows is therefore necessarily tentative, but the dearth of clear principle does not mean that the subject is not of vital importance as completing the armoury of remedies which the individual needs for his legal protection within the Communities.

Parenthetically, we may observe that the Court has also invoked the same concept of general principles, by way of analogy, in cases not involving liability under Article 215. This wider development of the concept, outside the context of non-contractual liability, calls for separate consideration (Chapter 14).

So far as non-contractual liability is concerned, "the general principles common to the laws of the Member States," to which Article 215(2) refers, provide no certain guide in this matter. There does not exist within the 10 countries of the Communities a common *corpus* of legal principles governing State liability in tort. Comparative study of the 10 national laws (or rather 11, as the Scottish law of reparation is distinct from the English law of tort) is a regular exercise of the Court in the preparation of cases and of the advocates general in their opinions; but, as Professors Kapteyn and VerLoren van Themaat well remark (*Introduction to the Law of the European Communities* (1973), p. 94):

> "This use of the comparative technique is not governed by an *a priori* intent to find the greatest common denominator; rather is it governed by an intent to trace elements from which such legal

> principles and rules can be built up for the Community as will offer an adequate, fair, and fruitful solution for the questions with which the Court is confronted."

In this free-ranging enquiry the Court has established certain essential elements for Community liability: there must be damage, an illegal act on the part of the Community, and a causal link between the damage and the act complained of. A number of leading cases illustrate these elements.

In Cases 5, 7 and 13–24/66 *Kampffmeyer* v. *Commission* [1967] ECR 245, a group of cereal importers, K and others, sued the Commission for damages in respect of its decision to authorise the German Government to take certain "safeguard measures" in the cereal market. Such measures could only be taken legally if there was a threat of "serious disturbances" in the market. In an earlier case of *Toepfer* (Cases 106 and 107/63, p. 98 above) the Court had held that this particular decision of the Commission must be annulled as the Commission had had no grounds to expect serious disturbances. K and the other importers proved that they had been prejudiced by the illegal decision and claimed damages accordingly. The Court found there was liability in principle on the part of the Commission arising from what it categorised as a "faute de service." But the Court deferred a decision on the amount of damages until the plaintiffs had exhausted any remedy they might have against the German Government in the German courts (this latter aspect of the case is returned to later).

As this case shows, although Article 215(2) EEC refers simply to the Community making good any damage caused by its institutions or by its servants in the course of their duties, the practice of the Court appears to require a finding of fault on the part of the Community. The importation of the concept of *faute* into the interpretation of Article 215(2) was no doubt influenced by the fact that the corresponding Article in the earlier ECSC Treaty (Art. 40) specifically based liability upon fault. The Court has usually adopted the distinction known to French administrative law between a *faute de service* and a *faute personnelle,* that is a fault in the functioning of the system as distinct from a purely personal fault by the individual Community servant not linked with his official functions. The former concept of French law is wide enough to overlap what an English lawyer would regard simply as maladministration, to be redressed, if at all, through the Parliamentary Commissioner for Administration: the more narrow English rules which curtail the scope of actions for damages against administrative authorities are therefore little guide to the French-inspired principles governing Community liability.

What constitutes a *faute de service* so as to impose liability on the Community was further examined in Case 4/69 *Lütticke* v. *Commission* [1971] ECR 325. There the Court held that under the general principles referred to in Article 215(2) the liability of the Community presupposed the combination of a number of conditions relating to (a) the reality of the damage, (b) the existence of a causal link between the injury relied upon and the behaviour of the institution complained of, and (c) the illegality of this behaviour. L complained that they were being required by the German Government to pay a tax on imports of powdered milk at too high a rate. After recourse to various remedies without success, they sued the Commission for damages under Article 215(2) on the ground it had a duty to intervene with a Member State who (allegedly) was imposing a tax offending Community law; accordingly, the Commission had defaulted in its duty. On the facts the Court held that the Commission had done all that could be expected of it in its extensive negotiations with the German Government: there had been no failure in its duty. Accordingly, the action was dismissed on the merits, no *faute de service* being established.

By contrast, a *faute de service* was established by the

applicants in Cases 19, 20, 25, 30/69 *Richez-Parise* v. *Commission* [1970] ECR 325. The applicants were Community officials who, on the basis of incorrect information given by the Commission concerning their pensions, had resigned from the service and elected to take their pensions in a certain form; subsequently, the Commission discovered that their advice was misleading but did not immediately inform the applicants to this effect. The Court held that, while the initial information supplied did not constitute a wrongful act, the failure to correct it as soon as the Commission discovered their mistake was a *faute de service.*

Liability arising from legislation

Liability under the terms of Article 215(2) can extend to liability in respect of legislation—what has been referred to in the context of Community law as "normative injustice." Normative is here used to describe an act such as a regulation, laying down a rule, as opposed to an individual decision. The notion that administrative rule-making may give rise to an action for damages is a novelty in English law, but Lord Wilberforce did canvass the possible need for such a remedy in *Hoffman-La Roche & Co.* v. *Secretary of State for Trade and Industry,* [1975] A.C. 295 (H.L.) at 359. Case 5/71 the *Zuckerfabrik Schöppenstedt* case [1971] ECR 975 explored the nature of this normative injustice in Community law. It arises where a Community institution (in this case the Council) has taken a measure of a legislative or normative character, such as a regulation, which measure is subsequently proved to be in breach of the Treaties or other provisions of Community law. But the Court requires, as it stated in the case, "a sufficiently flagrant breach of a superior rule of law protecting individuals." This stringent test was held not to be satisfied in the case. It is enough however that the provision allegedly violated was for the protection of individuals generally rather than for the protection of the particular plaintiffs: there is no equivalent under Article

215 of the requirement of "direct and individual concern" under Article 173. At least the balance of cases appears so to decide (compare Cases 9 and 12/60 *Vloeberghs* [1961] ECR 197, *Meroni*, p. 105, above, *Kampffmeyer*, p. 124, above, *Zuckerfabrik Schöppenstedt*, p. 126, above, and *Compagnie d'Approvisionnement*, p. 132, below).

The *Schöppenstedt* formula cited above was applied by the Court in Cases 83, 94/76, 4, 15, 40/77 *HNL* v. *Council and Commission* [1978] ECR 1209 (part of a series of *Skimmed-Milk Powder* cases).

Over-production of milk in the Community had led to the creation of a skimmed-milk powder "mountain," to reduce which the Council made a regulation requiring animal feed producers to buy skimmed-milk powder from the intervention agencies; the powder would be mixed with the feed to supply protein in place of soya. But as the powder was more expensive than soya, live-stock farmers had to pay more for their animal feed.

The farmers brought various actions to challenge the legality of the Council regulation. One group of actions were brought in the national courts, and the question of the validity of the regulation referred to the Court of Justice under Article 177 (*e.g.* Case 114/76 *Bergmann* v. *Grows-Farm* [1977] ECR 1211; Case 116/76 *Granaria* [1977] ECR 1247). Another group were actions for damages brought directly before the Court of Justice under Article 215(2) EEC: the *HNL* case was in this category.

Judgment was given first in the cases under Article 177. The Court ruled the regulation to be invalid as offending the principle of proportionality so as to produce discrimination between the different agricultural sectors contrary to Article 40(3) EEC.

In the action by *HNL* under Article 215(2) the Court had no difficulty in finding that there had been an infringement of a superior rule of law: the previous ruling under Article 177 had established that the regulation infringed the principles both of proportionality and non-discrimination. The principles were also intended for the protection of individuals. But had there been a sufficiently flagrant breach to justify an award of damages? In the circumstances, the Court held that there had not: where the Community institution was charged, as here, with wide discretionary power to legislate on matters involving choices of economic policy, it would not be liable unless it had manifestly and gravely disregarded the limits on the exercise of its powers. In the Court's view the Council had not shown such disregard, nor was the effect of the invalid regulation upon *HNL* sufficiently serious.

Subsequent cases falling on either side of the line are exemplified by the so-called *Quellmehl, Gritz* and *Isoglucose* cases, all involving Council regulations ruled invalid as discriminatory. In the *Quellmehl* and *Gritz* cases the Court found the Council's violation sufficiently flagrant and awarded damages under Article 215(2) EEC (Cases 64, 113/76, 167, 239/78, 27, 28, 45/79 *Dumortier* [1979] ECR 3091; Case 238/78 *Ireks-Arkady* [1979] ECR 2955; Cases 241, 242, 245–250/78 *DGV* [1979] ECR 3017; Cases 261, 262/78 *Interquell* [1979] ECR 3045); on the other hand, this test was held not to be satisfied in the *Isoglucose* cases (Cases 116, 124/77 *Amylum and Tunnel Refineries* [1979] ECR 3497; Case 143/77 *KSH* v. *Council and Commission* [1979] ECR 3583), in which a gloss appeared to be added to the *Schöppenstedt* formula, the Court stating that liability thereunder could only arise "in exceptional cases where the institution concerned has manifestly and gravely disregarded the limits on the exercise of its powers;" and grave meant "conduct verging on the arbitrary."

Limitation period

As well as being more generous in matters of *locus standi,* actions under Article 215 (or its equivalent in the other Treaties) are subject to a limitation period of five years (Article 43 of the Statute of the Court). This may be compared with the very short period of two months allowed for actions to annul under Article 173 EEC. Article 43 of the Statute makes the period of five years run from the occurrence of the event giving rise to the alleged liability; the period is interrupted if an application for relief is made to the Community institution concerned, in which case, if the institution has not defined its position (*e.g.* by accepting liability) the applicant will have two further months in which to commence proceedings (see Art. 175, p. 111, above).

Case 51/81 *De Franceschi S.p.A. Monfalcone* v. *Council and Commission* [1982] ECR 117 concerned these provisions. The applicant suffered loss through the operation of a Council regulation, published on March 4, 1975 and abolishing certain refunds, which was held invalid by the Court on October 19, 1977 in Joined Cases 124/76 and 20/77. The present action was commenced on March 9, 1981. The defendants argued that proceedings were time-barred, the five-years limitation period having begun to run on March 4, 1975. The Court, however, agreed with the applicant that the period only began to run from the moment when the damage became known: the injurious effects of the regulation were produced only with effect from October 19, 1977, on which date the measure was adjudged unlawful.

Distinctive nature of the remedy

The distinctive nature of the remedy under Article 215 was blurred in the earlier decision of Case 25/62 *Plaumann* v. *Commission* [1963] ECR 95. For there the Court pronounced that an administrative act which had not been annulled could not amount to a wrong founding liability in damages. This view has been rejected in several more recent cases: the Court now acknowledges that the two Articles have different objectives; Article 173 seeking to annul a particular act *erga omnes*; Article 215 providing compensation to the individual who has sustained damage through the faulty exercise of its functions by a Community institution. Thus, in *Zuckerfabrik Schöppenstedt* the plaintiffs sought damages for the loss they had suffered in consequence of a regulation of the Council fixing sugar prices. The Court was prepared to entertain the claim under Article 215 without action also being brought under Article 173, observing (at p. 984) that "in the present case, the non-contractual liability of the Community presupposes at the very least the unlawful nature of the act alleged to be the cause of the damage."

Subsequently, in Case 43/75 *Merkur* [1973] ECR 1055, the Court made explicit its readiness to rule on the illegality of an act in an action brought for damages. Thus, the two-months limitation period in Article 173 may be circumvented either by way of an action under Article 215(2) (subject to a five-years limitation period), or by resort to the plea of illegality under Article 184, or by a preliminary reference as to validity brought by a national court under Article 177 (neither Article 184 nor Article 177 being subject to any period of limitation).

Nevertheless, in several staff cases, claims for damages have been rejected on the ground that the plaintiffs could, by timely proceedings, have sought annulment of the allegedly illegal regulations; having failed to do so, they could not then complain of the damage caused them by such illegality: Case 4/67 *Muller-Collignon* [1967] ECR 365; Cases 15–33, etc., /73 *Schots-Kortner* [1974] ECR 177. The cases seem to illustrate a wider principle: the Court will not usually entertain a claim for damages by a plaintiff who could have sought annulment of the normative act in issue—*vigilantibus non dormientibus iura subveniunt.*

Damage, causation and liability without fault

The Court has avoided laying down firm principles as to the categories of damage which may be claimed or on what basis the actual damages will be calculated. Thus, it has admitted claims for such financial damage as loss of profit or loss due to currency fluctuations (see Cases 5, 7 and 13–24/66 *Kampffmeyer,* above; Case 74/74 *CNTA,* below); and in staff cases, damages may be claimed for anxiety and injured feelings by Community employees wrongfully dismissed or unfairly treated (*e.g.* Case 7/56, 3–7/57 *Algera* [1957 and 1958] ECR 39).

Actual damage must be proved, or at least imminent damage which is foreseeable with sufficient certainty (Cases 56–60/74 *Kampffmeyer* [1976] ECR 711). A mere expectation or likelihood of damage in the future will not suffice. Nor must the damage be too remote: the Court speaks of the need for there to be a causal link between the damage and the act complained of (Case 4/69 *Lütticke, above*).

This causal link was present in Case 74/74 *CNTA* [1975] ECR 533, where an exporter relied, as he claimed that he was entitled to do, on the fact that a payment from Community resources to offset the effects of the devaluation of the dollar would not be discontinued without due notice and, in such reliance, entered into certain binding contracts; the Commission suddenly suppressed the payments, thereby causing the exporter to sustain a quantifiable loss. The Court held him entitled to recover: in the absence of an overriding public interest, the Commission could not abolish the right to these payments without notice but must either provide transitional measures to cushion the effects of suppression or render itself liable in damages. In later proceedings, however, he failed to establish any damage.

Damage may be adjudged to be non-existent where the plaintiff is able to pass on the loss sustained to his customers: the Court so held in the *Quellmehl* and *Gritz* cases (Cases 64, 113/76, 167, 239/78, 27, 28, 45/79 *Dumortier* [1979] ECR 3091; Case 238/78 *Ireks-Arkady* [1979] ECR 2955; Cases 241, 242, 245–250/78 *DGV* [1979] ECR 3017; Cases 261, 262/78 *Interquell* [1979] ECR 3045), but for criticism of this view, see Rudden and Bishop (1981) 6 *European Law Review* 243.

Lord Mackenzie Stuart, speaking extra-judicially, has expressed the view that in the Court's more recent decisions "there can be detected a change of emphasis from the culpability of the administration to the protection of the legitimate interests of the administered," and he raises the question whether Community liability can arise without fault and without illegality. "Can a normative act competently made under the powers contained in the Treaties and justifiable in the Community interest form the basis of a claim for damages if injury has been sustained as its consequence?" (Maccabaean Lecture in Jurisprudence 1975, 20). Two cases touch on this important question.

In Cases 9 and 11/71 *Compagnie d'Approvisionnement* v. *Commission* [1972] ECR 391, certain French importers alleged not only fault on the part of the Commission in that it had acted illegally in fixing certain payments at too low a level, but also that, even in the absence of any illegality on its part, the Commission was liable to them in damages as they had suffered "abnormal and special loss" in comparison with Dutch and German importers. The Court rejected their argument on the ground that the measures in question had been taken in the general economic interest to reduce the consequence of devaluation for the whole body of French importers. Nevertheless, Advocate General Dutheillet de Lamothe left open the possibility that the principle of "equality in the face of public burdens," to which, in effect, the plaintiffs were appealing, might be applied in Community law, as it undoubtedly has in French administrative law, to cover an appropriate case (which this was not).

It should be pointed out, however, that if the French analogy were adopted, breach of the principle would constitute the violation of a general principle of law and, as such, amount in French eyes to an illegality. The *Compagnie d'Approvisionnement* case therefore does not resolve the problem whether the Community can be liable without fault and without illegality.

No less ambiguous in this respect is Case 169/73 *Compagnie Continentale France* v. *Council* [1975] ECR

117. The applicants were exporters of wheat who, in September 1972, had contracted to sell wheat to British customers for delivery in early 1973. They did so in the expectation of being entitled to certain compensatory payments for which the Treaty of Accession made provision. The amount of these payments had been fixed in advance by a draft regulation approved by the Council in July 1972; the regulation would be formally adopted after the Treaty of Accession came into force. This unusual step, as the Council explained, was taken so that dealers in the products covered by the proposed regulation should know with certainty what payments to expect from the beginning of 1973. However, the actual regulation which was adopted in January 1973 contained a modification permitted by the Treaty but having the effect of substantially reducing the value of the compensatory payments due to the applicants, a reduction made all the more substantial by the general rise in the price of wheat on the world market.

The advocate general advised the Court that, in his view, the Council's resolution of July 1972 which approved the regulation amounted to a promise to all interested parties that the text would be applied. It therefore had the consequence in law of imposing liability on the Community, because "the protection of confidence is a principle recognised in the Community legal system."

The Court rejected the applicants' claim for want of the necessary causal link between the acts of the Community and the damage suffered. It differed from the advocate general by holding that Community liability might have arisen, not because of reliance upon the Council's promise, but rather because of the Council's failure to give warning that it must act in accordance with the Treaty of Accession and that the application of the Treaty depended upon prevailing world prices for wheat. On either view, liability would have been based upon fault, that is a *faute de service*.

In the Coal and Steel Treaty Article 34 provides

specifically that, where a decision or recommendation of the High Authority is annulled in circumstances involving a *faute de service* on the part of the Community, undertakings which have suffered direct and special harm in consequence have the right to damages. As the Article is not limited to individual decisions, liability appears to extend to normative injustice, provided that the legislative measure has been annulled. The undertakings referred to in the Article are the limited category of coal and steel *producers* defined in Article 80 ECSC.

In Case 9, 12/60 *Vloeberghs* v. *High Authority* [1961] ECR 197, the applicant was a Belgium firm of coal *distributors*. It claimed damages from the High Authority on the ground that the latter had refused to bring an enforcement action against France under Article 88 ECSC, although the French Government had banned Vloeberghs from bringing into France coal which it had imported into Belgium from outside the Community, thereby causing it loss. The Court rejected the High Authority's argument that Article 34 was an exhaustive statement of the right to damages in these circumstances, and that Vloeberghs, as a distributor, could sue neither under that Article nor under Article 40. The Court allowed the action under Article 40, although it rejected as inadmissible the parallel action brought by Vloeberghs under Article 35 for the High Authority's failure to act (Article 35 being only available to coal and steel *producers*).

Acts of Community Servants

Often the wrongful or illegal act of a Community institution is anonymous in that it cannot be ascribed to any particular civil servant of the Communities. Sometimes, however, the fault can be laid at the door of an individual servant. In this event, EEC Article 215(2), like ECSC Article 40, limits the non-contractual liability of the Community to acts of servants in the performance of their duties. For such acts the party injured can claim damages against the Communities in the Court of Justice. If he attempted to sue the civil servant in the servant's personal capacity in the appropriate national court, he could expect to be met by a plea of immunity. For the Treaties confer upon Community servants immunity from legal proceedings "in respect of acts performed by them in their official capacity." Such official acts, however, may give rise to internal disciplinary action, which in turn may be challenged by the civil servant before the Court of Justice (under EEC Art. 179). Only where the civil servant was acting completely outside the scope of his duties ("on a frolic of his own," as English law might express it), would he lose his immunity, and in such a case only he and not the Communities could be sued.

The exact nature of the Communities' vicarious liability (as an English lawyer would regard it) for the acts of civil servants depends upon the interpretation to be given to the phrase "in the performance of their duties."

In the two *Sayag* cases (Case 5/68 [1968] ECR 395 and Case 9/69 [1969] ECR 329) the Court had to consider this question when S, an engineer employed by Euratom, was driving in his private car to a destination in Belgium to visit an atomic plant in connection with his work. He caused an accident on the way and was the subject of both criminal and civil proceedings in the Belgian courts. The Belgian Court of Cassation referred to the Court of Justice the question of possible immunity and of the meaning of the phrase "in the performance of their duties." The Court ruled that the use of a private car by a Community servant could only be considered as constituting the performance of his duties in the case of *force majeure* or exceptional circumstances of such compelling nature that the Community could not otherwise perform its functions. In the event, therefore, the Belgian courts had jurisdiction. It would have been otherwise, it seems, if a serious emergency at the atomic plant had required the immediate presence of the engineer at a time when neither official transport nor public transport was available.

The *Sayag* cases indicate a conservative attitude on the part of the Court of Justice. The vicarious liability of the Communities should not be extended so as to make the Community purse an insurance fund for the victims of any wrongful act of a Community servant.

The present state of the law, however, is open to several criticisms. In the first place, there is the risk of the civil servant invoking immunity for acts which are *not* committed in the performance of his duties. This risk is partly removed by the power of the Community institution which employs him to waive the immunity. If the immunity is not waived, then the Community would be impliedly admitting the official nature of the act in question. This would invite an action against it. But in such an action the Court of Justice might hold that the act fell outside the performance of the servant's duties. The aggrieved plaintiff would be left without further remedy, unless the immunity was at this stage withdrawn, which would mean the plaintiff having to recommence an action in the national court against the civil servant personally.

A second criticism is that the Community might improperly waive immunity in order to leave the civil servant, rather than itself, exposed to the action for damages. In the first *Sayag* case (above) the Court made clear that the mere waiver of immunity could not affect any possible liability on the part of the Community itself.

A third criticism arises from the lack of uniformity of the principles governing non-contractual liability in the laws of the Member States. Thus, assuming immunity has been properly waived, a plaintiff who sued the civil servant in State A might succeed in his suit, whereas in State B he might fail because of a difference, for example, in the principles of limitation of actions or remoteness of damage or contributory negligence.

Concurrent fault on part of Member States

The nature of the European Communities requires that Member States may be called upon to collaborate with

Community institutions in certain tasks. In other words, the execution of Community law may be entrusted to the Member States. Without this help from national administrations the relatively small Community civil service would be overwhelmed by its work-load. Moreover, members of the public may feel themselves better served by the more accessible, more familiar officials of their own governments.

In carrying out a function on behalf of the Communities, a Member State (that is, its government, officials or civil servants) may itself commit a wrongful or illegal act. Occasionally this may be deliberate; more often it will be a case of simple error—for example, a mistaken application of Community law.

Does then the principle of vicarious liability apply where a Member State is cast in the role of an agent, so as to attach liability to the Communities. An English lawyer might well see the State's relationship as analogous to that of an independent contractor, since the Communities exercise no real control over the Member States even when they perform Community functions; in which case, vicarious liability could not arise, although State and Communities might be joint tortfeasors. On such questions, the Treaties are silent. The problem has arisen, however, before the Court of Justice on several occasions. Thus, in a typical case, the plaintiff complains that his own government, acting on behalf of the Communities, is refusing to pay him money allegedly due under Community law, but he elects to bring his suit against the Communities in the Court of Justice rather than to sue his own government in the national court, prompted perhaps by the likelihood of a more speedy decision from Luxembourg.

Faced with this kind of problem the Court has proceeded by way of the following analysis. Firstly, is there joint liability on the part both of the Community and the Member State? If there is, then, second, is the Member State to be considered primarily liable so that it would be reasonable for it rather than the Communities to pay compensation? If so, then, third, the plaintiff must pursue his remedy in the national courts, before the Court of Justice can further entertain his claim. If, of course, he succeeds in his national court, the Member State may be entitled to recoup itself, wholly or in part, against the Communities in separate proceedings before the Court.

Thus, in *Kampffmeyer* v. *Commission* (p. 124, above), as we have seen, the Court found liability established against the Community on account of the Commission's decision, held illegal, authorising the German Government to take safeguard measures. But the Court refused to settle the amount of damages until the plaintiffs had completed proceedings against their government in the German courts: "final judgment cannot be given before the applicants have produced the decision of the national court.".

Critique

The principle that normally the plaintiff should first pursue his remedy in the national courts has been upheld by the Court in a series of cases beginning with Case 96/71 *Haegeman* v. *Commission* [1972] ECR 1005. More recent cases have been Case 99/74 *Société des Grands Moulins des Antilles* v. *Commission* [1975] ECR 1531, Case 46/75 *Importazione Bestiame Carni* v. *Commission* [1976] ECR 65, and Cases 67–85/75 *Lesieur Cotelle S.A.* v. *Commission* [1976] ECR 391. Behind the very complicated facts of the three later cases was the common basic feature that, as the plaintiffs alleged, their national government was refusing them certain payments to which they believed themselves entitled under Community regulations (relating in the instant cases to cereals, cattle and meat, and colza seeds, respectively). In each case the Court decided there was a concurrent remedy in the national courts which had therefore to be pursued first before any action would be admissible against the Community.

This approach by the Court is open to criticism. In the first place, as Mr. Hartley has pointed out (T. Hartley in [1976] 1 *European Law Review* 299–304, 396–399), the Court's own jurisdiction is made to turn on the presence or absence of a remedy under national law, and this is not a question on which the Court can give an authoritative ruling, should the parties disagree on the point. Presumably, if the Court did take the view that a remedy existed in the national court, and then, in subsequent proceedings, the national court decided otherwise, the matter would have to come back to the Court at Luxembourg—a process both dilatory and expensive.

A second criticism arises from the considerable variations in the scope of the remedy which the national laws provide to recover damages against public authorities. Differences exist on such matters as the heads of damages, the modes of assessing these, the periods of limitation, and the recovery of money paid under a mistake of law. Because of such differences an applicant in one Member State might well fare better than one in another, although both applicants were complaining, in effect, of the same fault on the part of the Community. Such lack of uniformity within the Community seems intolerable.

Again, the remedy in the Court of Justice may be more generous than that available in the national court, as, for instance, in Case 96/71 *Haegeman* (see above), where Belgian law did not permit recovery of loss of profit although this was recoverable under Community law (as held by the Court of Justice): hence the applicant was told by the Court that he could come back to the Court to obtain compensation under this head after he had sued in the Belgian court for the refund which he was claiming from the Belgian authorities (in respect of customs duties paid on imported Greek wine). This kind of circuity of actions seems also quite intolerable.

A procedure so dilatory and circuitous is hard to justify. A partial justification for it may be found in the fact that, if the Community is sued, rather than the Member State, and is then adjudged liable for the whole damages, no provision exists in the Treaties whereby the Community may recoup itself against the Member State, even though the latter bears joint liability for the plaintiff's loss. Professor Schermers suggests however that such a right of action might be deduced from the general principles referred to in Article 215(2) (Henry G. Schermers in *Legal Issues of European Integration*, 1975/1, 113).

A subsequent case suggests that the Court may be ready to relax its restrictive approach of requiring the prior exhaustion of the national remedy, at least where the action under Article 215(2) is for damages in tort rather than a claim in quasi-contract for money unlawfully exacted (as it alleged) by the national authorities on behalf of the Community. Thus, in Case 126/76 *Dietz* v. *Commission* [1977] ECR 2431, the applicant was a German exporter who contracted to export certain goods from Germany to Italy. After the contract was made, certain charges were introduced by the Community on the imported goods, which resulted in Dietz making an unexpected loss on the transaction. He sued the Commission under Article 215(2) for his actual loss on the ground that the sudden imposition of the charges was a violation of the principle of the protection of legitimate expectations. The Commission argued that the claim was inadmissible since Dietz should first be required to proceed in his national court against the national authority imposing the charges. In fact such an action by Dietz was pending. But the Court of Justice held the action before it to be admissible; for the alleged loss stemmed from the act of the Community itself rather than from the measures adopted by the national authorities in applying Community law. In the event, however, the action failed on the merits.

Whether the Court can work out solutions to these (and other) problems simply by way of its case law—hanging its decisions on the peg of "general principles" provided by Article 215(2) EEC—is an intriguing question. The drastic alternative would be a revision of the Treaties so as to confer jurisdiction upon the Court of Justice in respect of actions against Member States for non-contractual liability arising out of the administration of Community law by national authorities. The Communities and the Member States could then be sued jointly in the one Community Court, which could allocate liability between them as it thought fit. If the Communities alone were sued (and the plaintiff might often prefer to proceed thus) then the Communities would be able to join the Member State as a party and claim a contribution or even a complete indemnity from it, as appropriate.

APPENDIX

METHODS TO CHALLENGE THE VALIDITY OF A REGULATION

In the light of the discussion in this and the preceding chapter, it may be helpful to gather together, in summary form, the various methods by which, directly or indirectly, the validity of a Community regulation may be called in question before the Court at the suit of the individual. These are:

(a) Action to annul the regulation as a disguised decision (Article 173 EEC);

(b) Action for damages for "normative injustice" where the regulation constitutes a sufficiently flagrant breach of a superior rule of law protecting individuals (Article 215(2) EEC);

(c) Plea of illegality in respect of the regulation (Article 184 EEC);

(d) Reference from a national court or tribunal for a preliminary ruling on the validity of the regulation (Article 177 EEC: see Chapter 9 below).

The consequences of the challenge to the validity of the regulation, even if it be successful, will vary according to which method is adopted. Thus, a successful action under Article 173 ((a) above) will result in the quashing of the regulation: it is annulled *erga omnes* and (unless the Court rules otherwise) retrospectively. The award of damages under Article 215(2) necessarily imports a decision on the invalidity of the regulation in issue: although not formally annulled by the Court, *erga omnes,* the regulation will, in practice, cease prospectively to be applied until such time as it is revoked or replaced by its authors. Similar consequences flow from an indirect challenge under Article 184 or a preliminary ruling of invalidity under Article 177 ((c) and (d) above).

Chapter 8

STAFF CASES

Introduction

"Staff cases," *i.e.* actions by employees of the Community institutions who have complaints concerning their employment, are often omitted from general works on Community law as being too specialised a topic. Dealing with such matters as salaries, pensions, allowances, promotions, and disciplinary measures, they may seem of limited interest and perhaps even unworthy of the august attention of the Court. Yet they represent, as we shall see, a not unimportant aspect of the Court's jurisdiction.

Staff cases also have a special human interest and importance, since they are virtually the only cases where a private individual (as distinct from a legal person) goes directly to the Court. In all other cases, the only access of the individual to the Court in practice is the indirect route by way of a reference for a preliminary ruling from a national court as described in the next chapter.

The fact that the Court should have been given jurisdiction in such cases is perhaps a reflection of the influence of French administrative law, since the French *Conseil d'Etat* has a similar jurisdiction in respect of the higher ranks of the French civil service. The British tradition, by contrast, has been to deny civil servants access to the courts and to favour non-judicial arbitration, through Whitley Councils, of staff disputes over pay, promotion and conditions of service, although a civil servant may now sue for wrongful dismissal.

But international organisations generally have adopted the French conception of the status and conditions of service of public servants being regulated by detailed statutory provisions and subject to judicial control; thus,

within the United Nations an Administrative Tribunal was
set up in 1949 for the purpose of hearing staff disputes,
and the Administrative Tribunal of the International
Labour Organisation, set up in 1946, has jurisdiction not
only over the International Labour Office but also over
various specialised agencies of the United Nations (including the World Health Organisation, FAO, and UNESCO)
and other international organisations. In yet other organisations, a special domestic tribunal has been established.

The Court's jurisdiction

Within the European Communities it was appropriate,
in accordance with the principle of unity of jurisdiction,
that the Court of Justice, rather than a special tribunal,
should be the forum for staff disputes. Accordingly,
Article 179 EEC gives the Court jurisdiction in any
dispute between the Community and its servants within
the limits and under the conditions laid down in the Staff
Regulations or the Conditions of Employment. Thus the
staff of the Community institutions, including for this
purpose not only the four "institutions" so described in
Article 4 EEC but also the Economic and Social Committee, the Court of Auditors and the European Investment
Bank (p. 148), can bring their complaints against their
employing institution before the Court. The staffs of the
Community institutions are very small, compared with a
national civil service, ranging from about 11,000 in the
Commission to a few hundred in the Court and other
smaller bodies. There are two main categories of employee, the established "officials" of the European Communities, whose status and conditions of service are laid
down in the Staff Regulations, and "other servants,"
often engaged under contract for a limited period of time,
who are subject to the "Conditions of employment of
other servants of the Communities"; both these Conditions and the Staff Regulations are enacted by regulation
of the Council on a proposal from the Commission, and

the provisions in the Staff Regulations conferring jurisdiction on the Court apply to all employees alike. This is one case, therefore, where the jurisdiction of the Court can be altered, without amendment of the Treaties, by a decision of the Council acting by a qualified majority. Another unusual feature of staff cases is that the Court can adjudicate in cases brought by its own employees against the Court itself; such cases, apparent exceptions to the principle *nemo iudex in causa sua,* are rare but have occasionally arisen: see *e.g.* Case 15/60 *Simon* v. *Court of Justice* [1961] ECR 115 and Case 2/80 *Dautzenberg* v. *Court of Justice* [1980] ECR 3107. In the latter case the Court, sitting judicially, annulled its own administrative act refusing a promotion to a librarian at the Court.

In terms of numbers alone staff cases have contributed substantially to the Court's case-load, and in the first years after the establishment of the Court, when other business was sometimes slack, they provided grist for the judicial mill. These early cases provided the Court with the opportunity to start its work of building up a body of case-law where the texts provided little guidance. In particular, they enabled the Court to develop the principles of Community law on the nature and scope of judicial review of administrative action, principles which were subsequently applied to full-scale actions under Article 173 EEC; and despite the specialised nature of the disputes, despite the apparent lack of merit of some complaints which have been entertained, and despite the fact that staff cases are heard by a Chamber of three judges, rather than by the full Court, the judgments in these cases remain authoritative and can be cited equally with decisions given by the full Court in cases of less parochial concern.

Thus one of the earliest staff cases, which occupies no less than one-third of the volume of reports for 1957, raised the constitutional issue of the balance of power between the authorities set up under the ECSC Treaty: Cases 7/56 and 3–7/57 *Algera and others* v. *Assembly*

[1957 and 1958] ECR 39. Legislative authority in staff matters was originally conferred under the ECSC Treaty on a Commission composed of the Presidents of the four Institutions (the Court, the High Authority, the Assembly and the Council) in order to maintain a balance of power among the institutions. The ECSC Assembly, the precursor of the European Parliament, had taken certain decisions admitting the applicants to the protection of the Staff Regulations, and appointing them at certain grades and at certain levels of seniority. Subsequently those decisions were revoked, and the applicants challenged that revocation as being unlawful. The Court's judgment laid down important principles governing the circumstances in which an administrative act can lawfully be revoked, referring, in the absence of express provisions of Community law, to the laws of the Member States as a source of general principles of law: this aspect of the case is returned to below, p. 253. The case was the first authority for the principle that compensation could be given, under Community law, for non-material damage (*dommage moral*); and also, although with less precision, for the degree of negligence required to establish liability for damages.

The jurisdiction of the Court in staff cases is wider than that of many staff tribunals in international organisations, since it can pronounce on the legality of the Staff Regulations themselves as well as on particular decisions taken in application of those Regulations. This may arise on a plea of illegality under Article 184 EEC (p. 112, above), whereby any party challenging a particular decision before the Court may plead the inapplicability of the parent regulation. An example is a case considered more fully in Chapter 14, Case 20/71 *Sabbatini* v. *European Parliament* [1972] ECR 345. Signora Sabbatini complained of discrimination on grounds of sex, since she lost her expatriation allowance on marriage, while men in the same circumstances did not. Although the decision was taken in conformity with the Staff Regulations, it was annulled by the Court, which held that the relevant provisions of the Regulations were discriminatory and unlawful. The Regulations were subsequently amended on this point by the Council so as to apply equally to men and women. Henceforth they were entitled to the allowance under the same conditions, but subsequent attempts by other women to claim arrears of payment of the allowances were unsuccessful, the applications being rejected as out of time: Cases 15–33, etc., /73 *Schots-Kortner* [1974] ECR 177.

As well as the jurisdiction to rule on the validity of the Staff Regulations, it will be recalled that in staff cases the Court has plenary jurisdiction in the sense described in Chapter 7 (above, p. 118). The effect of this may be illustrated by Case 32/62 *Alvis* v. *Council* [1963] ECR 49, where the applicant claimed wrongful dismissal. The facts of the case were unusual and, it might be added, uncharacteristic of the behaviour both of Community servants and of the administration. The applicant was not an established official but had been engaged under contract. He had been dismissed for alleged misconduct; among other incidents, it was said that on one occasion he had reported for duty in a state of intoxication and that on another occasion, when he was also intoxicated, glasses were thrown from the ninth floor of his office block into the street below. He claimed that he had been dismissed without being given any opportunity of submitting his defence, and had not been informed of the incidents on which his dismissal was based. The Court, applying a generally accepted principle of administrative law in force in the Member States, held that the administration must allow its servants the opportunity of replying to allegations before any disciplinary decision is taken. That had not been done. However, the Court exercised its plenary jurisdiction, and ruled that, in this case, the failure to observe this principle was not such as to render the dismissal void. Nor did the failure justify the award of damages to the applicant; but it did justify ordering the

Council to pay a substantial proportion of the applicant's costs.

The Court's plenary jurisdiction thus enabled it to substitute, in effect, its own judgment for that of the administration. Although the decision to dismiss the applicant was technically vitiated by the denial of his right to be heard, it was considered that the decision should stand on its merits. Indeed the Court went on, in its judgment, to review the decision on its merits and held that the facts which had been established, with the assistance of witnesses summoned by the Court (see below, p. 201), justified the dismissal, revealing "an attitude and conduct incompatible with the functioning of the European institutions."

Procedure in staff cases

In most respects the procedure in staff cases is similar to that described in Chapter 11 below for any other direct action; but staff cases do have a number of special features.

The complaint must first be brought before the appropriate superior in the institution concerned; in other words, domestic remedies must be exhausted. If the complainant is not satisfied by the response, or if there is no response within four months (in which case there is deemed to be an implied decision rejecting the complaint), then he can appeal to the Court against the decision of rejection. The time-limit for the appeal is three months, as compared with two months under Article 173.

Staff cases are normally heard by a Chamber rather than by the full Court, although the Chamber may, under Article 95(3) of the Rules of Procedure, refer a case to the full Court. Thus in one case the full Court was called upon to decide whether it could entertain an action brought against the European Investment Bank, whose officials are not subject to the Community Staff Regulations; the Court held that it could do so: Case 110/75 *Mills* v. *European Investment Bank* [1976] ECR 955.

Staff cases also differ from other types of case in that, under Article 70 of the Rules of Procedure, the defendant institution normally has to pay its own costs, even if the action is unsuccessful.

If the action succeeds, the decision complained of is annulled; the applicant may also be awarded damages. Thus, in the *Algera* case mentioned above, the Court awarded damages for non-material harm (*dommage moral*) although only at the modest rate of 100 units of account (approximately £50) per applicant. In other cases, more substantial damages have been awarded; in one such case, the Commission was ordered to pay the applicant some 77,000 Belgian Francs (approximately £1,000), as compensation for leave which he had been unable to take "owing to the requirements of the service": Case 39/69 *Fournier* v. *Commission* [1970] ECR 267. In general, the amounts awarded for mental distress or injured feelings have been small.

A special feature of staff cases is that, as will already be apparent, the Court is frequently confronted with disputes concerning the facts of the case. Accordingly preparatory inquiries, and the calling of witnesses, are more frequent here than in other cases; and the burden on the Court is correspondingly greater, especially, perhaps, because the procedures available to it for the establishment of the facts of a case are not entirely satisfactory—a matter to which we return in the chapter on procedure. With the increasing pressure of its other work, especially the increase in references for preliminary rulings, proposals have been made for the setting up for staff cases of a tribunal of first instance which would find the facts and decide the dispute, this decision being subject to review by the Court but only on a point of law. These proposals, which had the blessing, in principle, of the Council as long ago as November 1974, would make the Community jurisdiction for staff cases more comparable with that for UN and ILO officials (see p. 144 above).

The problem of case-load is aggravated by the generous

approach of the Court to *locus standi* under Article 179 EEC: even unsuccessful candidates for posts in the Community service may sue, because, although not "servants" within Article 179, they are "person(s) to whom [the] Staff Regulations apply" within Article 91 of the Staff Regulations: see *e.g.* Case 130/75 *Prais* v. *Council* [1976] ECR 1589.

Chapter 9

PRELIMINARY RULINGS

Introduction

In many ways the most important aspect of the work of the Court is its jurisdiction to give "preliminary rulings" under Article 177 EEC and corresponding provisions of the other Treaties (Art. 41 ECSC, Art. 150 Euratom).

As we have seen, disputes involving Community law, between individuals or companies, or between private parties and the national authorities of the Member States, never come directly before the Court of Justice, but before the courts and tribunals of the Member States. The treaty provisions enable the Court of Justice, at the request of the national court, to rule on questions of Community law which arise in such litigation.

The preliminary ruling has proved a particularly effective means of securing rights claimed under Community law. Signora Leonesio claimed a premium for the slaughter of her cows which had been refused her under Italian law; Mme Defrenne claimed arrears of salary from the Belgian air-line on the ground that air hostesses and male members of the cabin crew performing identical duties did not receive equal pay; Mr. Kenny claimed sickness benefit in England, notwithstanding that he had been in prison in the Irish Republic during the qualifying period; Signor Bonsignore challenged a deportation order made by the German authorities: Case 93/71 *Leonesio* [1972] ECR 287; Case 43/75 *Defrenne* [1976] ECR 455; Case 1/78 *Kenny* v. *Insurance Officer* [1978] ECR 1489; Case 67/74 *Bonsignore* [1975] ECR 297. The type of claim varies considerably, as does the nature of the procedure before the national court; but in essence, in all these cases, the mechanism is the same. The right is claimed under

Community law, despite the absence of any provision of national law, or in opposition to national law. The remedy is before the national court, but the scope of the right is determined by the Court of Justice.

Conversely, Community law may be invoked by the defendant, whether in civil or in criminal proceedings. In an action for infringement of patent or trade mark rights, or in a prosecution for importing medicinal drugs without complying with requirements laid down by national law, the defendant may rely on the treaty provisions on the free movement of goods, Articles 30–36 EEC: Cases 15 and 16/74 *Centrafarm* [1974] ECR 1147 and 1183; Case 104/75 *De Peijper* [1976] ECR 613. The defence is raised in the proceedings before the national court; its scope is determined by the Court of Justice by means of a preliminary ruling. The Court will of course have regard to the exceptions set out in Article 36, *e.g.* public morality, as where on a reference from the House of Lords the English importers of Danish pornography from Holland, prosecuted before the Ipswich Crown Court, pleaded unavailingly the principle of free movement of goods: Case 34/79 *R.* v. *Henn and Darby* [1979] ECR 3795.

The term "preliminary ruling" is something of a misnomer. The ruling is requested and given, not before the case comes to the national court, but in the course of the proceedings before it. It is therefore an interlocutory ruling, a step in the proceedings before the national court. But it is a step which may be taken, and is frequently best taken, before the case comes to trial. Thus references are commonly made in the course of interlocutory proceedings: see, *e.g.* Cases 51, 86, 96/75 *EMI* v. *CBS* [1976] ECR 811, references from English, Danish and German courts.

Under the ECSC Treaty (Art. 41) the Court has jurisdiction to give preliminary rulings only on the validity of Community acts; under the EEC (and Euratom) Treaty it has jurisdiction on questions of interpretation as well as validity. While Article 41 ECSC has proved virtually a

dead letter (because of the readier availability of the
direct action under Article 33), it provided a model for
expansion in the later Treaties. Article 177 EEC provides
that

> "The Court of Justice shall have jurisdiction to give
> preliminary rulings concerning:
> (a) the interpretation of this Treaty;
> (b) the validity and interpretation of acts of the
>   institutions of the Community;
> (c) the interpretation of the statutes of bodies
>   established by an act of the Council, where those
>   statutes so provide.
>   Where such a question is raised before any court or
> tribunal of a Member State, that court or tribunal
> may, if it considers that a decision on the question is
> necessary to enable it to give judgment, request the
> Court of Justice to give a ruling thereon.
>   Where any such question is raised in a case pending
> before a court or tribunal of a Member State, against
> whose decisions there is no judicial remedy under
> national law, that court or tribunal shall bring the
> matter before the Court of Justice."

The effect is that any question of EEC law in issue
before a national court may be authoritatively determined
by the Court of Justice if that question is referred to it;
that a national court is in all cases entitled, and in some
cases obliged, to make such a reference; and that the
Court of Justice may thus be the final arbiter on matters of
Community law although the case is heard in the national
forum. Moreover, a question of interpretation may also
extend to the question of the direct applicability or direct
effect of the Community provision in issue.

The need for a system of preliminary rulings can be seen
most clearly in relation to questions of validity. Plainly it
would lead to intolerable confusion if national courts were
to declare Community legislation invalid: for example, to
hold that a Council regulation was *ultra vires*. Under

Article 41 ECSC, indeed, the Court of Justice was expressly given "sole jurisdiction" to rule on the validity of acts of the High Authority and of the Council. Although the Court is not expressly given exclusive jurisdiction on questions of validity under Article 177 EEC, it would clearly be improper for a national court to pronounce on the validity of Community acts, not least because a court in another Member State might come to a contrary conclusion. Thus any serious challenge in the national courts to the validity of such acts should be referred to the Court of Justice.

Illustrations of references on the validity of Community law, as opposed to its interpretation, may be found in the legislation on the social security of migrant workers. Article 51 EEC requires the Council to "adopt such measures in the field of social security as are necessary to provide freedom of movement for workers." Hence regulations of the Council provide, for example, that periods spent in different Member States should qualify for the calculation of the worker's retirement pension. While the detailed provisions of the legislation are inevitably complex, the essential principle underlying it, derived from Article 51, is that a person who has worked successively in different Member States should not be deprived of social security benefits that he would have secured if he had always worked in the same Member State. In some cases, a claimant has been faced with a calculation, purportedly based on the regulations, which would have the result of depriving him of the benefits to which he would have been entitled on the basis of national law taken alone. Here the Court has ruled that the provisions of the regulations, to the extent to which they lead to that result, are, in effect, *ultra vires* Article 51 and void: Case 191/73 *Niemann* [1974] ECR 571; Case 24/75 *Petroni* [1975] ECR 1149. Such decisions, invalidating Community legislation and so requiring the Council to enact amending provisions, could not properly have been taken by national courts.

A moment's reflection will show, however, that a similar line of reasoning may apply equally to questions of interpretation as well as validity. The applicability of Community law in particular situations may depend as much upon its interpretation as upon its validity. A restrictive interpretation of legislation might be tantamount to holding it invalid; or the actual validity of a provision may depend upon its precise construction. Thus the uniform interpretation of the law is necessary to secure its uniform application. As the Court itself has stated:

> "Article 177 is essential for the preservation of the Community character of the law established by the Treaty and has the object of ensuring that in all circumstances this law is the same in all States of the Community":

Case 166/73 *Rheinmühlen* [1974] ECR 33 at 38. Uniform application of the law is the basis of the common market and without it Community law, applied by the national courts, would be liable to fragment and become overlaid by the national legal systems. In the absence of a federal structure or of any Community appellate court, the preliminary ruling is the only means by which uniform application of Community law can be attained.

Moreover, the provisions of the Treaty and the measures taken by the Community institutions cannot readily be interpreted by national courts without assistance. They have to be interpreted in the light of the purposes for which they were drafted, they are often broad and general in scope, and texts in the different official languages may have to be compared. These problems of interpretation are examined in Chapter 13. Again, if the courts of each Member State were to take it upon themselves to construe Community law, it is probably not too much of an exaggeration to say that there would be as many systems of Community law as there are national legal systems within the EEC.

The need for uniform interpretation applies equally to other areas of Community law which do not fall within the categories listed in the founding Treaties. This is the case with two conventions concluded pursuant to Article 220 EEC: the Convention of February 29, 1968 on the Mutual Recognition of Companies, Firms and Legal Persons, and the Convention of September 27, 1968 on Jurisdiction and the Enforcement of Judgments in Civil and Commercial Matters. As these Conventions are not Community acts, but treaties requiring ratification by Member States, they fall outside Article 177. In each case, a separate Protocol gives the Court jurisdiction to give preliminary rulings on the interpretation of the Convention. The detailed provisions differ in some important respects from the scheme laid down by Article 177. While the Companies Convention is not yet in force, the Judgments Convention has given rise to a substantial and growing body of case law.

Provisions for preliminary rulings are also contained in the Community Patent Convention, concluded on December 15, 1975 under the title "Convention for the European Patent for the Common Market"; when in force, this Convention will establish a Community patent system, under which it will be possible to take out a single patent for the whole of the EEC, within the framework of the Convention on the grant of European patents.

The Companies Convention, the Judgments Convention, and the Patent Convention are likely to be followed by others; a draft Bankruptcy Convention is at an advanced stage of negotiation, and an instrument for a Community trade mark is also in preparation. These instruments are progressively extending the jurisdiction of the Court and the implications of this increasing workload will be considered in the concluding chapter.

The procedure on a reference is in all cases the same; it is described in Chapter 11. Here it is necessary to mention only certain points of procedure which are relevant to the subject of this chapter. Firstly it should be noted that a decision to refer can be taken only by the national court.

In practice such a decision will usually be taken at the instance of the parties or of one of them; but the court may also take the step of its own motion, and even contrary to the express wishes of the parties. When a reference is made, the proceedings before the national court are stayed for the period, about 12 months in most cases, until the ruling is given. The procedure before the Court of Justice is, as we have seen, an interlocutory step in the action before the national court; but the Community institutions concerned (that is, the Commission in all cases, and the Council if a Council act is involved, but not the Parliament) and all the Member States, as well as the parties to the action before the national court, have the opportunity of submitting observations, both in writing and at an oral hearing, before the Court of Justice. When the ruling has been given, it is sent to the national court, and the proceedings there are resumed.

The system of preliminary rulings has its origins in analogous procedures in the legal systems of the original Member States, such as the reference in France from the civil to the administrative courts, and these analogies have been used where procedural difficulties have arisen. Thus, the analogies in French and German law were considered by Advocate General Lagrange in the *Bosch* case, Case 13/61 [1962] ECR 45 at 59–60, and by Advocate General Warner in the *Rheinmühlen* cases, Cases 146 and 166/73 [1974] ECR 33 at 44. In English law perhaps the closest analogies are the appeal by way of case stated and the motion for the determination of a preliminary point of law. Although these analogies with national law may sometimes be helpful, the Community system is perhaps better considered as *sui generis*.

Indeed the function of the preliminary ruling is best explained by the special character of Community law itself. Community law is by its nature a common internal law in the Member States rather than a law governing relations between them; and in the absence of a developed federal structure it is natural that Community policies should fall to be implemented primarily by the authorities of the Member States and Community law to be applied by their courts. So it is to be expected that, in the normal way, Community law is enforced through the national courts, which, as mentioned above, have an exclusive jurisdiction to apply it in disputes between individuals, and between the individual and the authorities of the Member States.

Conflicts of jurisdiction between a national court and the Court of Justice can therefore rarely arise, but the exact demarcation line may be a delicate one to draw. The following sections illustrate the relationship between the two courts and the limits to their respective jurisdiction. These sections show also the pains taken by the Court of Justice both to preserve its own jurisdiction and at the same time to respect what is sometimes described as the "judicial sovereignty" of the national courts.

The decision to refer

It is for the national court alone to judge whether a decision on the question is necessary to enable it to give judgment. That was established in Case 6/64 *Costa* v. *ENEL* [1964] ECR 585 when objections were raised to the admissibility of the reference: it was argued that the Court could not entertain the reference (see on this concept of admissibility Chapter 11 below). The argument was that the Milan court had requested an interpretation of the Treaty which was not "necessary" for the solution of the dispute before it. The Court of Justice simply replied to these objections that, since Article 177 is based upon a clear separation of functions between itself and the national courts, it could not investigate the facts of the case or criticise the grounds and purpose of the request for interpretation. The Court's concern was clearly to respect the exclusive competence of the national court to decide whether a reference should be made, and at the same time to obviate the risk of challenge to the admissibility of a reference. This approach is undoubtedly correct.

It is important to note that Article 177 does not require that the reference should be necessary, but only that the national court should consider that it cannot give judgment without deciding the point of Community law. If that condition is satisfied, then the court, unless it is a court of last instance, has a discretion whether or not to make a reference, and the exercise of that discretion is a matter for the national court alone, subject to the possibility of an appeal: Cases 146 and 166/73 *Rhein-mühlen*, below, p. 283.

Nevertheless, the Court will not entertain a collusive action brought in one Member State with the intention of challenging the law of another Member State as contrary to Community law. Case 104/79 *Foglia* v. *Novello* [1980] ECR 745 was a reference by the Pretore of Bra where the parties before the Italian court both contested the compatibility with Community law of a tax imposed by the French customs authorities on a consignment of Italian liqueur wine. The Court of Justice held, however, that, in the absence of a genuine dispute between the parties, it had no jurisdiction to give a ruling on the questions raised by the Pretore of Bra touching as they did the compatibility of French fiscal measures with Community law.

The holding of the Court has been criticised as introducing a kind of preliminary censorship of the motives of the parties and the judge in the national proceedings: Barav (1980) 5 E.L.Rev. 443. Certainly, the previous case law seemed to be well settled that (as was said in Case 10/69 *Portelange* [1969] ECR 309 at 315) "Article 177 does not give the Court jurisdiction to take cognisance of the facts of the case or to criticise the reason for the reference." Nor does the Court normally object to being asked to rule at the request of a judge in one Member State upon legislative measures or administrative acts in another Member State: see *e.g.* Case 22/76 *Import Gadgets* [1976] ECR 1371, pp. 46–53 above. From the laconic judgment in *Foglia* v. *Novello*, read in the light of the advocate-general's opinion, it seems that the Court wished to curb what it saw as a *détournement de procédure* by the referring judge.

In a subsequent reference in the same proceedings (Case 244/80 *Foglia* v. *Novello* [1981] ECR 3045) the Pretore sought clarification of the Court's judgment in the first reference. The Court reaffirmed its authority to question of its own motion the admissibility of any preliminary reference: it must retain what has been well described as this "valuable long-stop against abuse of process in exceptional cases" (Wyatt in (1981) 6 E.L.Rev. 449). But the Court did soften its attitude somewhat by inviting the Pretore to resubmit a reference if he could lay before the Court any new and relevant factors not present in the original reference: Article 177 being based upon co-operation between the national court and the Court of Justice, the latter could require the former to explain, where they were not obvious, the reasons why the national judge considered an answer to the question of Community law to be necessary in order to resolve the dispute.

The question referred

The formulation of the question or questions referred is a matter for the national court alone. If the question is formulated in such a way as to relate to the application, rather than the interpretation or validity, of Community law, the reference will not be inadmissible on that ground, but the Court will confine its ruling to any issues of interpretation or validity which do arise. If, for example, the question referred is whether a provision of national law is incompatible with a rule of Community law, the Court will rule only on the interpretation of the latter, leaving it to the national court to decide whether, in the light of that interpretation, and of the national court's interpretation of national law, the provision of national law should not be applied.

Here again the Court has sought to preserve its own jurisdiction without trespassing on that of the national court. To put the point in a different way, it has sought to provide an answer helpful to the national court while remaining within the limits of its competence.

Thus in the very first Article 177 reference, the *Bosch* case, objections were made to the jurisdiction of the Court on the ground, among others, that the question related not only to the interpretation but to the application of the Treaty. The Court had been asked to rule on the question whether the prohibition on export imposed by the Bosch company on its customers was void by virtue of Article 85(2) EEC as far as exports to the Netherlands were concerned. To answer that question would have involved not merely interpreting, but applying, Article 85. The Court held, however, following Advocate General Lagrange, that " . . . it is permissible for the national court to formulate its request in a simple and direct way leaving to this Court the duty of rendering a decision on that request only in so far as it has jurisdiction to do so, that is to say, only in so far as the decision relates to the interpretation of the Treaty. The direct form in which the request in the present case has been drawn up enables this Court to abstract from it without difficulty the questions of interpretation which it contains.": Case 13/61 [1962] ECR 45 at 50. As it has frequently done in subsequent cases, the Court proceeded to extract from the material presented to it the questions of law which it was competent to answer.

Only where Community law has no bearing on the question referred will the Court hold that it cannot give an answer to the question referred. Thus in Case 93/75 *Adlerblum* [1975] ECR 2147, the classification under French law of a pension paid under German law to a victim of Nazi persecution was held to be a matter of national law alone. However, even in such cases the Court does not reject the reference by a preliminary decision on admissibility. Instead, the proceedings follow their normal course and result in a ruling to the effect that the Court has no jurisdiction to answer the question referred.

In the historic case *Van Gend en Loos*, where the Court for the first time held that a provision of Community law "produces direct effects and creates individual rights which national courts must protect" (Case 26/62 [1963] ECR 1 at 16) the plaintiff had challenged a Dutch law as contravening Article 12 of the EEC Treaty. The Dutch and Belgian Governments submitted, *inter alia*, that the Court had no jurisdiction to decide whether the provisions of the EEC Treaty prevail over Dutch legislation, and that the solution to this question fell within the exclusive jurisdiction of the national courts, subject to an application under Articles 169 and 170 of the Treaty. The argument was that an alleged infringement of the Treaty by a Member State could not be brought before the Court under Article 177, at the instance of an individual party to proceedings before a national court, but only in proceedings instituted before the Court directly by the Commission or by another Member State under Article 169 and Article 170 respectively.

The Court rejected this argument as misconceived. "A restriction of the guarantees against an infringement of Article 12 by Member States to the procedures under Article 169 and 170 would remove all direct legal protection of the individual rights of their nationals." The decision is illuminating on the relation between the Court's jurisdiction under Article 177 and its jurisdiction in a direct action. It is plain on reading the judgment why a remedy in the hands of the Commission and the Member States was considered ineffective. Such an action on their part is purely discretionary and will be affected by political calculation. The notion of the direct effect of Community law, coupled with the jurisdiction of the Court to give a preliminary ruling and so to determine the scope of the individual's rights and obligations, is a more powerful weapon. The individual has no direct remedy, before the Court, against the default of a State. The remedy lies with the national court, with the use of Article 177 where necessary.

Questions of Community law

The Court has taken a wide view, also, of the questions of Community law which may be the subject of a reference. It will be recalled that under the ECSC Treaty (Art. 41), the Court's jurisdiction is limited to the validity of acts of the High Authority and of the Council; under the EEC Treaty (Art. 177) and the Euratom Treaty (Art. 150) it extends to the interpretation of the Treaties themselves and the validity and interpretation of the acts of the institutions. As well as the EEC and Euratom Treaties, the Court can interpret the Merger Treaty and the Treaty of Accession (by virtue of Art. 30 and Art. 1(3) respectively). Thus, apart from the ECSC Treaty, which by its nature is less likely to be invoked before the national courts, the Court can deal with any questions involving interpretation of the Treaties.

What "acts" of the Community institutions are subject to interpretation? The Court, as has been said, has taken a liberal view. In Case 181/73 *Haegeman* [1974] ECR 449, it interpreted certain provisions of the Agreement of Association between the EEC and Greece, on the ground that such an agreement, concluded by the Council under Articles 228 and 238 of the EEC Treaty, was an act of one of the Community institutions within the meaning of Article 177: see also Case 87/75 *Bresciani* [1976] ECR 129 and Case 270/80 *Polydor* [1982] ECR 329.

Although international agreements with non-member States can thus be interpreted by the Court, questions can of course be referred only by the courts and tribunals of the Member States, and not by the judicial bodies of other States parties to the agreements.

Courts and tribunals of Member States

The question of what constitutes "a court or tribunal of a Member State" (in the French simply "une juridiction nationale") arose in *Vaassen-Göbbels* (Case 61/65 [1966] ECR 261), on a reference from a Dutch social security tribunal. The tribunal, in making the reference, suggested that it was competent to do so. It stated that although it could not be considered as a court or tribunal under Dutch law, nevertheless this did not exclude the possibility that it should be regarded as a "court or tribunal" within the meaning of Article 177. The defendant, a social security fund set up under private law by organisations representing employers and wage-earners in the mining industry, submitted that the tribunal gave "binding opinions" rather than decisions and was therefore not competent to make a reference.

The Court held that the tribunal should be considered as a court or tribunal of a Member State for the purposes of Article 177. It took account of the fact that the responsible minister had to appoint the members of the tribunal, to designate its chairman and to lay down its rules of procedure; the tribunal was a permanent body which heard disputes according to an adversary procedure and was bound to apply rules of law.

This case illustrates the interaction of national law and Community law as well as the broad view taken by the Court of its Article 177 jurisdiction. The general question of what constitutes a court or tribunal of a Member State under Article 177 is a question of Community law and must be answered by reference to general criteria applicable to all Member States rather than by reference to national law. But to determine whether those criteria are satisfied in a particular case it is necessary to look at the rules of national law governing the composition, status and functions of the body in question. Thus, although the Court is normally concerned on a reference only with questions of Community law, it may have to consider questions of national law for the purposes of determining its jurisdiction.

In another Dutch case, a reference from the Dutch Council of State (*Raad van State*), Advocate General Mayras examined at some length the question whether that body, whose functions were strictly only advisory, was to be regarded as a court or tribunal; but the Court gave its ruling without adverting to this question and presumably entertained no doubts about the answer: Case 36/73 *Nederlandse Spoorwegen* [1973] ECR 1299.

In Case 138/80 *Borker* [1980] ECR 1975 the Court declined to give a ruling on a reference from the Paris *Chambre des Avocats* on the ground that the Chamber was not exercising a judicial function; and in Case 65/77 *Razanatsimba* [1977] ECR 2229 the *Cour d'appel* of Douai declared that the *Conseil de l'Ordre des Avocats* of Lille was not a tribunal which could refer questions to the Court of Justice, a view with which, in *Borker*, the Court appeared to concur.

So far as the United Kingdom is concerned, Article 177 obviously applies, not only to the ordinary courts, but also to tribunals established by statute, *e.g.* a National Insurance Commissioner (Case 17/76 *Brack* [1976] ECR 1429) or the Special Commissioners of Income Tax (Case 208/80 *Lord Bruce of Donington* [1981] ECR 2205).

A problem might, however, arise in relation to what English lawyers term domestic tribunals. In the United Kingdom such tribunals are very numerous and diverse, ranging from the Judicial Committee of the Privy Council, exercising a disciplinary jurisdiction in relation to doctors, or a statutory body like the Solicitors' Disciplinary Tribunal, to membership or disciplinary committees of such voluntary associations as the Jockey Club or the Football Association. Would they all qualify as tribunals "of" a Member State, or does the preposition denote some relationship of the tribunal to state authority or what Mr. Hartley terms "a measure of official recognition" (in *The Foundations of Community Law*, 1981, p. 258)? Nor is it far-fetched to suggest issues could arise before such tribunals upon which a reference under Article 177 might be appropriate. Thus, if the facts of *Russell* v. *Duke of Norfolk* [1949] 1 All E.R. 109 had not arisen until 1973, the Jockey Club might have wished to refer to Luxembourg the question whether they could continue to deny women the right to be professional jockeys.

The approach of the Court of Justice to such problems may be illustrated by comparing two recent decisions: Case 246/80 *Broekmeulen* [1981] ECR 2311 and Case 102/81 *Nordsee* [1982] ECR 1095. Broekmeulen was a Dutch citizen holding Belgian medical qualifications and duly authorised to practise medicine in Holland. The Dutch medical authorities refused to place him on the Dutch medical register of general practitioners on the ground of his not having had one year's experience in general practice; as a result, he was not qualified to treat patients under the Dutch social security scheme. Broekmeulen appealed to the Dutch Appeal Committee for General Practice, which body made a reference under Article 177 to ascertain whether Broekmeulen could rely on the right of establishment and the freedom to provide services conferred by Community law. On the preliminary point whether the Appeal Committee was entitled to refer under Article 177, the Court held that it was, despite its being a body set up under the rules of the Dutch Medical Association, a private association. The Court decided that the Appeal Committee was exercising a public or quasi-public jurisdiction which could affect the exercise of Community rights; it also had regard to the adversarial and quasi-judicial nature of proceedings before it. Moreover such cases did not, in practice, come before the ordinary courts.

In *Nordsee* a group of German companies made an agreement for the pooling between them of an EEC grant for the construction of new ships. They subsequently were in dispute as to how the grant should be allocated and, under a clause in the agreement, submitted their dispute to an arbitrator appointed by the Bremen Chamber of Commerce. The Chamber appointed the President of the Bremen Oberlandesgericht who decided to make a reference under Article 177 EEC on points of Community law relevant to the dispute. The Court decided, however, that the arbitration tribunal, which was established pursuant to a contract between private individuals, was not a court or tribunal of a Member State: consequently the Court had no jurisdiction to rule on the substantive issues referred to it. In reaching this decision, the Court found it significant that there was no obligation on the parties to submit their dispute to arbitration; in contrast with the position in the *Broekmeulen* case, they could have taken their case to the ordinary courts, which could also review the decision of the arbitrator and, if necessary, themselves make a reference to the Court of Justice.

Courts and tribunals obliged to refer

Under the last paragraph of Article 177, as we have seen, a court or tribunal against whose decisions there is no judicial remedy under national law is not merely entitled, but obliged, to refer a question, if it considers that a decision on that question is necessary to enable it to give judgment. A reference in such a case is not discretionary but mandatory. The question arises whether the obligation to refer is restricted to those courts and tribunals whose decisions are never subject to appeal, or whether it extends to any court or tribunal whose decision in the particular case is not subject to appeal. On the first (or "abstract") view (adopted *per incuriam* by Lord Denning M.R. in *Bulmer* v. *Bollinger* [1974] Ch. 401) only the House of Lords in England (as to Scotland, see below), and the highest courts of the other Member States, would be obliged to refer. On the second (or "concrete") view even a quite lowly tribunal would be in the same position; on this view even the Milan magistrate in *Costa* v. *ENEL* (above, p. 158) was obliged to refer since his judgment was not subject to appeal in Italian law because of the small amount involved in the claim. A literal interpretation might support the first view, since the text refers to "decisions" in the plural, but as the question is one of interpretation of the Treaty, such an approach seems unlikely to commend itself to the Court. More pertinent is a consideration of the purposes of the provision. Here the first view might be supported by the argument that the decisions of the highest national courts carry a special authority, and should therefore be subject to a special provision to ensure the uniform application of Community law at the highest level. On the other hand it could be argued that what is important is for the individual litigant to have the opportunity of a reference before a final decision is given in his case.

Here too the Court, although not expressly invited to rule on this question, has adopted the wider view, stating in *Costa* v. *ENEL* [1964] ECR 585 at 592 that the magistrate was under an obligation to make a reference in that case as there was no appeal against his decision.

In relation to the United Kingdom, the view sometimes expressed that only the House of Lords would be obliged to refer is an over-simplification even if one adopts the "abstract" view (see above). For the House of Lords is the ultimate appellate jurisdiction in the United Kingdom as a whole only for civil matters. In criminal matters, there is no appeal to the House of Lords from the Scottish criminal courts of last instance, which therefore would rank as final courts for the purpose of the last paragraph of Article 177.

A complication in determining which courts or tribunals fall within Article 177(3) arises from the English habit of permitting an appeal, not as of right, but by leave only. Thus, an appeal from the Court of Appeal to the House of Lords requires either the leave of that court or, if it be refused, the leave the Appeals Committee of the House of Lords. The parties therefore do not know until after the Court of Appeal has delivered judgment, and leave to appeal from that judgment has been refused, that the Court of Appeal was the court of last instance in their case. By then, it is not possible to invoke Article 177(3) and to insist on a reference: the national court has become *functus officio*, and any ruling obtained would be retrospective, not preliminary.

To this dilemma, the only logical solution and one which the spirit and intendment of Article 177(3) dictate, is to regard that court as the court of last resort from whose decisions no appeal lies as of right (but see the ingenious suggestion of T.C. Hartley, *op. cit.* p. 262).

Again, in English procedure the prerogative orders of certiorari, prohibition or mandamus, or the new-style application for judicial review, pose problems by reason of these remedies being discretionary in character and conducted in two stages. In the first stage, an *ex parte* application must be made for leave to apply for the order. These remedies are not therefore available as of right, and, by analogy with what was said in relation to appeals (above), a court whose judgment is final, except for possible review by way of certiorari, etc., should, logically, be considered to fall within Article 177(3). British writers differ on this question, but a National Insurance Commissioner has held himself to be outside Article 177(3) and to have a discretion whether or not to refer under Article 177(2) because his judgment, although "final," was reviewable by way of certiorari: see *Re a Holiday in Italy* [1975] 1 CMLR 184, *per* Mr. J.G. Monroe.

In practice the problem of which courts are obliged to refer will be less acute where the courts both of first instance and appellate exercise correctly their discretion.

Approach of the national courts

The success of the preliminary ruling system plainly depends on a close co-operation between the Court and the national courts. With a view to fostering this co-operation, the Court has in recent years arranged regular meetings in Luxembourg with judges and lawyers from the Member States, and has also visited the courts of the Member States; on occasion, members of the Court have sat on the bench in the national courts. Individual members of the Court have also maintained contact with the Bench and Bar of their respective countries, and regularly give talks and lectures at conferences and meetings of lawyers.

Such efforts, however, must be fully reciprocal to be effective, and it cannot be said that the readiness of the Court to receive references, and to give prompt and helpful answers to the questions referred, has been met with equal enthusiasm. Judges are generally cautious and conservative by temperament, and it was not to be expected that so radical an innovation in the European legal scene would flourish very rapidly. In the earliest years of the EEC Treaty, the Court received little but an occasional reference from a Dutch court, and subsequently only the German courts have made the fullest use of the procedure. Although it is now more widely used, there have been striking differences in the approach of the courts of different Member States, as appears from Table 7 of the Judicial Statistics (below, p. 191). In view of the importance of the preliminary ruling in the Community legal system, the approach by national courts to the exercise of their discretion to refer is crucial and has received much attention.

Those courts which have been reluctant to refer have not been very successful in their attempts to rationalise that reluctance. The French courts sought in the early days to rely on the doctrine of "acte clair," so that even a final court such as the *Conseil d'Etat* could avoid Article 177 on the ground that no "question" of interpretation arose because the answer was clear; but this argument is open to abuse (see Judge Pescatore in *Legal Problems of an Enlarged European Community,* 1972, at p. 27, and now *Cohn-Bendit* [1980] 1 CMLR 543, below p. 171; and contrast the more faithful approach of Lord Diplock in *Garland* v. *British Rail Engineering* [1982] 2 CMLR 174).

In England, when Article 177 first came before the Court of Appeal Lord Denning M.R. in *Bulmer* v. *Bollinger* [1974] Ch. 401, sought to lay down certain "guide-lines" in an apparent attempt to restrict the use of references. The attempt was marred by some confusion of thought and met a very critical reception from the late J.D.B. Mitchell, Mrs Elizabeth Freeman, and others (see

Bibliography, p. 298). Broadly the chief criticism is that, while the exercise of its discretion is a matter for the national court, that discretion must be exercised in the light of the purposes of Article 177; and, as the Court of Justice itself has held, its exercise cannot be limited by any considerations of national law (the *Rheinmühlen* cases, below, p. 284). Thus the "guide-lines" have no authority as a matter of law; but emanating from so eminent a source they have had some influence in practice: see, *e.g. Concorde Express Transport* v. *Traffic Examiner Metropolitan Police*, Kingston Crown Court [1980] 2 CMLR 221. They have, however, been expressly rejected by an Irish court: see F. Murphy, (1982) 7 E.L.Rev. 331 at 337.

Proposals have been made to remedy the problem where a final court wrongly decides not to refer; for example, a direct right of appeal to the Court could be conferred in such cases. This possibility is mentioned by the Commission in its report on European Union (below, p. 290 at para. 125. But the answer probably lies with the national courts themselves, and the statistics show that they have progressively adjusted to the system. Theoretically an action by the Commission under Article 169 would lie against a Member State whose courts were in breach of their obligation under Article 177, since the courts, although constitutionally independent, are nonetheless organs of the State for the purposes of State responsibility: see to this effect the Opinion of Advocate General Warner in *Meyer-Burckhardt* [1975] ECR 1171 at 1187. But such an enforcement procedure seems inappropriate except for a flagrant breach, and even then the Commission may decide not to bring the matter before the Court for fear of exacerbating a politically sensitive situation (as, for instance, when the French *Conseil d'Etat* refused to refer on the ground that the Community law was clear, although the *Conseil's* view of that law was directly contrary to the established case-law of the Court of Justice: *Cohn-Bendit* [1980] 1 CMLR 543).

Manifestly, the *Conseil d'Etat*, in contrast with the

French civil courts, is not presently imbued with that "spirit of judicial co-operation" which the Court of Justice sees as implicit in the reference procedure. Confrontation will only be avoided if national courts regard themselves also, no less than the Court of Justice, as Community courts.

Recently, in what some may see as a conciliatory gesture, the Court of Justice has conceded that the obligation to refer under Article 177(3) still leaves the national judge free not to do so where he believes the point is sufficiently clear not to require an interpretation; the Court accepted that the *acte clair* doctrine is not limited to where the point in question has already been the subject of interpretation at Luxembourg in a previous case: Case 283/81, *C.I.L.F.I.T.* At the same time the national judge was warned against assuming that the point is clear in all the language versions of the text in issue.

Effects of preliminary rulings

Firstly, we must distinguish between the effect of the ruling in the instant case and its effect in subsequent cases. The ruling is binding upon the referring court or tribunal in the sense that the interpretation or validity of the Community law in question has been authoritatively and finally determined in Luxembourg: the national judge has consulted the oracle and must accept the reply as what indeed the Treaties say it is: a ruling, not an opinion: see Case 29/68 *Milchkontor* [1969] ECR 165. It is then for the national judge to apply the Community law to the facts of the case.

The next question is whether the ruling is binding in future cases in which the same point of Community law arises; or, as an English lawyer might ask, is it a precedent? The whole question of precedent in the Court of Justice is discussed later in Chapter 15. Here we must anticipate the conclusion there reached, namely, that the Court prefers to follow its own previous decisions (including rulings) but that it does not hesitate to depart from them where necessary. Hence, the Court has held that a

national court, at whatever level, is always free to seek a
new preliminary ruling instead of following an old one: in
Joined Cases 28–30/62 *Da Costa* [1963] ECR 31 the Dutch
Tax Court put exactly the same question to the Court as it
had already put in the previous case of *Van Gend en Loos*
(Case 26/62 [1963] ECR 1), and the Court endorsed its
freedom to do so. In practice, however, national courts
frequently accept previous rulings as clarifying the question of Community law in issue now before them so as to
render otiose a further reference: see, *e.g.* the *Terrapin*
case before the German Federal Supreme Court [1978] 3
CMLR 102; and a United Kingdom court is bound by
statute to accept not only the ruling in a case which it has
referred but also the principles laid down by the Court and
any relevant previous decision: see the European Communities Act 1972, s.3(1) and below, p. 283.

The doctrine of precedent is concerned with the
prospective effect of a judgment (or ruling). Whether a
ruling has *retrospective* effect is a different matter and
requires us to distinguish between (a) a ruling on
interpretation, and (b) a ruling on validity (or invalidity).

1. *Rulings on interpretation*

It is the characteristic of an oracle to make plain what
has always been. Thus, when in 1963 the Court of Justice
ruled in *Van Gend en Loos* (above), that Article 12 EEC
had direct effect, it was declaring what had always been
the correct interpretation of that Article since the Treaty
became applicable on January 1, 1958.

However, in exceptional cases where the interest of
legal certainty so demands, the Court has been prepared
to limit the general retrospective effect of its ruling on
interpretation: see Case 43/75 *Defrenne* [1976] ECR 455,
fully discussed below, p. 257.

2. *Rulings on validity*

It is only common sense that provisions of Community
law enjoy a presumption of validity. Rulings on invalidity,

therefore, are much less frequent than rulings on interpretation: Community law is often obscure, seldom invalid.

Where the Court rules that a Community measure is valid or invalid, the ruling is binding upon the referring court in the same way as we have seen a ruling on interpretation binds that court. Similarly, the ruling has force as a precedent: if, however, the Court has ruled that no factors indicating invalidity have appeared, then new factors may be suggested in a future case, while of course if the measure has been held invalid the question cannot arise again.

When ruling a measure to be invalid, the Court has treated it as being void *erga omnes*: the ruling under Article 177 EEC is therefore different from a decision under Article 184 EEC which merely declares the measure to be inapplicable in the instant case (for Art. 184 and the plea of illegality, see p. 112, above).

Ratione temporis, however, the Court may decide to limit the retrospective effect of its ruling in order to leave previous transactions unaffected. We have already seen in *Defrenne* above how it did this when ruling upon interpretation, but the same concern for legal certainty may operate *a fortiori* when it rules a Community measure to be void.

Thus, in Cases 4, 109 and 145/79, *Providence Agricole de la Champagne and others* (the *Maize and Starch* cases) [1980] ECR 2823, the Court held a Council regulation to be void which had caused the applicants (and other processors of the same products) to receive lower payments for their products than they would otherwise have done. Nevertheless, the Court went on to hold that the applicants should not be entitled to claim against their national authorities the extra sums which would be due to them if transactions concluded prior to the date of the ruling were to be re-opened; the Court claimed jurisdiction to do this in proceedings under Article 177, by analogy with the power conferred upon it by Article

174(2) (whereby the Court may state which of the effects of the regulation which it has declared void in proceedings under Article 173 shall be considered as definitive).

In the result, the Court evolved a doctrine of great flexibility akin to that of prospective overruling in the United States. Whereas, in *Defrenne,* the applicant—but not *future* applicants—was able to benefit from the ruling, in the *Maize and Starch* cases not even the applicants could benefit from the ruling. In reality, of course, the applicants (and all fellow processors) would be better off in the future by reason of the offending regulation being held void.

Conclusions

Earlier chapters have shown the narrow limits within which the individual can bring a case directly before the Court: limits which the Court itself has strictly construed. In contrast, the Court's policy, as this chapter has shown, has been to welcome references from national courts; and it has availed itself of the opportunity presented by such references to develop the law in ways which are explored in Part Four.

Characteristically, in cases referred under Article 177, what is at stake between the parties in the action before the national court is relatively little; but the case often raises wider principles concerning the impact of the Communities on the sovereignty of the Member States; and the ruling of the Court is such as to determine authoritatively, and with binding force, the conflict between Community law and national law. In addition, other principles of a constitutional character have been laid down.

The two classic illustrations are the judgments in *Van Gend en Loos* in 1963 and in *Costa* v. *ENEL* in 1964. In the former case, as we have seen, the question concerned a tariff classification made under Dutch law which the plaintiff challenged in the Dutch court as contrary to

Article 12 of the EEC Treaty. The action raised the issue of conflict between national legislation and the provisions of the Treaty. The Court not only resolved this issue in favour of the primacy of Community law, but also formulated the doctrine of direct effect, thus providing for a direct guarantee of rights arising under Community law before the national courts, and ensuring, incidentally, that the future development of the law would be the responsibility of the national courts acting, where appropriate, under the guidance of the Court through the use of Article 177.

In *Costa* v. *ENEL* the sum involved, the amount of the plaintiff's electricity bill, was trivial—little more than £1; but by challenging its legality before the Italian magistrate he put in issue the validity, under the EEC Treaty, of State measures of nationalisation. While leaving the magistrate to apply its ruling as he thought fit (he, in fact, upheld the plaintiff's submission), the Court took the opportunity, in this most famous of its judgments, of elaborating its doctrine that membership of the Community limited the sovereignty of the Member States:

"By contrast with ordinary international treaties, the EEC Treaty has created its own legal system which, on the entry into force of the Treaty, became an integral part of the legal systems of the Member States and which their courts are bound to apply.

By creating a Community of unlimited duration, having its own institutions, its own personality, its own legal capacity and capacity of representation on the international plane and, more particularly, real powers stemming from a limitation of sovereignty or a transfer of powers from the States to the Community, the Member States have limited their sovereign rights, albeit within limited fields, and have thus created a body of law which binds both their nationals and themselves": [1964] ECR 585 at 593.

In another reference from Italy (Case 106/77 *Simmen-*

thal [1978] ECR 629) the Court was faced with a conflict between a directly applicable Community rule and a later national law. Developing the doctrine in *Costa* v. *ENEL* of the Community as a new legal order and of the paramountcy of Community law, the Court was careful not to rule that the Community rule had made the subsequent Italian law void; rather, it precluded the valid adoption of new legislative measures to the extent to which they would be incompatible with Community provisions. The Court declared (in a passage which stimulated several letters to *The Times*):

> "A national court which is called upon, within the limits of its jurisdiction, to apply provisions of Community law is under a duty to give full effect to those provisions, if necessary refusing of its own motion to apply any conflicting provision of national legislation, even if adopted subsequently, and it is not necessary for the court to request or await a prior setting aside of such provisions by legislative or other constitutional means."

Professor Hood Phillips has commented on this passage that it would not prevent the British Parliament from repealing the whole or part of the European Communities Act 1972 so as to deprive British courts of the relevant jurisdiction referred to above (see (1979) LQR p. 167); but see *contra*, Usher, *European Community Law and National Law: The Irreversible Transfer?* (1981).

Quite apart from the content of its rulings, this aspect of the jurisdiction of the Court of Justice is of constitutional significance in other respects. In the first place, if a reference is made on the validity of, for example, a Council regulation, the Court may be required to consider the compatibility of the Community enactment with the founding Treaties in the same way as a constitutional court is required to consider the constitutionality of national legislation. Second, the ruling of the Court is final in a sense unknown in systems which have a sovereign legislature. Thus in the United Kingdom a decision of even the highest court can, in the last resort, be reversed by an Act of Parliament. In the Communities, however, a ruling on the interpretation of the Treaties could be reversed only by an amendment of them; and such an amendment, requiring the unanimous approval of the Member States in accordance with their respective constitutional provisions, is almost impossible to attain. Here too therefore the Court is more comparable to a constitutional court than to an ordinary court. Moreover, as the normal law-making processes in the Community have been partially paralysed by the lack of power and influence of the Parliament and by the unanimity rule of practice in the Council, the Court has assumed a creative law-making role for which the Article 177 system is the principal vehicle.

Chapter 10

OPINIONS: EXTERNAL RELATIONS

As well as the judgments which it gives in direct actions, and the rulings which it delivers on references from national courts, the Court has an advisory jurisdiction to give "Opinions" under Article 228 of the EEC Treaty. Article 228 concerns the negotiation and conclusion of agreements between the Community and non-Member States or international organisations. It provides that, where such an agreement is envisaged, the Council, the Commission or any Member State may seek, before the agreement is entered into, the opinion of the Court as to whether the agreement is compatible with the provisions of the Treaty. There is a corresponding provision under Article 103 of the Euratom Treaty. Article 228 further provides that, where the opinion of the Court is adverse, the agreement may enter into force only by an amendment to the EEC Treaty in accordance with the process prescribed by Article 236, a process which has not been used, apart from the accession treaties enlarging the Communities, since the Budgetary Treaties of 1970 and 1975. Thus although this aspect of the Court's jurisdiction is advisory, and it gives only an "Opinion," it does rule definitively under Article 228 on the vital question of the treaty-making power of the Community.

That power has been very widely construed, although the provisions of the EEC Treaty are rudimentary. Remarkably, the Treaty leaves the general question as to the scope of the Community's treaty-making powers unanswered; in particular, it fails to specify the dividing line between the treaty-making powers of the Community and those of the Member States. There are only three relevant articles. Firstly, Article 113 provides for a "common commercial policy" governing the Commun-

ity's trade with non-Member States and covering in
particular "changes in tariff rates, the conclusion of tariff
and trade agreements, the achievement of uniformity of
liberalisation, export policy and measures to protect trade
such as those to be taken in case of dumping and
subsidies." By Article 113(3), where agreements with
third countries need to be negotiated, the Commission is
to conduct the negotiations under the general supervision
of the Council. Second, Article 229 instructs the Commission to ensure the maintenance of "all appropriate
relations" with the United Nations, with the GATT, and
with international organisations generally. Lastly, Article
238 empowers the Community to conclude association
agreements. Here the outstanding achievement has been
the conclusion of a succession of agreements with African,
Caribbean, and Pacific States, currently under the title of
the Second Lomé Convention.

The division of competences between the Community
institutions is governed by Article 228. According to that
Article, where the Treaty provides for the conclusion of
international agreements by the Community, the Commission generally negotiates and the Council concludes
the agreements. It might be thought, from a reading of
Article 228, that the treaty-making powers of the Community are limited to those enumerated in Article 113
(common commercial policy), Article 229 (relations with
international organisations) and Article 238 (association
agreements). That view has been roundly rejected by the
Court of Justice, which has progressively expanded the
Community's external competence over the past ten
years. In the *ERTA* case which, as we have seen (p. 94),
came before the Court under Article 173 and not under
Article 228, the Court held that the Community had the
capacity to establish treaty relations with non-Member
States over the whole field of objectives specified in Part
One of the Treaty. In order to determine whether the
Community had such capacity in a particular case, the
Court looked to the whole scheme of the Treaty, as well as

to its specific provisions. The capacity was found to arise not only where it was expressly conferred, as by Articles 113 and 238, but also from other provisions of the Treaty, or from measures taken by the Community institutions within the framework of such provisions. In particular, whenever the Community implemented a common internal policy, Member States were deprived of the right to undertake separately any obligations in their external relations which might affect the Community's common rules. As the Court said in the *ERTA* judgment (at p. 274): "As and when such common rules come into being, the Community alone is in a position to assume and carry out contractual obligations toward third countries affecting the whole sphere of application of the Community legal system."

The Court has developed this approach in a succession of cases, usually at the instigation of the Commission, and often in the face of opposition from the Member States. In this way, the external competence of the Community has been progressively expanded.

The next step in the development of the Court's case law was taken in 1975 in the *Export Credits* case: Opinion 1/75 [1975] ECR 1355. Here an agreement on export credits was being prepared within the OECD in the form of a draft "Understanding on a Local Cost Standard." The Commission recommended the Council to take a decision under Article 113 of the Treaty according to which the attitude of the Community would be expressed by the Commission. When doubts arose about the Community's competence in the matter, the Commission asked the Court for an Opinion pursuant to Article 228(1). The Court took the view not only that the Community was competent to participate in the agreement but that its competence was exclusive: Member States had no concurrent power. Elsewhere the Court has recognised the possibility of "mixed agreements" where the competence to negotiate and to conclude a treaty may be shared between the Community and the Member States: Opinion

1/78 [1979] ECR 2811, concerning a commodity agreement, the International Agreement on Natural Rubber.

The division of competences between the Community and the Member States came before the Court again in Joined Cases 3, 4 and 6/76 *Kramer* [1976] ECR 1279. Here the question arose under Article 177 when Dutch fishermen were prosecuted in a Dutch court for infringing Dutch conservation measures designed to conserve stocks of sole and plaice in the North East Atlantic. The connection with Community law was not immediately apparent since the Dutch measures had been adopted pursuant to the North East Atlantic Fisheries Convention, which was not a Community treaty: the parties to the Convention were seven Member States and seven non-member States. But the Dutch court asked, among other questions, whether the Member States were still competent to assume commitments on the international plane, or whether the Community alone had authority to enter into such commitments. The Court of Justice answered that, since there was not yet a fully developed Community policy on conservation, the Member States did have, at the time, the competence to assume the commitments in question, but that their competence was only temporary and would expire at the end of the transitional period laid down by Article 102 of the Act of Accession, *viz.*: at the end of 1978.

The international competence of the Community was further explored, under Article 228, in Opinion 1/76 [1977] ECR 741, which concerned an international agreement on a laying-up fund for barges on the Rhine, and in Ruling 1/78 [1978] ECR 2151, concerning a draft convention on the protection of nuclear materials. The latter ruling, given under Article 103 of the Euratom Treaty, provoked an extraordinarily virulent reaction in France, where two parliamentarians introduced a Bill seeking to have the judgment declared illegal on the ground of "fraud," and seeking to provide, in terms designed to recall the re-establishment of French independence after the end of the German occupation in 1944, that any French authority submitting to the Court's ruling should be guilty of the crime of "forfeiture." The Bill did not become law; but the strength of political reactions to the judgments of the Court raises questions to which we must return in the concluding chapter.

Here it may be appropriate to consider why the Court was given this somewhat unusual advisory jurisdiction. Normally, courts do not have, and do not like exercising, advisory functions, nor jurisdiction to rule on measures which are merely proposals or other hypothetical questions. The purpose of this jurisdiction, according to the *Export Credits* case, is to forestall complications which might arise subsequently if the question of compatibility with the Treaty were raised after the Community had concluded an international agreement. It is noteworthy that, under international law, the relations between the parties to a treaty cannot normally be affected, once the treaty is concluded, by a ruling of a court of one of the parties that the treaty is, in its view, invalid: *cf.* Article 46 of the Vienna Convention on the Law of Treaties. As we have seen, the Court has gone well beyond the original purpose of its jurisdiction under Article 228 in order to prevent the Member States from encroaching on the international competence of the Community.

Procedure

Requests for an opinion under Article 228 have usually come from the Commission. The Commission's request is served on the Council and the Member States, and the President of the Court fixes a period within which the institutions and the Member States may submit their written observations. There are no public proceedings; all the advocates general (and sometimes also Member States) are heard in private, and the Court then delivers a reasoned opinion. The Court's Rules of Procedure appear, somewhat unusually, to enlarge the Court's jurisdiction, by providing that the opinion may deal, not only with the question whether the envisaged agreement is compatible with the provisions of the Treaty, but also with the question whether the Community or any Community institution has the power to enter into that agreement.

APPENDIX

JUDICIAL STATISTICS

1. Cases brought

	1953–1981	1981	1980	1979	1978	1977	1976	1975	1974	1973	1972	1971	1970	1969	1968	1967	1966	1965	1964	1963	1962	1961	1960	1959	1958	1957	1956	1955	1954	1953
Preliminary Rulings	949	109	99	106	123	84	75	69	39	61	40	37	32	17	9	23	1	7	6	6	5	1	—	—	—	—	—	—	—	—
Direct actions	941	120	64	53	123	50	32	35	22	31	19	13	12	35	6	4	24	20	19	63	28	22	18	38	43	14	9	7	10	4
Staff cases	1,894	94	116	1163	22	24	19	26	41	100	23	46	35	25	17	9	6	35	30	36	2	3	4	9	—	5	2	2	—	—
Interim measures	142	17	12	8	14	6	6	5	8	7	2	1	—	2	1	—	2	4	4	8	3	—	—	9	17	2	2	2	—	—
Total:	3,926	340	291	1330	282	164	132	135	110	199	84	97	79	79	33	36	33	66	59	113	38	26	22	56	60	21	13	11	10	4

	2. *Direct actions brought by*	1953–1981	3. *Direct actions brought against*	1953–1981
	Belgium	3	Belgium	30
	Denmark	—	Denmark	4
	Germany	14	Germany	9
	Greece	—	Greece	—
	France	10	France	27
	Ireland	2	Ireland	6
	Italy	17	Italy	70
	Luxembourg	2	Luxembourg	8
	Netherlands	8	Netherlands	8
	United Kingdom	3	United Kingdom	9
	Total Member States	59	Total Member States	171
	Commission	173	Commission	643
	Natural or legal persons	709	Council	48
			Commission and Council	75
	Total:	941	Total:	937

4. Judgments and interim orders

	1953–1981	1981	1980	1979	1978	1977	1976	1975	1974	1973	1972	1971	1970	1969	1968	1967	1966	1965	1964	1963	1962	1961	1960	1959	1958	1957	1956	1955	1954	1953
Cases completed	1,921	154	175	223	114	113	113	114	146	89	90	77	70	32	26	34	39	62	44	31	39	27	58	18	10	10	8	5	2	—
Judgments given in cases completed	1,355	122	130	135	97	100	85	76	60	79	61	59	64	29	26	22	24	50	31	17	20	11	19	13	10	4	5	5	2	—
Interlocutory judgments	27	6	2	3	—	—	3	2	2	1	—	1	—	1	—	2	1	2	—	—	—	—	—	—	—	—	1	—	—	—
Total judgments	1,382	128	132	138	97	100	88	78	62	80	61	60	64	30	26	24	25	52	31	17	20	11	19	13	10	4	6	5	2	—
Interim orders	119	6	12	6	6	5	5	5	7	7	2	1	—	1	1	—	2	4	4	8	3	—	—	10	17	2	2	1	—	—

5. *Subject matter of direct actions*

	1953–1981		1953–1981
a. EEC		Non-contractual liability (Tr. Art. 215)	159
Customs duties (Tr. Arts. 12–17)	18	Protective measures (Tr. Art. 226)	28
Common customs tariff (Tr. Arts. 18–29)	4	b. EAEC	
Quantitative restrictions (Tr. Arts. 30–35)	29	Supply (Tr. Arts. 52–76)	1
Industrial property (Tr. Art. 36)	5	Arbitration clause (Art. 153)	2
Agriculture (Tr. Arts. 38–47)	203	c. ECSC	
Agricultural guidance fund (Tr. Art. 40)	9	Coal market	15
Freedom of movement for workers (Tr. Art. 48)	2	Control by the High Authority	2
Right of establishment (Tr. Arts. 52–58)	5	Aids granted by States (Tr. Art. 4c)	4
Freedom to provide services (Tr. Arts. 59–60)	1	Consultative Committee (Tr. Art. 18)	1
Transport (Tr. Arts. 74–84)	7	Non-contractual liability (Tr. Art. 40)	64
Cartel agreements dominant positions (Tr. Arts. 85–90)	136	Levies (Tr. Arts. 49–50)	8
Aids granted by States (Tr. Arts. 92–94)	17	Equalisation of scrap metal (Tr. Art. 53)	167
Internal taxation (Tr. Arts. 95–99)	25	Investments (Tr. Art. 54)	2
Approximation of laws (Tr. Arts. 100–102)	66	Prices (Tr. Arts. 60–64)	37
Conjunctural Policy (Tr. Art. 103)	5	Cartels and concentrations (Tr. Arts. 65–66)	22
European Social Fund (Tr. Arts. 123–128)	4	Transport (Tr. Art. 70)	35
		d. Privileges and Immunities	2
		e. Staff Cases	1,894
		f. Functioning of the Communities	5

6. *Subject matter of preliminary rulings*

	1961–1981		1961–1981
EEC		Aids granted by States (Tr. Arts. 92–94)	13
Common customs tariff (Tr. Art. 3)	82	Internal taxation (Tr. Arts. 95–99)	50
Free movement of goods (Tr. Arts. 9–11)	37	Approximation of laws (Tr. Arts. 100–102)	27
Customs duties (Tr. Arts. 12–17)	73	Conjunctural policy (Tr. Art. 103)	4
Quantitative restrictions (Tr. Arts. 30–35)	53	Balance of payments (Tr. Arts. 104–109)	1
Industrial property (Tr. Art. 36)	24	Social policy (Tr. Arts. 119–122)	9
National monopolies (Tr. Art. 37)	16	Procedural questions (Tr. Art. 177)	15
Agriculture (Tr. Arts. 38–47)	364	Non-contractual liability (Tr. Art. 215)	2
Agricultural Guidance (& Guarantee) Fund (Tr. Art. 40)	4	Protective measures (Tr. Art. 226)	5
Free movement of workers (Tr. Art. 48)	32	Functioning of the Communities	8
Social security for migrant workers (Tr. Art. 51)	163	Associations between EEC & third countries	8
Right of establishment (Tr. Arts. 52–58)	15	Privileges and Immunities	8
Services (Tr. Arts. 59–60)	13	Convention on jurisdiction (27.9.1968)	33
Transport (Tr. Arts. 74–84)	18		
Cartel agreements, dominant positions (Tr. Arts. 85–90)	50		

7. *Courts which have requested a preliminary ruling*

	1961–1981		1961–1981
BELGIUM		**ITALY**	
Cour de Cassation	21	Corte Costituzionale	—
Conseil d'Etat	6	Corte Suprema di Cassazione	26
Others	86	Consiglio di Stato	—
		Others	92
Total:	113		
		Total:	118
DENMARK			
Højesteret	2	**LUXEMBOURG**	
Others	7	Cour Supérieure de Justice	6
		Conseil d'Etat	1
Total:	9	Others	4
GERMANY			
Bundesverfassungs-		Total:	11
gericht	—		
Bundesgerichtshof	19	**NETHERLANDS**	
Bundesarbeitsgericht	3	Raad van State	4
Bundesverwaltungs-		Hoge Raad	16
gericht	10	Centrale Raad van Beroep	22
Bundesfinanzhof	61	College van Beroep voor het	
Bundessozialgericht	19	Bedrijfsleven	42
Others	257	Tariefcommissie	9
		Others	69
Total:	369	Total:	164
GREECE	—	**UNITED KINGDOM**	
		House of Lords	2
FRANCE		Privy Council	—
Cour de Cassation	17	Court of Appeal	5
Conseil d'Etat	5	Inner House of Court of	
Others	102	Session	—
		Court of Appeal of Northern	
Total:	124	Ireland	—
		Others	25
IRELAND			
An Chúirt Uachtarach	—		
An Ard-Chúirt (High			
Court)	7		
An Chúirt Chúarda	1		
An Chúirt Dúiche	1		
Others	—		
Total:	9	Total:	32

8. *Actions brought alleging failure by a Member State to fulfil its obligations under the Treaties*

	1953–1981
Belgium	29
Denmark	4
Germany	8
Greece	—
France	26
Ireland	6
Italy	69
Luxembourg	8
Netherlands	8
United Kingdom	8
Total:	166

PART THREE: PROCEDURE AND PRACTICE

Introductory

It is a lawyer's commonplace that procedure often counts
for more than substantive law. But the role of procedure
in the Court of Justice is in some ways more limited than
in national legal systems. The procedure has no long
tradition behind it. It was devised for lawyers from the
differing legal backgrounds of the six original Member
States and therefore was not tied to any particular
national system. Thus, although it was modelled broadly
on the procedure of the French *Conseil d'Etat*, the copy
was not slavish and has diverged further from that model
as the years pass. Modifications in the procedure have
been few, although minor amendments were introduced
after the enlargement of the Communities in 1973 and
again in 1979. It remains, as we shall see in the next
chapter, relatively straightforward, flexible and swift.

Yet a lawyer from the British Isles is likely to find the
procedure very strange. The oral and adversary character
of English civil procedure (and its Scottish and Irish counter-
parts) is in marked contrast with the written and inquisitorial features of the Luxembourg procedure, features
which cause the continental lawyer little or no surprise.

The emphasis on written procedure is explicable on two
grounds, historical and practical. In continental civil
procedure there is a very long tradition of a written or
documentary process, derived from Roman and canon law
models; the absence of the English-type institution of the
lay jury meant there was little pressure to evolve towards
a more oral process. With this shared background, it was
natural for the original framers of the procedure at
Luxembourg to devise a process with more emphasis on
written argument to persuade the legal mind than on
forensic flourishes to impress a jury.

In practical terms, a mainly written procedure makes good sense. For the administration of Community justice is ultimately controlled by its single supreme court at Luxembourg which has to serve a territory stretching from the Shetlands to Sicily, from the Atlantic Ocean to the Aegean Sea. The geographical isolation of Luxembourg from the other capitals (and principal legal centres) of the Member States means that lawyers will not wish to prolong their visits to the Court and burden their clients with additional costs. By the time the oral stage is reached the main work has been done on paper by the lawyers working in the convenience of their own offices or chambers.

The Rules of Procedure binding upon the Court were revised in 1974 and published in the Official Journal of December 28, 1974; amendments, unconsolidated, were published in the Official Journal of September 21, 1979. The Rules are drawn up by the Court itself but submitted for approval to the Council: as Article 188 EEC states: "The Court of Justice shall adopt its rules of procedure. These shall require the unanimous approval of the Council." The Rules themselves fill out and amplify the organisational and procedural framework set out in the Protocols on the Statute of the Court of Justice which are annexed to the three founding Treaties.

However, the Rules themselves are relatively brief and give only schematic guidance: there is much less detail than, for example, in the English Rules of the Supreme Court and although there is a handy compendium of texts, "Selected Instruments Relating to the Organisation, Jurisdiction and Procedure of the Court," published by the Court itself, there is no semi-official practitioner's manual equivalent to the English Supreme Court Practice. Within the framework of the Rules, decisions on procedural questions are taken by the Court, on the advice of the judge-rapporteur and advocate general, but often without the parties being consulted. Such decisions are taken at regular "Administrative Meetings" of the Court, held in private in the Deliberation Room. The decisions are communicated to the parties but are not normally reported, so that a lawyer who needs to know the practice of the Court on a particular point can only inquire of the Registry.

Chapter 11

PROCEDURE AND PRACTICE

Introduction

Within the categories of cases coming before the Court a broad distinction is drawn between direct actions and references for preliminary rulings. The latter involves a reference by a national court to Luxembourg for a preliminary ruling on a point of Community law; the procedure is distinctive and forms the subject of a separate section (p. 214, below). The account which follows is confined to direct actions, that is those where a private individual, a company, a Member State or a Community institution is bringing proceedings directly before the Court—usually with a Member State or a Community institution as the defendant.

A. *The Usual Stages in Procedure*

The procedure has four stages, of which the second stage is sometimes omitted. These stages are (1) the written proceedings; (2) the investigation or preparatory inquiry; (3) the oral proceedings; (4) judgment. The first and second stages are essentially private, in contrast to the third which takes place publicly in open court.

Despite the number of stages, and the heavy case-load, the procedure moves along with relative despatch; indeed, by continental standards, it is quite swift. Thus, a straightforward direct action usually takes a year to 18 months from commencement of proceedings to judgment; a preliminary reference takes a year or rather less, as the Court always gives priority to such cases, taking the view that time is here of the essence in order to enable the national court to resume its own adjourned proceedings as soon as possible.

1. *Written proceedings*

Proceedings are begun by the filing of an application (*requête*) with the Registrar. No set form is required for the application but under the Rules it must contain certain information. Thus, the plaintiff (in the Rules, "the applicant") must set out the subject matter of the dispute and the grounds upon which the application is based. He must also state the form of order that is being sought (*e.g.* an order to quash or for damages) and the nature of the evidence being relied upon. Any claim for costs must be included in the application

These are the minimum requirements, but the successful drafting of an application requires considerable skill. The document is the equivalent neither of an English writ nor of a statement of claim, although it performs the function of both. It is much more, for it contains, in effect, the whole of the applicant's case. It should include a full statement of the facts, of the nature of the complaint, and of the arguments of law upon which the applicant relies; any documentary evidence should be annexed. Moreover since the form of order sought cannot normally be amended, and since the Court cannot adjudicate *ultra petita*, the contents of the application circumscribe the scope of the action. The case can be expanded in the reply to the defence or at the oral hearing, but no substantial modification is permitted at these later stages.

Other, more technical information required in the application includes an address for service in Luxembourg: usually, this is the office of a Luxembourg *avocat* but the address may be "of any person enjoying the confidence" of the applicant. In addition, the lawyer acting for the applicant must file a certificate of his entitlement to practise before the courts of a Member State. The question of the right of audience is considered in the next chapter. It should be noted that legal representation is obligatory in direct actions, (below, p. 224), but a preliminary application for legal aid may be made without the services of a lawyer (below, p. 208).

The language in which an application is drafted will normally be taken to be the language of the case. Where the applicant is a private individual (or company) who is proceeding against a Community institution, the general rule is that he has the choice among the eight languages allowed by the Court: Danish, Dutch, English, French, German, Greek, Irish or Italian. But where the action is against a Member State (or, as may exceptionally arise, an individual or company in a Member State), the choice of language belongs to the defendant. As a matter of practical convenience, however, the Court has settled (at least for the present) upon French as its working language. Accordingly, whatever language is chosen for the particular case, the documents will always be translated at least into French for internal use.

The application, if in satisfactory form, is then served upon the defendant. Service of this, as of all other documents, is effected by the Registrar by registered post.

The defendant has one month in which to file his defence. The defence is of similar scope to the application, and should set out the considerations of fact and law on which the defendant relies, an indication of the supporting evidence—again annexed to the pleading— and also any counterclaim or other relief sought. The time for filing a defence can be extended for good reason by the President of the Court.

The Court has adopted the practice, common to many legal systems, of distinguishing generally between the admissibility of the action and its merits or substance. Questions of admissibility include all questions which go to the jurisdiction of the Court: they may include, for example, the question whether the applicant has the necessary standing to challenge the measure in issue, whether the action has not been brought out of time, or whether the "conclusion" or form of relief sought by the applicant is one which the Court can grant.

Accordingly the defendant often sets out his submissions under two heads, admissibility and substance; or he may make a "preliminary objection" to the admissibility of the action, and ask the Court to take a decision on that alone, which may obviate the need for a decision on the substance. The Court may also consider, of its own motion and at any time, whether there is an "absolute bar" to proceeding with a case, what the French term *un moyen d'ordre public*, that is, a bar which does not require to be pleaded by the parties and cannot be waived by them.

In the absence of a defence, judgment can be given in default. Usually, however, a defence is lodged. This allows the applicant to put in a reply, to which the defendant in turn can respond by a rejoinder. Although not obligatory, both reply and rejoinder are common steps in the pleading of a case at Luxembourg. The time limits for each are usually one month. With the rejoinder the pleadings are closed.

2. *Investigation or preparatory inquiry*

Meanwhile, upon the lodging of the application, the case will have been assigned by the President to one of the three Chambers, and he will nominate one of the judges from that Chamber to act as rapporteur while the First Advocate General will designate the advocate general for the case.

All the papers relating to the case will have been distributed to all members of the Court, but at this stage, they will only have been studied closely by the judge-rapporteur and the advocate general to whom the case is assigned—and their legal secretaries.

The pleadings being closed, the Court now takes over the direction of the proceedings. Up to this point the procedure has been adversary; it now becomes inquisitorial, if the Court decides an *instruction* of the case is needed. (This term of French procedure has become "preparatory inquiry" in the English version of the Rules).

This and other procedural decisions are based upon the preliminary report (*rapport préalable*) of the judge-rapporteur. Guided by this report and any views expressed by the advocate general, the Court decides what (if any) issues of fact need to be proved and what evidence is to be adduced for the purpose including whether witnesses (and if so, which) are to be summoned to testify. This decision is made at an Administrative Meeting (see above, p. 194) held in private in the Deliberation Room. An order setting out any measures of inquiry is served upon the parties. The Court may also decide at this stage whether the case will be heard by the Chamber to which it was assigned, or whether it should be heard by the full Court (above, p. 26).

The investigation may include all or any of the following: the personal appearance of the parties; the production of documents or the supply of information by the parties; the summoning of witnesses to appear and give evidence; the commissioning of a report by an expert; or the arranging of a visit or inspection. The Rules permit these measures, where appropriate, to be assigned by the Court either to the Chamber for the case or to the judge-rapporteur individually.

It should be noted that the hearing of witnesses is part of the investigation, not part of the oral proceedings; moreover, the witnesses or the expert are witnesses of the *Court*, not of the parties. It is possible for the parties to request the Court to hear a witness in order to prove certain specified facts; if there is good reason for this request, the Court will accede to it, and the witness then becomes the Court's witness.

The taking of evidence from a witness conforms, for the most part, with the normal practice of continental courts—practice which common lawyers generally regard as much inferior to their own for the establishment of facts where this depends on the credibility of a witness. The order sets out what facts are to be established. The witness is heard by the Chamber in the presence of the parties or their representatives. The presiding judge examines the witness. Until the revision of the Rules of Procedure in 1974, the parties' lawyers could only put questions through the medium of the judge, but now they may be permitted to put their questions directly, as in cross-examination—although the different context of the Luxembourg questioning makes it no more than a pale shadow of the English original. The other judges and the advocate general may also put questions. The statement of the witness, attested on oath, is recorded and later transcribed.

A formal investigation or preparatory inquiry is relatively rare. Thus, up to January 1, 1982 (some 29 years after the Court came into existence) the Court had heard only 120 witnesses in 28 cases and had appointed only 11 experts in eight cases; there had been three instances of an inspection, all under the ECSC Treaty where it was necessary to ascertain conditions of production in the iron and steel industry. If witnesses are to be heard, the inquiry may be fixed on the day preceding, or the same day as, the oral proceedings in order to save the lawyers a double journey to Luxembourg.

More commonly, the Court at its Administrative Meeting may decide, at the prompting of the judge-rapporteur, to ask the parties, or the Commission, to produce documents, or to reply, either in writing or at the oral hearing, to questions put by the Court in advance of the hearing.

Whatever material is added to the court file of the case as a result of a preparatory inquiry or the informal requests just mentioned, it must be made freely available to the parties, who have then the right to make written submissions upon its content. In this respect, the procedure conforms with the requirement that it be (as the French would say) *une procédure contradictoire*, that is, one in which the arguments and evidence of each party are made available to, and can be commented upon by, the other.

3. *Oral proceedings*

Once the pleadings have been exchanged and the preparatory inquiry (if any) has been conducted, the President of the Court fixes the earliest convenient date for the public hearing. The parties and their lawyers are given at least three weeks' notice to attend. With the current congestion of the Court's time-table, hearings are now often fixed months in advance. Once fixed, the date cannot readily be changed. In England it has been accepted that a barrister's obligation to attend a hearing before the Court of Justice takes precedence over obligations before all courts save the House of Lords.

A few days before the hearing the judge-rapporteur issues his report for the hearing (*rapport d'audience*). This sets out the facts of the case and summarises the respective arguments of the parties. The original purpose of the report was that it should be read aloud at the start of the oral hearing to inform the public and preserve the public character of the proceedings. But it is now always taken as read. It now serves different purposes, including the instruction of members of the Court who may be less familiar with the full contents of the file than the judge-rapporteur and advocate general. It is distributed very shortly before the hearing to the parties' lawyers so that they can make any comments either formally at the hearing or otherwise. Immediately before the hearing, copies of the report are placed on a table outside the Courtroom for interested members of the public. And the report makes it easier to produce the eventual judgment, which usually reproduces, with any corrections and a brief reference to the oral proceedings (see *Import Gadgets*), the full text of the report, to which the Court's decision on the law is appended (see above, p. 46).

The oral proceedings are reduced in practice to the

204   *Procedure and Practice*

addresses by the opposing lawyers and the opinion submitted by the advocate general. This opinion, as we shall see, is almost always delivered at a subsequent sitting of the Court.

So far as the lawyers' addresses are concerned, counsel at Luxembourg have learnt not to waste the Court's time by going over again the facts and arguments already fully set out in the written proceedings and so known to the Court. Instead, they show their skill in marshalling the salient points of their case and the weaknesses of the other side. High-flown rhetoric is eschewed. Unless the language of the case is English or French, some members of the Court will be dependent upon their earphones for simultaneous translation, a barrier which not even the oratory of a Demosthenes could surmount.

Counsel are encouraged, in Notes for the Guidance of Counsel issued by the Court (see Appendix to this chapter), to bring a text of their speeches for the benefit of the interpreters: such a text may also limit any tendency to digress, or to go beyond the length of time they will have indicated to the Court in advance of the hearing.

It is not customary to interrupt the main speeches. Each side is allowed a brief right of reply to the other. In recent years the judges and the advocate general have increasingly exercised their right to put questions.

After counsel have had their say, the President states that the advocate general will deliver his opinion at a date to be announced and then adjourns the case. Only very rarely might the opinion be delivered forthwith, for example, where the case is already exactly covered by a previous decision of the Court to which the advocate general might then simply refer. Usually, the opinion is delivered in open court at a hearing some weeks later. The advocate general stands to address the Court as an indication that he is in no sense a member of the tribunal of judgment but rather their impartial adviser. His opinion closes the oral proceedings, so that it is he, and not the parties, who has the last word. Exceptionally, the

Court may order further investigative steps to be taken, which may mean the advocate general has to deliver a second opinion. The same situation may arise if the advocate general delivers a first opinion which urges the Court to decide the case upon a preliminary point without entering into the merits: if the Court decides against him on the preliminary point, it will ask him to deliver a second opinion on the substance.

An illustration of the re-opening of oral proceedings is provided by Case 155/79 *AM & S Europe Limited* v. *Commission* [1982] 2 CMLR 264, which raised the question of the scope of legal professional privilege in Community law. In the course of an investigation by the Commission under the competition rules, AM & S claimed privilege for certain documents which they refused to make available to the Commission. The Commission did not accept the claim and AM & S took the matter to court. After the oral procedure had been completed, with a very full opinion by Advocate General Warner, the Court decided that the oral procedure should be re-opened: it decided itself to look at the documents for which privilege had been claimed, and for this purpose ordered the applicant to produce them under seal, and decided also to hold a further hearing, after which Advocate General Sir Gordon Slynn gave a further opinion.

4. *Judgment*

The Court always reserves its judgment. Following continental traditions, the Court preserves strictly the principle of the secrecy of its deliberations. Thus, only the judges are admitted to the Deliberation Room, a large room, elegant in the modern style and with a panoramic view of the City of Luxembourg; neither the advocate general for the case nor the Registrar is present. The principle also entails the exclusion of interpreters, so that the judges have had to settle upon a language which they all understand. In the result, the deliberations of the Court are normally conducted in French.

The principle of secrecy of deliberations has an additional consequence. Dissenting judgments cannot be permitted. Where the Court finds itself divided, a majority view must be determined by vote and this will then emerge as the judgment of the Court. The outside world has no way of knowing whether the judgment was unanimous or by a majority. The interesting implications of the single collegiate judgment are discussed in Part Four (p. 234, below).

Where a vote has to be taken the Rules of Procedure require votes be cast in the reverse order to the order of precedence of the judges; as Professor Schermers explains "Voting in the reverse order to the order of seniority is an old judicial custom in European courts and is designed to prevent the votes of the older and more experienced judges from influencing their younger colleagues" (*Judicial Protection in the European Communities* (2nd ed., 1979), p. 396).

The Statute requires that judgments should state the reasons on which they are based and give the names of the judges who took part in the deliberations. The judgment is signed by all the judges sitting and authenticated by the signatures of the President (who may not necessarily have sat on the case) and the Registrar.

The operative part of the judgment (what the French term *le dispositif*) is read out at the next available public hearing of the Court, either by the President (or President of Chamber) or the judge-rapporteur or as linguistic convenience may dictate; thus, if the language of the case is Danish or Greek, the Danish or Greek judge, as the case may be, may read out the judgment.

The *dispositif* must then be published in the Official Journal, in all the different language series. The judgment in its entirety is also published in the special series of the Court's reports, accompanied by the advocate-general's opinion. The official version in English is that in the European Court Reports. The citation before the Court of other series of reports became improper as soon as the

English version of the cases prior to 1973 was published. In the event of some discrepancy having legal significance between the different language versions, the version in the language of the case is to be regarded as authentic and must prevail.

B. *Execution and Enforcement*

The Court has no powers to enforce its judgment. It has no criminal jurisdiction whatsoever, nor does it have the power to commit for contempt which is the peculiar weapon at the disposal of the English judge. This has led to certain problems, theoretical rather than practical, for dealing with perjury by witnesses at Luxembourg.

It will be appreciated from what has been said in previous chapters about the effects of judgments of the Court that questions of execution or enforcement rarely arise. The implementation of preliminary rulings is a matter for the national courts. In actions against Community institutions, the consequences of a judgment given against them are either automatic, as in the case of annulment, or at any rate unlikely to raise problems of non-compliance. A judgment against a Member State is declaratory. There is no provision for enforcement of judgments against Member States or Community institutions, although as we have seen (p. 76) the ECSC Treaty contains provisions for sanctions against Member States. The EEC Treaty merely places the State or institution under an obligation to take the necessary measures to comply with the Court's judgment.

So far as the execution of a judgment is concerned, a problem only arises where the judgment imposes a pecuniary obligation on a private individual or company (as distinct from a Member State). By Article 192 EEC it is only such a judgment which has enforceable effect. The same Article then provides that enforcement shall be governed by the rules of civil procedure in the Member State where enforcement is being sought. In other words, the successful party, armed with an authenticated copy of the judgment, is left to pursue his judgment debtor in the national forum.

C. *Costs*

This is a subject of great practical importance. It is linked with the subject of legal aid, to be dealt with in the next chapter.

One preliminary difference between the Luxembourg Court and most national courts is that there are no court fees, because of the principle that procedure before the former is free of charge. A further saving follows from the principle that the service of pleadings is effected by the Registry of the Court. A minor qualification to the gratuitous principle is that the Court may order a party to pay court costs which could have been avoided or where the proceedings are deemed vexatious.

Regarding party and party costs, the Court is bound by rule to include in its judgment a decision as to costs. The general principle is that the unsuccessful party is ordered to pay the costs if they have been asked for by the successful party in his application (or defence). There are however a number of exceptions, real or apparent, to this principle.

Thus, in staff cases, the Community institution, as "the employer" concerned, has normally to bear its own costs, even if the employee loses his action.

Again, one party may be only partly successful; for example, the Court may grant his application to annul a Community decision but refuse his claim for damages. Or there may be several parties suing jointly, some of whom succeed while others fail. In such cases the Court may apportion the costs as it thinks fit or simply leave each party to bear his own costs.

If a party withdraws or discontinues proceedings, he may be ordered to pay all the costs, unless the withdrawal or discontinuance is justified by the conduct of the other party.

The question of costs on references for preliminary rulings is dealt with below.

What items are included under costs may give rise to dispute. They appear to cover the travelling and subsistence expenses of parties and their lawyers, the fees of lawyers or other specialist advisers, and the costs involved in providing an address for service in Luxembourg. If the parties cannot agree the items, the Rules provide that one of the parties may apply for costs to be taxed by the Court. This is done by one of the Chambers, whose order is not subject to appeal. In the history of the Court there have only been 32 applications for taxation.

Taxation in Luxembourg is quite different from taxation in London: the Court will make a rough assessment of the appropriate level of fees, based on what it considers reasonable in the circumstances.

Decisions on taxation are not normally reported, but Case 126/76 *Dietz* v. *Commission* [1979] ECR 2131 established a point of principle. The Commission claimed from the unsuccessful plaintiff the sum of 75,000 Belgian Francs (rather less than £1,000) for the conduct of the case by its agent, a member of its Legal Service. The Court upheld the applicant's challenge to this claim and ruled that, although the Community institutions could recover fees paid to outside counsel, the position was different where they chose to be represented by one of their own officials acting as agent: they could then recover only the travel and subsistence expenses incurred in attending the hearing in Luxembourg.

D. *Some Special Matters of Procedure*

1. *Interim measures*

Occasionally, a party involved in litigation before the Court may apply to the President for interim relief (a procedure known in French as *le référé*). For example, the party may wish to obtain a stay of execution of the decision which is being challenged in the principal suit.

The circumstances must justify such a stay, and this condition has been strictly construed so as to limit it to cases where there is a risk of irreparable damage or serious prejudice to the applicant. This reluctance to grant stays of execution is in accordance with French practice where *le référé* is seldom successful before the administrative courts.

As we saw in Chapter 5, the Court has even been prepared to order interim measures in proceedings brought by the Commission against Member States under Article 169 EEC. A recent example occurred in the continuing "Wine war" between France and Italy (above, p. 83), where the President made an order against France: Case 42/82R [1982] ECR 841 (the letter R after the case number denoted *référé*). Interim relief may also be granted to a company appealing against a Commission decision in competition proceedings. Thus in Case 27/76R *United Brands* v. *Commission* [1976] ECR 425, the President suspended two provisions of a Commission decision (requiring UB to cease to charge dissimilar and unfair prices and to cease prohibiting the resale of green bananas) until the Court had given judgment on the appeal from that decision; UB had pleaded that there was a threat to it of irreversible damage and financial disaster.

The application for interim relief is dealt with separately from the principal suit to which it is, in a sense, ancillary. It is made in writing, and the document must set out the grounds of fact and law so as to establish a prima facie case for the relief being sought. A copy of the application is served on the other side, which may then submit written observations within a short time limit. The parties may attend before the President to reply to his questions. He then arrives at his decision to grant or refuse the relief sought. Exceptionally, he may refer an application to the full Court.

Applications for interim relief have averaged some half dozen a year, of which only about 10 per cent. have been successful.

2. *Preliminary objections to admissibility*

In a direct action the defendant, usually a Community institution, may wish to contest the admissibility of the action, without entering into the substance of the case (see above, pp. 199–200). For example in an action for annulment brought by a natural or legal person against the Council or Commission under Article 173(2) EEC, the Council or Commission may contend that the measure at issue is a regulation which the applicant has no *locus standi* to attack (see above, p. 97 *et seq.*). The defendant may then, without entering a full defence, make a preliminary objection to admissibility. The applicant will then reply and the hearing will be limited to the question of admissibility. Only if the Court finds the action admissible, or decides to reserve the issue of admissibility, will the action continue on the substance in the usual way.

3. *Interventions by third parties*

The Protocols on the Statute of the Court of Justice under both the ECSC and the EEC Treaties permit the intervention in proceedings of third parties provided they have a sufficient interest in the suit between the principal parties. Notice to potential third parties (and to the world at large) of all proceedings before the Court is given by publication in the Official Journal, as required by the Rules, of every application to originate proceedings. An application to intervene must be made within three months of such publication.

Under the ECSC Statute, a Community institution, a Member State, or a private individual or a company may intervene upon proof of sufficient interest, in order to argue for or against the cases put forward by the principal parties. In the EEC Statute it is presumed that a Community institution or Member State has a sufficient interest to intervene: only a private individual or company is put to proof of their interest, but their intervention is never permitted in suits between Member States or between Member States and Community institutions.

Where permitted, the intervention may only support the submissions of one of the principal parties.

As we have seen, the intervention of the European Parliament was accepted by the Court in proceedings against the Council in the *Roquette* and *Maizena* cases (above, p. 106), despite the Council's objection that the Parliament was seeking to use the intervention procedure to circumvent its lack of a direct right of action under Article 173. The Court has sometimes been liberal in admitting interventions: for example, by a national consumers' association in the Sugar Cartel case (Joined Cases 40, etc., /73 *Suiker Unie and Others* v. *Commission* [1975] ECR 1663); and by the CCBE, a body representing the Bars and Law Societies of the Member States, in the *AM & S* case concerning the scope of legal professional privilege in Community law (above, p. 205).

4. *Joinder of actions*

Where two (or more) actions are concerned with similar or closely related matters, they may be joined at any stage of the proceedings. This is done by an order of the Court, either on the initiative of the Court itself or at the request of one of the parties.

Joinder of actions is quite a frequent occurrence, as will be apparent from the number of cases cited in this book which bear more than one serial number. But even without a formal joinder, the Court may arrange administratively for suits which are proceeding concurrently and have a common subject matter to come for oral hearing on the same day, or again the advocate general may deliver a single opinion—a sensible economy in time and effort.

5. *Can judgments be appealed against?*

A judgment of the Court is final and not subject to any appeal. There are, however, five special procedures which may be invoked with reference to a judgment that has already been delivered.

The first is an application for an interpretation by the Court of its judgment. Thus, a party or a Community institution with a sufficient interest may so apply if difficulty arises in understanding the meaning or scope of a judgment of the Court. But the Court has been severe in restricting such applications to cases where there is a real ambiguity in the judgment.

Second, there is a procedure for rectification of a judgment: the Court may, of its own motion or on application by a party made within two weeks after the delivery of a judgment, rectify clerical mistakes, errors in calculation and obvious slips: see *e.g.* Case 27/76 *United Brands* v. *Commission* [1976] ECR 446 and 450, and Case 158/80 *Rewe* [1981] ECR 1805 (the "butter boats" case (1982) 7 E.L.Rev. 316 at 322).

Third, there is the application for a judgment to be reconsidered: the French term is *révision*. A party may apply for this reconsideration if the judgment was given in ignorance of facts which subsequently came to light and which would have had a decisive influence. The new facts may even be subsequent to the judgment of the Court: see Case 56/75-rev. *Elz* v. *Commission* [1977] ECR 1617; but the procedure must not be abused as an attempt to appeal: see Case 116/78 *Bellintani* v. *Commission* [1980] ECR 23. Three months are allowed for the lodging of the application from the date when the party learns of the new facts; no application can be brought after the expiration of 10 years from the date of the judgment.

Fourthly, there is the procedure known in French as *tierce opposition*. This is an application for reconsideration of a judgment brought by a third party not involved in the original proceedings. The third party may be a private individual or company, a Member State or a Community institution. It must be shown that the judgment adversely affects their interests and that the proceedings had not been brought to their notice. The Rules of Procedure reduce the scope of this procedure by requiring the applicant to show that the judgment would occasion actual

damage to the applicant. The application has to be
notified to all the original parties and may include a
request for a stay of execution. Two months are allowed
for such applications from the date of the publication of
the judgment in the Official Journal.

Finally, if a judgment by default has been given against
a defendant who was properly served with the application
but who did not duly enter an appearance, the defendant
is allowed one month from the service of the judgment in
which to lodge an application for it to be set aside for
cause shown.

E. *Preliminary Rulings*

The procedure that we have considered so far is the
procedure in direct actions, which are brought directly
before the Court, and which originate and terminate
there. The procedure in preliminary rulings is different:
here the Court is ruling, at the request of a national court,
on a question of Community law in issue before the
national court. The procedure is incidental to, or, in the
Court's words (above, p. 52), a step in, the action before
the national court. Before the Court of Justice the
proceedings on such a reference are not, strictly speaking,
contentious, and there are formally no parties to such
proceedings. As we saw in Chapter 9, it is regarded as
more in the nature of a dialogue between the national
court and the Court of Justice. This has important
consequences for the character of the procedure.

When the order for reference has reached the Court
from the national court, a copy is sent by the Registry to
the parties to the action before the national court, to the
Member States, to the Commission and, where a measure
of the Council is in issue, to the Council. These may all
submit written observations within a single period of two
months; they have no obligation to do so. They may also
submit oral observations at the hearing of the case; in
practice, the Commission always attends such hearings,

the parties usually do so, and sometimes also one or more Governments. After the hearing, the advocate-general's opinion and the ruling of the Court follow in the usual way, as in direct actions.

The Court deals with references as expeditiously as possible. Sometimes there is a delay in the transmission of the reference to the Court but, once received, the questions were, until recently, answered within about six months, which includes the two month period for the submission of written observations. Thus the judgment in the *Import Gadgets* case (Chapter 3, Appendix) records that the order for reference was made on January 22 and received on March 5, 1976; the ruling was given on September 22, 1976. In recent years the great increase in the Court's case-load has led to considerable delays, the average period rising to a year; but efforts are being made to reduce these delays.

Although in principle the same Rules of Procedure apply to both direct actions and preliminary rulings, the various special features of procedure in direct actions which have been described under head D above are inapplicable to preliminary rulings. Thus in one case where the plaintiff before the German court asked the Court of Justice to supplement its ruling, the Court said that "Article 177 of the EEC Treaty establishes a direct form of cooperation between the Court of Justice and the national courts or tribunals by means of a non-contentious procedure, in which the parties to the main action cannot take any initiative and during the course of which they are only invited to submit their observations within the legal context outlined by the court making the reference": Case 13/67 *Becker* v. *Hauptzollamt München* [1968] ECR 187 at 197. Accordingly a further ruling could be given only if a further reference were made by the national court.

Similarly an application by the Edison electricity company to intervene in Case 6/64 *Costa* v. *ENEL* was rejected by the Court which stated that

"Article 177 of the EEC Treaty does not envisage
contentious proceedings designed to settle a dispute
but prescribes a special procedure whose aim is to
ensure a uniform interpretation of Community law by
cooperation between the Court of Justice and the
national courts and which enables the latter to seek
the interpretation of Community provisions which
they have to apply in disputes brought before them":
[1964] ECR 585 at 614.

The character of the proceedings also determines many
other aspects of the procedure which differ from direct
actions. No address for service in Luxembourg is necessary. The language of the case is that of the national court
or tribunal which made the reference, although a Member
State retains the right to submit observations in its own
language, and the advocate general will normally deliver
his opinion in his own language. Again, in contrast to
direct actions, the ruling will *ex hypothesi* be concerned
only with an abstract question of law; normally therefore
there will be no occasion for any preparatory inquiries.

Objections to the admissibility of a reference, or to the
jurisdiction of the Court, also have a more limited scope
than in a direct action. As we saw in Chapter 9, the Court
will not normally allow such objections as that a decision
on the question referred is not necessary to enable the
national court to give judgment. Apart from special
circumstances such as those of *Foglia* v. *Novello* (above,
p. 159), the Court has consistently held that its jurisdiction
is dependent on the mere existence of a reference. Thus a
question of admissibility is likely to arise only if the very
existence of the reference is itself in doubt, as when for
example the order for reference has been set aside on
appeal in the national courts. But the practice of the Court
is to discontinue its proceedings only if the order for
reference is withdrawn by the court making it or quashed
by a higher court; otherwise the Court proceeds to judgment: Case 127/73 *B.R.T.* v. *S.A.B.A.M.* [1974] ECR 51.

The position on costs is also different. The costs of the parties are always reserved to the national court, the Court's decision on costs invariably stating, as the reason for this, that the proceedings are, insofar as the parties to the main action are concerned, in the nature of a step in the action pending before the national court: see *Import Gadgets*, above, p. 52. The costs incurred by the Member States and by the Community institutions in submitting observations, whether written or oral, are not recoverable. When the national court comes to rule on the costs incurred by the parties in connection with the reference, it must do so, as the law now stands, in the context of its own national law: Case 62/72 *Paul G. Bollmann* v. *Hauptzollamt Hamburg-Waltershof* [1973] ECR 269. However the Court of Justice can itself grant legal aid for the purposes of the preliminary ruling procedure. This is laid down in one of the very few provisions in the Rules of Procedure specifically concerned with preliminary rulings. Another provision in the same Article, Article 104, deals with legal representation. We revert to this and to legal aid in the next chapter.

APPENDIX

NOTES FOR THE GUIDANCE OF COUNSEL AT ORAL HEARINGS

These notes are issued by the Court with the object of making it possible, with the assistance of Counsel for the parties, to ensure that the Court can dispose of its business in the most effective and expeditious manner possible.

1. *Estimates of time.* The Registrar of the Court always requests from Counsel an estimate in writing of the length of time for which they wish to address the Court. It is most important that this request be promptly complied with so that the Court may arrange its time-table. Moreover, the Court finds that Counsel frequently underestimate the time likely to be taken by their address—sometimes by as much as 100 per cent. Mistaken estimates of this kind make it difficult for the Court to draw up a precise schedule of work and to fulfil all its commitments in an orderly manner. Counsel are accordingly asked to be as accurate as possible in their estimates, bearing in mind that they may have to speak more slowly before this Court than before a national court for the reasons set out in point 5 below.

2. *Length of address to the Court.* This inevitably must vary according to the complexity of the case but Counsel are requested to remember that:

    (i) The Members of the Court will have read the papers;

    (ii) The essentials of the arguments presented to the Court will have been summarised in the Report for the Hearing; and

    (iii) The object of the oral hearing is, for the most part, to enable Counsel to comment on matters which they were unable to treat in their written pleadings or observations.

Accordingly, the Court would be grateful if Counsel would keep the above considerations in mind. This should enable Counsel to limit their address to the essential minimum. Counsel are also requested to endeavour not to take up with their address the whole of the time fixed for the hearing, so that the Court may have the opportunity to ask questions.

3. *The Report for the Hearing.* As this document will normally form the first part of the Court's judgment Counsel are asked to read it with care and, if they find any inaccuracies, to inform the Registrar before the hearing. At the hearing they will be able to put forward any amendment which they propose for the drafting of the part of the judgment headed "Facts and Issues."

4. *Written texts.* If Counsel have prepared a written text of their address it assists the simultaneous translation if the interpreters can be given a copy some days before the hearing. It goes without saying that this recommendation does not in any way affect Counsel's freedom to abridge, or supplement their prepared text (if any) or to put their points to the Court as they see fit.

5. *Simultaneous translation.* Only some Members of the Court in any given case will be able to listen directly to Counsel. The remainder will be listening to an interpreter. The interpreters are highly skilled but their task is a difficult one and Counsel are particularly asked, in the interest of justice, to speak *slowly* and into the microphone. Counsel are also asked so far as possible to simplify their presentation in order to avoid any ambiguities or mistranslations. A series of short sentences in place of one long and complicated sentence is always to be preferred. It is also helpful to the Court and eliminates misunderstanding if, in approaching any topic, Counsel first states very briefly the tenor of his argument, and, in an appropriate case, the number and nature of his

supporting points, before developing the argument more fully.

6. *Citations*. Counsel are requested, when citing in argument a previous judgment of the Court, to indicate not merely the number of the case in point but also the names of the parties and the reference to it in the Reports of Cases Before the Court (the ECR). In addition, when citing a passage from the Court's judgment or from the opinion of its Advocate General, Counsel should specify the number of the page on which the passage in question appears.

7. *Documents*. The Court wishes to point out that under Article 37 of the Rules of Procedure all documents relied on by the parties must be annexed to a pleading. Save in exceptional circumstances and with the agreement of the parties, the Court will not admit any documents produced after the close of pleadings, except those produced at its own request; this also applies to any documents submitted at the hearing.

Since all the oral arguments are recorded, the Court also does not allow notes of oral arguments to be lodged.

Chapter 12

LAWYERS IN THE COURT

Introduction

In this chapter we consider the role of the lawyer representing his client before the Court of Justice. For the English or Scottish lawyer, this role may seem different, in some respects, from that which he plays before the national courts.

In the first place, the nature of the procedure, as described in the previous chapter, is such as to give a different emphasis to the lawyer's task. In the written proceedings, as we have seen, the drafting of the pleadings requires considerable skill; the lawyer will also have to set out in writing the substance of his arguments. In the oral procedure, which has a more limited scope, the opportunity for forensic talents is correspondingly reduced.

Second, the advocate general plays a crucial role which supplements that of the parties' representatives. Indeed, the parties may feel that the judges will be more influenced by the advocate-general's opinion than by anything their own representatives may say. But the advocate general will himself have a full opportunity to consider the submissions of the parties, both written and oral, since the proceedings are adjourned before he delivers his opinion. By contrast, in the French *Conseil d'Etat*, the advocate general's counterpart, the *commissaire du gouvernement*, gives his view of the case immediately after the oral submissions, if any.

Third, in the Court of Justice, the judges themselves see their role as an active rather than a passive one. Their function is not only to adjudicate on the basis of the respective strength of the parties' submissions, but (as we shall see in Part Four) to develop the law and to give due weight to the interest of the Communities. Here the lawyer can both serve his client and assist the Court by relating his submissions to those wider interests.

Perhaps the most important limitation for the lawyer arises from the novelty of the Community legal system. In principle, as we shall see, any lawyer qualified to practise before the courts of a Member State is entitled to appear before the Court of Justice. Inevitably, the lawyer trained in his own legal system faces new problems. He will often be unfamiliar with Community law and the procedure of the Court, since even in the original Member States those subjects are not widely known or taught. He may have to acquaint himself, not merely with a new branch of law, but with a fundamentally new approach to law, with what is in effect a new legal system having, for example, its own principles of interpretation which differ to a greater or lesser extent from those of his own national law, and which derive in part from the plurilingual character of Community law. Indeed, the lawyer must always appreciate that this plurilingual character adds a dimension to Community law not present in his own law: thus, the British lawyer must shed the blinkers interposed by the English language when reading a Community text, or at least be aware of their presence.

Considerable efforts have been and are being made to overcome these problems. The Court for its part regularly invites, and receives visits from, groups of lawyers from the Member States, but out of the enormous total of perhaps a quarter of a million lawyers in the Communities, only a very small proportion can be reached in this way.

Within the Member States, lawyers have set up their own organisations to encourage interest in and knowledge of Community law. A leading part has been played by the International Federation for European Law (*Fédération Internationale pour le Droit Européen*—FIDE), with its national groups such as the United Kingdom Association for European Law, which include both practising and academic lawyers. Practitioners have formed their own associations, such as the Scottish Lawyers European Group, and the Solicitors' European Group and the Bar European Group in England. A Community forum for problems of mutual interest to practitioners is provided by the Consultative Committee of the Bar and Law Societies of the Member States (usually referred to by its French initials CCBE).

In some respects, indeed, more progress has probably been made in the United Kingdom than in other Member States. Long before the United Kingdom joined the Communities the British Institute of International and Comparative Law had organised extensive programmes of lectures and conferences to acquaint British lawyers with developments in Community law. Community law is now widely taught in the universities and in other law schools, and features also, as an optional subject, in the English Bar examinations. New degree courses combining the study of law with another European language are being developed. The lawyer of the future will therefore be better equipped to meet the demands of Community law, but much remains to be done if the lawyer is to play the fullest part and to have a truly European perspective.

The role of the lawyer in the Court of Justice is only one aspect of this wider perspective. Articles 52 to 58 EEC envisage, as part of the right of establishment, the right of nationals of Member States to practise a profession throughout the EEC, while Articles 59 to 66 envisage the right to provide services, including professional services, across national boundaries. (See on the right of establishment of lawyers Case 2/74 *Reyners* [1974] ECR 631 and on the provision of legal services Case 33/74 *van Binsbergen* [1974] ECR 1299). In 1977 a Directive on Lawyers' Services was issued by the Council to facilitate these developments: in the preparation of this Directive an active role was played by CCBE (for a critique of the Directive, see Walters (1978) 3 E.L.Rev 265). In this chapter, however, we are concerned not with cross-frontier legal services but only with the practice of the lawyer before the Court of Justice.

Legal representation

Parties before the Court must normally be represented by a lawyer. This rule is laid down in the Statute of the Court. So in general a litigant cannot plead his own case. The only exception is that, possibly in order to widen the rights of audience on a reference from a national court, the Rules of Procedure (Art. 104) require account to be taken of the rules of procedure of the national court concerning the representation of the parties. So where there was a litigant in person before the national court, he may appear in person before the Court of Justice; this happened, for example, on a reference from a Dutch court in Case 39/75 *Coenen* [1975] ECR 1547. It has also been suggested that this Article imposes an obligation, on a reference from an English court where barristers have an exclusive right of audience, that a barrister (as opposed to a solicitor) be instructed before the Court of Justice; but the Court has, as we shall see (p. 226), been prepared to accept that the proceedings in Luxembourg be conducted even by a lawyer from a different jurisdiction.

A Member State or a Community institution is represented by an agent appointed for the case, assisted, as necessary, by an adviser or lawyer. Member States appear quite frequently; apart from their role as parties in direct actions, usually as defendants in proceedings by the Commission under Article 169 EEC, Member States frequently make use of their right to submit observations in references from national courts. The British, German and Italian Governments have been particularly active in exercising this right. The practice on representation varies in the different Member States. The Italian Government has frequently been represented by a member of the diplomatic service, the German Government by an official from a Government department who is also a lawyer. In the United Kingdom the practice in some cases has been to instruct counsel in practice at the Bar, and in this way a number of barristers have gained experience of the workings of the Court. In other cases, the Government has been represented by lawyers employed in the Treasury Solicitor's Department or in the Government department directly concerned.

The Council and the Commission are usually represented by a member of their Legal Services, although they occasionally instruct private practitioners. The role of the Legal Service of the Commission is particularly important. The Commission, apart from appearing as applicant or defendant in most contentious cases, always submits observations in references from national courts, and can assist the Court by explaining the background to the particular Community instrument in question, which it will often have been responsible for drafting. It can also supply information on the economic context of a provision, or on the way in which it has been implemented in the Member States. Because of the Commission's special expertise it quite often happens that the Court adopts the interpretation proposed by the Commission, although at other times, of course, the Court adopts a more restrictive, or a more adventurous response. An illustration of a more restrictive approach can be found by comparing the observations of the Commission, the opinion of Advocate General Trabucchi, and the judgment of the Court in Case 118/75 *Watson and Belmann* [1976] ECR 1185; and an illustration of a more adventurous approach can be found by means of a similar comparison in Case 43/75 *Defrenne* [1976] ECR 455. For an interesting analysis, see Eric Stein (1981) *Am. Journal of International Law 1*.

Right of audience

No special qualifications are required of a lawyer to appear before the Court. The only requirement is that he is a "lawyer entitled to practise before a court of a Member State" (Art. 18 of the Statute of the Court); he must lodge with the Registrar a certificate to this effect when submitting an application or defence (Art. 38(3) of the Rules of Procedure): for this purpose, the Registrar accepts a CCBE identity card issued or validated within the previous year. On a reference for a preliminary ruling, the parties will normally be represented by the lawyers who acted in the national court and who may have had no previous encounter with Community law. In a direct action, the parties are more likely to instruct a lawyer with some experience of the Court, but, perhaps because of the diversity of the Court's jurisdiction, there is little sign at present, with the exception of a few lawyers who appear regularly, of the development of a specialist Bar. As a result, there cannot be the same kind of relationship between Bench and Bar as exists in the English High Court or the Scottish Court of Session. The relations, and also the style of the proceedings, are necessarily less personal.

Moreover, the Court has apparently accepted that a lawyer entitled to practise before a court of *any* Member State has the right of audience in both direct actions and references for preliminary rulings; thus, a French lawyer could, it seems, appear in Luxembourg on a reference from an English court. In Case 234/81 *du Pont* [1982] ECR, a reference from the English High Court, the proceedings in Luxembourg were conducted by an advocate of the Scots Bar practising in Brussels. However, in some cases a broadening of the right of audience could give rise to difficulties. For example, in a case referred by a German court in which questions of German law as well as Community law arose, a lawyer from outside Germany might be at a disadvantage, and might also place the Court of Justice at a disadvantage when it sought to put questions for guidance on German law. Moreover, the national court, when the case returned to it with the ruling of the Court of Justice, might be surprised to discover that proceedings which are, as we have seen (p. 214, above), a step in the proceedings before the national court, had been conducted by a lawyer who had not appeared, and might not be entitled to appear, before it. There might even be difficulties about which rules of professional conduct were applicable in respect of the Luxembourg proceedings, or how they were to be enforced. And where legal aid has been granted by the national authorities for the purpose of those proceedings, it might be doubtful whether public funds could be used to pay the fees of a lawyer from a different jurisdiction who might not be subject to the local code of discipline or whose fees were customarily fixed on a much more generous scale. The Court's liberal approach to the right of audience accords with the literal wording of the Statute which, as we have seen, refers to a lawyer entitled to practise before a court of a Member State; but it may be questioned whether it accords with the requirement of Article 104 of the Rules of Procedure, mentioned above, that, on a reference from a national court, account must be taken of the rules of procedure of that court concerning the representation of the parties.

Special problems arising from a divided profession

Problems may arise in countries with a divided profession. Within the Communities those countries include England, Wales, Scotland, Northern Ireland, and the Republic of Ireland. Although the United Kingdom is a single entity as a Member State of the European Communities, for many domestic purposes England and Wales, Scotland, and Northern Ireland constitute three separate jurisdictions, and the legal profession is separately regulated in each jurisdiction.

The right of audience at Luxembourg is expressed so widely as to appear to include solicitors as well as barristers and advocates. Has then a solicitor a right of audience before the Court?

In Scotland and Northern Ireland there has been no formal arrangement between the two branches of the profession regarding audience at Luxembourg, and to date only one case, surprisingly, has come to the Court from these jurisdictions (Case 83/78 *Pigs Marketing Board* v. *Redmond* [1978] ECR 2347, in which members of the English and Irish Bars represented the parties).

In England and Wales a working agreement was reached by representatives of the Bar and of the Law Society in 1971 in anticipation of the United Kingdom's entry into the Communities. The general purport of the agreement was to give solicitors almost complete equality of opportunity with barristers to play a full part in the legal professional life of the enlarged Communities. To this end, solicitors as well as barristers were to be placed on equal terms with the French *avocat* and the equivalent categories of lawyers in the other countries of the original Six, wherever reference was made to *avocats* (or their equivalents) in the Treaties or other Community instruments.

The one important exception to such equality was to reserve to barristers the right of audience before the Court of Justice in preliminary references from the English High Court, the Court of Appeal or the House of Lords (these being courts, of course, in which the Bar enjoys an exclusive right of audience).

The 1971 agreement was never embodied into the English Practice Rules. Serious doubts were subsequently expressed as to its validity, at least under Community law, and in 1981 the whole agreement was quietly abandoned by the Law Society, the Bar *non obstante*. And since, as we have seen, the Court of Justice may be willing to extend the right of audience to lawyers from a *different* jurisdiction, it cannot be supposed that the Court would be concerned to uphold purely domestic demarcations. However, from an English perspective, it might still seem curious if a solicitor were to act alone on a reference from, say, the House of Lords.

The only appearance to date as advocate by a solicitor in private practice has been in a staff case, Case 175/80 *Tither* v. *Commission* [1981] ECR 2345. This was, of course, a direct action. It seems unlikely that solicitors will seek to specialise in advocacy at Luxembourg since (as we have seen) very real problems might arise in preliminary references from English (or Scottish) courts in which they have no right of audience.

Legal aid

Litigation is an expensive pursuit, although in the Court of Justice it is probably less expensive than, for example, in the High Court in England, because hearings are generally much shorter and the preliminary proceedings generally simpler.

The Court may grant legal aid; the decision is made by a Chamber, after considering the application and the written observations of the other party. The application for legal aid need not be made through a lawyer. Consequently anyone contemplating bringing an action may himself apply for legal aid, stating the subject of the proceedings which he intends to introduce. In practice, applications are few: in 1980 there were only three.

In granting legal aid the Court acts on the principle of *ex aequo et bono*: it considers the justice and equity of the matter. Acting on this basis it may, therefore, grant legal aid even where the applicant would not be eligible for legal aid in his own country (*e.g.* because he falls outside the financial conditions or because his own country in fact has no system of legal aid: see *Lee* v. *Minister for Agriculture*, below).

Legal aid takes the form of a cash grant in aid rather than the payment of a taxed bill of costs. Indeed the Court has no such English device as a taxing master. However, the rules appear to go so far as to provide that if a person is granted legal aid he may, if he loses the case, be ordered to repay the whole or part of the funds advanced to meet his costs, or if he succeeds, his opponent may be ordered to repay the Court, as in Case 175/80 *Tither* v. *Commission* [1981] ECR 2345.

This provision does not seem to apply to legal aid on a

reference for a preliminary ruling. Here there is a separate provision merely empowering the Court to provide funds, in special circumstances, to assist the representation and attendance of a party. Since the reference is to be regarded as a step in the proceedings before the national court, a party may also be able to obtain legal aid for this purpose under national law.

This question arose in England when a stipendiary magistrate's court made a reference in the case of Pierre Bouchereau. Bouchereau was a French national working in England who was convicted by the magistrate of unlawful possession of drugs. For these proceedings he had been granted legal aid. Before deciding whether to recommend deportation, the magistrate referred certain questions to the Court of Justice, but declined to extend the legal aid order to cover proceedings in the Court of Justice on the ground that he had no jurisdiction to do so. The Divisional Court, however, held that the existing legal aid certificate covered the proceedings before the Court of Justice, since these were a step in the proceedings before the national court: *R.* v. *Marlborough Street Stipendiary Magistrate, ex p. Bouchereau* [1977] 1 W.L.R. 414. But in civil proceedings the authority of the Area Committee is required before a legal aid certificate may extend to proceedings in the Court of Justice.

In other cases, the parties may be unable to obtain legal aid in the particular national proceedings. In the United Kingdom, for example, this may arise in claims before social security tribunals, where legal aid is not available. A person claiming pension rights under Community law would then not be eligible for legal aid before the national tribunals, but, if a reference were made, could apply to the Court of Justice for legal aid to meet the costs of the reference. Again, difficulty may arise where the reference is from a country which has no scheme of legal aid. Thus in Case 152/79 *Lee* v. *Minister for Agriculture* [1981] ECR 1495, a reference was brought from a court in the Irish Republic (where no general provision exists for civil legal aid). The plaintiff in the Irish proceedings then sought, and was granted, legal aid from the Court of Justice in respect of the reference. Although the eventual ruling was unfavourable to the plaintiff and the Irish court subsequently gave judgment against him, the Court of Justice did not seek to recover the funds advanced to him to meet his costs at Luxembourg.

PART FOUR: THE COURT AS LAW-MAKER

Introductory

In this Part we examine what may be termed judicial legislation by the Court. For the Court's decisions constitute a source of Community law in a number of ways. Firstly, in relation to the Treaties and legislation made thereunder, decisions of the Court provide author- itative interpretations, explaining and developing the texts by reference to concrete cases: as such they supply an essential gloss upon the *corpus* of Community *lex scripta,* which must always be read in the light of the Court's rulings, much as the English statute book (or the French Civil Code) is incomplete unless annotated with refer- ences to the relevant case law. The Court of Justice has evolved its own style of interpretation, and this forms the subject of Chapter 13.

Second, the Treaties refer to the general principles of law common to the Member States as a source of Community law. The elucidation of these principles is an important function of the Court and amounts (as we see in Chapter 14) to a creative act of judicial legislation. For whatever the fiction, the legal reality is that the Court largely creates, and does not merely declare, these general principles. Inevitably, a common lawyer will be reminded of the Blackstonian theory of the King's judges ("reposi- tories of the law, the living oracles") declaring the immemorial customs of the realm as the common law of England.

Third, in fulfilling its two previous functions, the Court has had to come to terms with the principle of *stare decisis.* Like any court, the Court of Justice seeks to be consistent, and to the extent that consistency prevails over the competing pressure to adjust Community law to ever- changing circumstances, the Court's decisions are "precedents" in the English sense—or (better) in the American sense, being at most persuasive and never binding upon the Court for the future. This topic forms the subject of Chapter 15.

We have seen in previous Parts the style in which the Court's judgments are drafted and the process by which they emerge. Here we consider how far their collegiate character is appropriate for the Court's law-making functions.

Undoubtedly, the great advantage of the single judgment is to enhance its authority. Whatever the hidden reservations or concealed dissents, the judgment moves, syllogistically, to its logical conclusion, to which the appearance of single-mindedness then attaches greater legal certainty. In 1952 it was practical wisdom to adopt the rule of unanimity for the new-born Court of the Coal and Steel Community. Now that the Court has come of age its authority seems assured, but the single judgment has special value for reinforcing the unity of Community law. For the need to prolong deliberation to secure, if at all possible, a collegiate judgment without recourse to a vote helps to produce an agreement (or compromise) which is truly *communautaire,* that is, one in which all the judges, with their differing viewpoints, bring forward and blend together in the eventual judgment various elements from all the national legal systems. In this way, as Professor Schermers points out, the inability openly to dissent "aids the amalgamation of rules from all the national legal orders and their assimilation into Community law" (*Judicial Protection in the European Communities* (2nd ed., 1979), p. 398).

The absence of individual judgments has also the advantage of not identifying a particular judge with a particular decision. To this extent it is made easier for the Court as a whole to adopt a new departure in its case law, without fear of the charge of inconsistency being laid at the door of one judge rather than another.

In addition, the single judgment is seen as a means of

strengthening judicial independence. The twin principles—of secrecy of deliberation and singleness of judgment—provide together an effective shield for the individual judge against pressure from his government or from public opinion in his own country.

Chapter 13

METHODS OF INTERPRETATION

Introduction

The judicial process is characteristically the two-fold one of the interpretation of the law and then its application to the case in hand. As we have seen, however, the Court of Justice may find its role limited to that of interpretation only; where a preliminary ruling is sought from it, the application of the law is reserved to the national court. Under its other heads of jurisdiction the Court has both to interpret and apply the law. This chapter will survey the methods adopted by the Court in interpreting Community law. Community law includes, of course, both the Treaties and the legislation made thereunder, but the methods of interpretation do not substantially differ as between the two categories of Community law.

The methods of interpretation employed by the Court have added importance for British lawyers since they constitute the "European way" which Lord Denning recognised the courts of England (and Scotland) should follow when called upon themselves to interpret Community law. In *Bulmer* v. *Bollinger* [1974] Ch. 401 at 425 Lord Denning declared:

"The (EEC) treaty is quite unlike any of the enactments to which we have become accustomed . . . It lays down general principles. It expresses its aim and purposes. All in sentences of moderate length and commendable style. But it lacks precision. It uses words and phrases without defining what they mean. An English lawyer would look for an interpretation clause, but he would look in vain. There is

none. All the way through the treaty there are gaps
and lacunae. These have to be filled in by the judges,
or by regulations or directives. It is the European
way . . . Seeing these differences, what are the
English courts to do when they are faced with a
problem of interpretation? They must follow the
European pattern. No longer must they argue about
the precise grammatical sense. They must look to the
purpose and intent . . . They must divine the spirit of
the treaty and gain inspiration from it. If they find a
gap, they must fill it as best they can . . . These are
the principles, as I understand it, on which the
European Court acts."

This view of Lord Denning is reinforced by the terms of
section 3(1) of the European Communities Act 1972,
which provides:

"For the purposes of all legal proceedings any
question as to the meaning or effect of any of the
Treaties, or as to the validity, meaning or effect of
any Community instrument, shall be treated as a
question of law (and, if not referred to the European
Court, be for determination as such in accordance
with the principles laid down by and any relevant
decision of the European Court)."

The reference here to "the principles laid down by the
European Court" is wide enough to include its methods of
interpretation.

Plurilingual dimension of Community law
A problem peculiar to interpreting Community law, as
distinct from English law, which we must add to those
mentioned by Lord Denning in the passage cited above, is
the Community's "linguistic regime." This term describes
the principle of linguistic equality which has been
accepted in the Communities since the EEC Treaty. With
each enlargement of the Communities the principle that

the languages of all the Member States should rank equally has been steadfastly upheld, no matter at what cost or inconvenience. In the result, Community law has a plurilingual dimension not encountered in English law nor, indeed, in most national legal systems. In particular, all the texts of Community law rank equally in the different official languages (since Greek entry, seven in number), so that the Court of Justice has had to evolve methods of interpretation appropriate to plurilingual texts.

The Court's own style of interpretation

Generally, the Court does not discuss in its judgments the methods of interpretation being employed, although its choice of phrase may sometimes serve as a signpost of the road it has followed to reach its conclusions. Fortunately, individual members of the Court have been less laconic in their extra-judicial speeches and writings, and a considerable literature now exists on the subject of interpretation, some of which must be considered authoritative having regard to its source.

Interpretation of law is in no way an exact science but rather a judicial art. In the end, it is a matter of judicial instinct, and because the judge proceeds instinctively, the process cannot be reduced to a series of mechanical rules. Writers sometimes refer to "canons of interpretation," but it is better to think in terms of varying *approaches*: sometimes one approach is preferred, sometimes another, sometimes a combination of several; or one approach may be followed by another as a check upon the result achieved by the first.

The Court of Justice has no special methods of its own but uses those with which national courts are familiar. But the Court's use of traditional methods should not deceive us: the distinctive nature of Community law, when compared with national laws on the one hand and international law on the other, as well as the manner in which the Treaties are drafted, have led the Court to evolve its own style of interpretation. Moreover, as we have emphasised above, the plurilingual character of Community law introduces an extra dimension not normally encountered in the courts of the Member States. In addition, resort to comparative law is more common in the sense that the Court may look to the national laws of the Member States for guidance. This is especially so when the Court is venturing beyond mere interpretation into creative law-making: of this a notable example is the Court's development of the doctrine of the general principles of law, to be discussed in the next chapter.

In the exposition which follows, four methods of interpretation are discussed *seriatim*. These are the literal, historical, contextual and teleological. Although this order has a certain logic and accords broadly with the way in which the approaches to interpretation by national courts are traditionally presented, it would be quite wrong to assume that the methods are placed in descending order of importance. As will become apparent, the dominant approaches of the Court of Justice are the contextual and teleological.

Literal interpretation

Every court must begin from the words of the text before it. If their meaning is plain, either in their ordinary connotation or in some special sense appropriate to the particular context, then for the national judge the task of interpretation is a light one and ends there. Usually, the same can be said for the Court of Justice, but exceptionally the Court may be led to disregard the plainest of wording in order to give effect to what it deems the overriding aims and objects of the Treaties. In other words the literal interpretation is displaced by the contextual or teleological approach, although the Court may speak rather in terms of looking to "the spirit" of the text in question.

Case 22/70 *ERTA* [1971] ECR 263 provides a good example. The Commission sought the annulment of a

Council discussion to co-ordinate the attitude to be adopted by the six Member States in certain international negotiations to revise the European Road Transport Agreement. The Council's defence included the plea that the discussion did not constitute an "act" subject to annulment within the meaning of that term in Article 173 EEC: any such act was limited to the categories of regulation, directive or decision as enumerated in Article 189. Despite the apparently exhaustive wording of Article l89, the Court found against the Council on this plea, holding that the aim of Article 173 was to subject to judicial review all measures taken by the institutions designed to have legal effect and declaring that "It would be inconsistent with this objective to interpret the conditions under which the action is admissible so restrictively as to limit the availability of this procedure merely to the categories of measures referred to by Article 189."

As Lord Denning has indicated, literal interpretation is made more difficult for the Court by the general absence in the Treaties of definitions of the terms used. An English or Scottish Court may often be able to resolve a question of interpretation by the help of the glossary or dictionary which the legislator has thoughtfully provided in the definition or interpretation section of the particular statute. Such definitions are rare in Community law. Rather, the Treaties adopt the opposing continental approach of preferring to leave to judicial interpretation (assisted by doctrinal opinion) the meaning of terms which have been deliberately left undefined in the texts. Examples from the EEC Treaty include:

> "charges having equivalent effect" (Arts. 9, 12, 13 and 16) (see the *Gingerbread* case below, p. 249);
> "public policy" (Art 48) (see *Van Duyn* v. *Home Office* below p. 242);
> "abuse of a dominant position" (Art. 86) (see *Continental Can* case below p. 255);

"general principles common to the laws of the Member States" (Art. 215(2)) (see Chapter 14.)

By contrast, although definitions do not normally feature in the Treaties, the different technique is used of providing either an exhaustive list or a number of examples which is deliberately left open-ended: for the former, see the list of products subject to the Common Agricultural Policy set out in Annex II to the EEC Treaty, and for the latter, see the five examples in Article 85(1) EEC of prohibited agreements under that Article.

By its very nature and purpose, secondary legislation under the Treaties is much more tightly drafted. Thus, the Common Customs Tariff (pursuant to Articles 19–29 EEC) is a detailed catalogue of nearly 3,000 items; it may still however give rise to problems of interpretation (see Case 22/76 *Import Gadgets* and the opinion of Advocate General Warner in the Appendix to Chapter 4 above.) But Community legislation also often makes use of vague terms: see, for example, Council Directive No. 64/221 which failed to clarify sufficiently the reference in Article 48 EEC to "grounds of public policy, public security or public health," a clarification which the Court had to supply in Case 41/74 *Van Duyn* v. *Home Office* [1974] ECR 1337.

Faced as it often is with texts which are vague, ambiguous or incomplete, the Court has recognised the limitations for itself of the literal method of interpretation. Particularly after 1958, when the Court was confronted with the more programmatic EEC Treaty, its interpretation shifted perceptibly towards the contextual and teleological, with emphasis on the *ratio legis* and the objectives of the Treaty. Thus, in Case 6/60 *Humblet* [1960] ECR 559 it declared at 575: "it is not sufficient for the Court to adopt the literal interpretation and the Court considers it necessary to examine the question whether this interpretation is confirmed by other criteria concerning in particular the common intention of the High

Contracting Parties and the *ratio legis*." Again in Case 26/62 *Van Gend en Loos* [1963] ECR at 12, the Court stated:

> "To ascertain whether the provisions of an international treaty [*viz.*: Article 12 EEC] extend so far in their effects it is necessary to consider the spirit, the general scheme and the wording of those provisions."

Significantly, the Court ranked the wording in third place, as it did in similar language in Case 6/72 *Continental Can* [1973] ECR at 243: "In order to answer this question, one has to go back to the spirit, general scheme and wording of Article 86 EEC, as well as to the system and objectives of the Treaty." But in its earlier decisions the Court gave greater emphasis to wording: thus in Case 9/56 *Meroni* v. *High Authority* [1958] ECR 133 at 140, it re-affirmed the view it had expressed in Case 8/55 *Fédéchar* [1954–1956] ECR 245, that an argument *a contrario* is only admissible if no other interpretation appears to be appropriate and compatible with the express wording, with the context and with the purpose of the provisions.

In comparison with a national court, the task of the Court of Justice is inevitably more difficult because, as we have seen, there will seldom be a single text before it. In the event of ambiguity it may have to consider the versions in the various Community languages, all equally authentic. Very real difficulties may arise from subtle differences between the alternative texts. Thus, Article 48(3) EEC uses, in the English text, the expression "public policy," to translate the French term "ordre public," a false equation with which Advocate General Warner wrestled valiantly to find the *mot juste* in Case 30/77 *Bouchereau* [1977] ECR 1999. Likewise, the French term "détournement de pouvoir" as used in Article 173 EEC has a more precise meaning than the vague English term "misuse of powers" employed in the English texts: the same expression in Article 33 ECSC has presented problems of interpretation for the Court because of its various shades of meaning in the original six Member

States: *e.g.* Case 3/54 ASSIDER [1954–1956] ECR 63. Again, in Case 29/69 *Stauder* [1969] ECR 419, the Court had to consider the different versions of a Commission decision addressed to the Member States permitting the sale of butter at reduced prices to persons in receipt of welfare benefits. The Dutch and German texts required the beneficiaries to receive their butter in exchange for a "coupon indicating their names." A German citizen challenged this in his national courts as an infringement of fundamental rights. The Court referred to the French and Italian versions which only stipulated the production of a "coupon referring to the person concerned." It adopted this more liberal version of the decision which would enable its objective to be achieved by other and unexceptionable methods of identifying the beneficiaries.

Faced thus by a disparity of texts the Court looks, where the context so permits, for that text which offers the most liberal solution in relation to the rights of the individual, being guided by the spirit and intention of the texts rather than by the verbal symbols in which they are expressed: this is an approach consistent with its own doctrine of proportionality whereby the Court requires a Community act to use the minimum of means to achieve the desired end (see p. 262, below). Other cases posing problems of textual disparity include: Case 9/79 *Koschniske* [1979] ECR 2717; Case 814/79 *Rüffer* [1980] ECR 3807; Case 131/79 *Santillo* [1980] ECR 1585: see generally Brown (1981) 15 *Valparaiso Univ. Law Rev.* 319.

Historical interpretation

By historical interpretation is usually meant the quest for the subjective intention of the author of the text. It may also mean the discovery of the objective intention of the measure in question, to be deduced from its purpose at the date of enactment. The English so-called "Mischief Rule" as laid down in *Heydon's Case* (1584) 3 Co.Rep. 7a confines the English judge to the objective legislative intent, whereas in most Continental countries the judge may examine the *travaux préparatoires* ("preparatory work") in pursuit of the subjective intention of the legislature. This is only a generalisation, for on both sides of the Channel there is movement towards a more intermediate position, limited access to certain *travaux préparatoires* becoming acceptable in England, while such materials are treated with increasing caution in some continental jurisdictions. (For a valuable survey, see Norman S. Marsh, *Interpretation in the National and International Context*, 1973).

Historical interpretation in either sense is little used by the Court of Justice. In regard to the Treaties, the negotiations have remained shrouded in secrecy by common agreement of the contracting States. Professor Pescatore, now a distinguished judge of the Court, was himself the head of the Luxembourg team which negotiated the EEC Treaty, and he has explained in a public lecture in 1963 the wisdom of excluding recourse to the records of the negotiations:

> "Treaties are not established unilaterally, they are negotiated. In order to interpret an international treaty correctly, account must therefore be taken of the actual conditions in which it was negotiated. However, it is precisely one of the rules of negotiation that one does not always reveal one's intentions. It is not, in actual fact, on the intentions of the contracting parties that agreement is reached, but on the written formulas of the treaties and only on that. It is by no means certain that agreement on a text in any way implies agreement as to intentions. On the contrary, divergent, even conflicting intentions may perfectly well underlie a given text and I would even go so far as to say . . . that the art of treaty-making is in part the art of disguising irresolvable differences between the contracting States."

The former President of the Court, Robert Lecourt, in his Geneva Lectures *Le juge devant le Marché commun*

(1970), confirms the view of Judge Pescatore that it is not the function of the Luxembourg Court to rediscover the intention of the parties in the manner which is traditional for interpreting treaties in international law. He explains (at p. 64) that:

> "In the Community the judge is the repository of the will of the authors of the Treaties, who moved into the background on the day of signature, to re-appear only at rare moments when they sign new agreements. They have made the judge the guardian of their common achievement, that is to say, of its objectives, institutions and law. They have carried so far the trust which they have placed in the judge as the custodian of their common will that they have even destroyed every official trace of their *travaux préparatoires*."

Somewhat greater freedom in resorting to *travaux préparatoires* is manifested by the advocates general of the Court in their opinions. In particular, they have occasionally referred to the record of proceedings in the national parliaments when the Treaties were being submitted for ratification. Thus, in Case 6/54 *Netherlands* v. *High Authority* [1954–1956] ECR 103 concerning the interpretation of Article 33 ECSC Advocate General Roemer suggested, after citing the explanations given to their national legislatures by the German and French Governments, that "the Court should examine the statement of reasons laid before the parliaments of the other countries." And the Court itself in Case 6/60 *Humblet* [1960] ECR 559 referred in its judgment to the fact that "the opinions of the governments put forward during the parliamentary debates on the ECSC Treaty do not touch on this question. The same is true of the parliamentary votes on the EEC and EAEC Treaties which contain a provision in substantially the same terms." In *Humblet* the Court had to determine the scope of the provision in the Protocol on the Privileges and Immunities which exempted the salaries of Community officials from national charges; having found the parliamentary debates silent on the point, the Court then resorted to a comparison of different national laws as an aid to interpretation of the Protocol.

Because of the dynamic character of the Treaties as laying down programmes for the future, such reference to *travaux préparatoires*, whether by the Court or its advocates general, tends to diminish as the dates of concluding the Treaties (or Protocols) recede into the past. President Kutscher has declared indeed that "It is useless to look at such pointers in the more recent judgments . . . interpretations based on the original situation would in no way be in keeping with a Community law orientated towards the future." (H. Kutscher, *Methods of Interpretation as seen by a judge of the Court of Justice* (1976), pp.21–22).

So far as Community legislation is concerned, both the Council and the Commission deliberate in secret, and especially in the Council hard bargaining is common. Accordingly, even if available, the records of deliberations in these bodies would be open to the same objections as those attached by MM. Pescatore and Lecourt to the negotiations of the Treaties. On the other hand, certain official *travaux préparatoires* are available for Community legislation. Thus, the Official Journal publishes all legislative proposals by the Commission as well as formal opinions of the European Parliament, which may relate to proposed legislation.

In addition, the regulations, directives and decisions of the Council and Commission are required by Article 190 EEC to state the reasons on which they are based and to refer to any proposals or opinions which were required to be obtained pursuant to the Treaty. These obligatory recitals in the preamble to such legislation throw light on the intention of the Council or Commission and are frequently referred to by the Court as a guide to the interpretation of their provisions. Thus, in Case 14/69

Markus v. *Hauptzollamt Hamburg-Jonas* [1969] ECR 349
the Court held that:

> "according to the seventh recital of the preamble to
> the regulation in question . . . the eighth recital of
> the same preamble states . . . It must therefore be
> assumed that the authors of the first paragraph of
> Article 16 intended . . . This solution is confirmed by
> the penultimate recital of the preamble to the said
> regulation according to which . . ."

Again, in Case 9/72 *Brunner* [1972] ECR 961 the Court
held that: "It is clear from the recitals of the preamble to
that regulation that . . ." And in the *Import Gadgets* case
(as we saw in the Appendix to Chapter 3, at p. 46 above),
the Court followed its normal practice of interpreting the
Common Customs Tariff by reference to the Explanatory
Notes to the Brussels Nomenclature, that is, notes relating
to the Convention of December 15, 1950 on nomenclature
for the classification of goods in customs tariffs, this
Nomenclature, which provides the historical basis for the
Common Customs Tariff, being legally binding as an
international obligation on all the Member States and, in
the view of the Court, on the Community itself.

Contextual interpretation
   This method is extensively used by the Court in
interpreting both the Treaties and Community legislation.
It involves placing the provision in issue within its context
and interpreting it in relation to other provisions of
Community law. The Treaties, in particular the EEC
Treaty, set out a grand design or programme, and it is
natural to stress the interrelationship of the individual
provisions as component parts of the total scheme. Not
seeing the wood for the trees is, for the Court, a cardinal
sin. Hence, its judgments abound with references such as:

> "the context of all the provisions establishing a
> common organisation of the market": Case 190/73

Van Haaster [1974] ECR 1123;
"the general scheme of the Treaty as a whole": Cases 2 and 3/62 *Gingerbread* case [1962] ECR 425;
"taking account of the fundamental nature, in the scheme of the Treaty, of the principles of freedom of movement and equality of treatment of workers": Case 152/73 *Sotgiu* [1974] ECR 153;
"one must have regard to the whole scheme of the Treaty no less than to its specific provisions": Case 22/70 *ERTA* case [1971] ECR 263;
"the context of the Treaty": Case 23/75 *Rey Soda* [1975] ECR 1279;
"the framework of Community law": Cases 90 and 91/63 *Dairy Products* case [1964] ECR 625; Case 6/64 *Costa* v. *ENEL* [1964] ECR 585.
"Article 37(1) EEC must be interpreted in its context in relation to the other provisions of the article and taking account of its place in the general scheme of the Treaty": Case 59/75 *Manghera* [1976] ECR 91.

A striking example of the effect of this systematic interpretation of the Treaty can be found in the Court's treatment of customs duties and charges having equivalent effect in Article 12 of the EEC Treaty. Article 12 provides that

"Member States shall refrain from introducing between themselves any new customs duties on imports or exports or any charges having equivalent effect, and from increasing those which they already apply in their trade with each other."

In the *Gingerbread* case, Cases 2 and 3/62 *Commission* v. *Luxembourg and Belgium* [1962] ECR 425 the Court held that

"The position of those Articles (Articles 9 and 12) towards the beginning of that Part of the Treaty dealing with the 'Foundations of the Community'— Article 9 being placed at the beginning of the Title relating to 'Free Movement of Goods,' and Article 12 at the beginning of the section dealing with the 'Elimination of Customs Duties'—is sufficient to emphasise the essential nature of the prohibitions which they impose."

Relying on, among other things, the "general scheme" of these provisions and of the Treaty as a whole, the Court went on to argue that there was evidence of "a general intention to prohibit not only measures which obviously take the form of the classic customs duty but also all those which, presented under other names or introduced by the indirect means of other procedures, would lead to the same discriminatory or protective results as customs duties."

It is interesting to compare the approach which an English court might adopt to the expression "customs duties and charges having equivalent effect." An English court would be likely to apply the more restrictive approach, according to which, when general words are used, they are to be confined to those kinds of things with which the context deals explicity or implicitly: the *eiusdem generis* rule is a specific instance of this approach where two examples of a category are given, followed by a general expression. An English court, therefore, would refer to the context of the provision "customs duties and charges having equivalent effect," but rather with a view to *limiting* the general expression in the light of that context. In the *Gingerbread* case, on the contrary, the Court uses the general expression "any charges having equivalent effect" as a "catch all" concept to cover not only charges of the *same* kind but charges of *all* kinds having the same effect. Hence it takes Chapter 1 of this Part of the Treaty as prohibiting all pecuniary obstacles to trade between Member States. In other cases, the same result is achieved in relation to Chapter 2, on the elimination of quantitative restrictions. All measures having equivalent effect to quotas, prohibited by Article 30, are taken to exclude, in effect, all non-pecuniary trade

barriers, subject only to the exceptions expressly provided
(and narrowly construed) in Article 36. Thus, by looking
at this Title of the Treaty as a whole, and construing its
very general provisions in the light of its supposed aims,
the Court takes it as abolishing at a stroke, with very
limited exceptions, all barriers, pecuniary or otherwise, to
trade between Member States.

In a characteristic passage in case 24/68 *Commission* v.
Italian Republic [1969] ECR 193, the Court held (at
200–201):

> "Thus, in order to ascribe to a charge an effect
> equivalent to a customs duty, it is important to
> consider this effect in the light of the objectives of the
> Treaty, in the Parts, Titles and Chapters in which
> Articles 9, 12, 13 and 16 are to be found, particularly
> in relation to the free movement of goods. Conse-
> quently, any pecuniary charge, however small and
> whatever its designation and mode of application,
> which is imposed unilaterally on domestic or foreign
> goods by reason of the fact that they cross a frontier,
> and which is not a customs duty in the strict sense,
> constitutes a charge having equivalent effect within
> the meaning of Articles 9, 12, 13 and 16 of the Treaty,
> even if it is not imposed for the benefit of the State, is
> not discriminatory or protective in effect and if the
> product on which the charge is imposed is not in
> competition with any domestic product."

Contextual interpretation is no less important in relation to Community legislation. Typically, the Court may
have to interpret a regulation of the Commission which
implements a regulation of the Council which itself is
issued pursuant to a provision in the Treaties: Case 64/69
Compagnie Française Commerciale et Financière v. *Commission* [1970] ECR 221 was such a case. The Court will
necessarily examine the subordinate regulation immediately in issue for its compatibility both with the
enabling regulation and with the superior law of the

treaty provision. Having examined the vertical context it will also consider the horizontal relationship of the regulation with other Commission regulations *in pari materia*. Again, the language of the Court's judgments is indicative of this approach, for example:

> "the Regulation (No. 3 on social security for migrant workers made pursuant to Article 51 EEC) must be interpreted in the context and within the bounds of this article and having regard to the fundamental principles which it lays down": Case 28/68 *Torrekens* [1969] ECR 125. And in Case 17/76 *Brack* v. *The Insurance Officer* [1976] ECR 1429 "The Regulation [No. 1408/71 which superseded No. 3 above] must be interpreted above all in the light of the spirit and of the objectives of the Treaty."

Comparative Law as aid to interpretation

Part of the context in which Community law operates is its interrelationship with the national laws of the Member States. The judges themselves of the Court bring to their task the conceptual background and instinctive reactions derived from previous careers in their own legal systems. Almost subconsciously, therefore, comparative law must be influencing their interpretative function.

In addition, Community law may use terms or concepts which are well known in the national laws, without itself defining them. In this case, the Community sense of the term may involve a comparison of the relevant national laws: see, for example, the opinion of Advocate General Lagrange in Case 3/54 *ASSIDER* v. *High Authority* [1954–1956] ECR 63 concerning the term *détournement de pouvoir* in the authentic French text and its Dutch, German and Italian equivalents in Article 33 ECSC. The Judgments Convention (p. 156, above) offers particular scope for the comparative method in its interpretation. To secure its uniform application in all the Member States, the Court has been persuaded to adopt autonomous Community meanings for legal terms and concepts employed in the Convention: the advocates general have demonstrated in several cases that such terms lack any consistent meaning in the various national laws (see, *e.g.* Case 29/76 *LTU* v. *Eurocontrol* [1976] ECR 1541 Opinion of Advocate General Reischl; Case 814/79 *Rüffer* [1980] ECR 3807 Opinion of Advocate General Warner).

Likewise, Community law may simply be silent on questions of principle which have received solutions in the laws of the Member States. Thus, the question whether Community law admitted the revocation of measures creating subjective rights was answered by the Court in Cases 7/56 and 3-7/57 *Algera* [1957–1958] ECR 39 "by reference to the rules acknowledged by the legislation, the learned writing and the case-law of the member countries," and there followed in the judgment "a comparative study of this problem of law" (for the facts of this case, see p. 145, above).

So extensive a comparative examination in an actual judgment is rare, indeed unique; but the opinions of the advocates general contain much comparative analysis. The judgment of the Court may then briefly adopt the result of such analysis, as, for example, in Case 32/62 *Alvis* [1963] ECR 49, which upheld in Community law the generally accepted principle of administrative law in the Member States whereby a civil servant must be allowed the opportunity to reply to allegations against him before being disciplined (see further p. 147 above). Again in Case 155/79 *AM & S* [1982] 2 CMLR 264 both Advocate General Warner and (in the re-opened oral proceedings) Advocate General Slynn included in their opinions extensive comparative analysis of the scope of legal professional privilege in all the Member States with a view to guiding the Court how far that privilege should extend as a general principle of Community law.

More specifically, as we have seen in Chapter 7, Article 215(2) EEC bases the non-contractual liability of the Community for damage caused by its institutions or by its servants in the performance of their duties upon "the general principles common to the laws of the Member States." In the earlier chapter we saw how the Court had drawn, by an eclectic process, upon the national legal systems to create a uniform Community law governing tortious liability or reparation.

Resort to a *ius commune Europaeum*, which is explicitly required by Article 215(2) EEC (Art. 188 Euratom), is also an underlying feature of the wider doctrine of "general principles of law" which the Court has developed as an additional source of Community law. This important topic is returned to more fully in Chapter 14, but it is relevant here as a further example of the Court's use of comparative law as an aid to interpretation. Of necessity, much comparative research is constantly undertaken on behalf of the members of the Court, and we have seen in Chapter 2 what internal arrangements exist to facilitate this. In addition, the Commission's Legal Service often includes comparative material in presenting its observations to the Court, or the Commission may be expressly requested by the Court to include such material in its observations (Pescatore (1980) *Revue Internationale de Droit Comparé* 337).

Teleological interpretation

The term teleological is applied to an interpretation which is based upon the purpose or object of the text facing the judge. This approach, which is increasingly favoured by the Court, is peculiarly appropriate in Community law where, as we have seen, the Treaties provide mainly a broad programme or design rather than a detailed blue-print. In setting forth the grand design the Treaties, both in their preambles and in certain Articles, express the objectives of the Communities in very general terms; in turn, these objectives are knit together by the underlying assumption that they will lead eventually to an economic and political union. Article 2 EEC is a striking example with its declaration of intent that:

"The Community shall have as its task, by establishing a common market and progressively approximating the economic policies of Member States, to promote throughout the Community a harmonious development of economic activities, a continuous and balanced expansion, an increase in stability, an accelerated raising of the standard of living and closer relations between the States belonging to it."

Faced with a body of law whose core is couched in such terms the Court of Justice has naturally adopted the teleological method in interpreting both the Treaties and the legislation derived from them. For Judge Pescatore, as for President Kutscher, the teleological and contextual methods assume greater importance than the historical or literal methods; see above p. 245 and p. 247.

From the case law of the Court we have already discussed one notable example, Case 22/70 *ERTA* [1971] ECR 263 (see p. 240, above). A further illustration is a leading case on Article 86 EEC, Case 6/72 *Europemballage Corporation and Continental Can Co. Inc.* v. *Commission* [1973] ECR 215. Article 86 prohibits any "abuse of a dominant position within the common market or in a substantial part of it . . . in so far as it may affect trade between Member States." The *Continental Can* case raised the question whether Article 86 could apply to take-overs or mergers.

According to a decision taken by the Commission, Continental Can Company Inc. of New York, which held, through the medium of its German subsidiary, a dominant position over a substantial part of the common market in certain packaging products, had abused that dominant position by acquiring, through a Belgian subsidiary Europemballage Corporation, a Dutch company which was the only significant competitor in those products.

The Commission's decision required Continental Can to put an end to its alleged infringement of Article 86 and to submit proposals to the Commission for that purpose by a specified date. The decision was challenged before the Court by Continental Can and by Europemballage, who argued that the Commission had wrongly interpreted Article 86 and was trying to introduce merger control in the EEC Treaty. The ECSC Treaty made express provision for merger control but there was no such express provision in the EEC Treaty. The Court rejected comparison with the ECSC Treaty as a method of interpretation and referred instead to "the spirit, general scheme and wording of Article 86, as well as to the system and objectives of the Treaty." It went on to examine the Article in the context of the other treaty provisions on competition and in the light of the principles and objectives set out in Articles 2 and 3. Ultimately it annulled the decision on other grounds, but it upheld the Commission's extensive interpretation of Article 86. ⟶▷

The use of the teleological method of filling gaps in codes or statutes is a familiar one in continental legal systems. It is expressly enjoined upon the Swiss courts by the Swiss Civil Code of 1922. In Community law the original Treaties were designed to have their details filled out by legislation of the Council and Commission. The political near-paralysis which has crippled the legislative institutions of the Communities in the last decade or more has left yawning gaps in the enacted Community law. The Court of Justice sees itself as charged by the Treaties with upholding Community law, and accordingly it must fill the gaps left in that law by the default of the other institutions or the inactivity of the Member States.

Thus, the adjustment of State monopolies of a commercial character was required of Member States under Article 37 EEC during the transitional period; in default of the adjustment by the Italian Government of its tobacco monopoly (albeit this default was with the tacit acquiescence of the Council), the Court, in Case 59/75 *Manghera* [1976] ECR 91, took upon itself to declare the incompatibility of that monopoly with the Treaty and to draw the necessary consequences.

Again, in the second *Defrenne* case (Case 43/75 [1976] ECR 455), the Court had to consider the application of the principle of equal pay for equal work imposed by Article 119 EEC, and whether that principle had become directly enforceable in the national courts at the end of the first stage of the transitional period (December 31, 1961), or whether the further period of grace granted by the Council to Member States for implementing Article 119 was valid. The Court held the Article to have come into operation on January 1, 1962 and to have direct effect. It supported this conclusion by reference to the nature of the equal pay principle and the objective of this principle and its place in the EEC Treaty. It combined the teleological with the contextual approach in emphasising not only the dual purpose (economic and social) of Article 119 but also its relationship to other provisions, particularly Article 117 concerning the need to promote improved working conditions and an improved standard of living for workers.

That the Court has consciously assumed a legislative role in this case is confirmed by the further (and controversial) component of its judgment in which, in the interest of legal certainty, it declined to give a general retrospective effect to its ruling on Article 119: only those who had already commenced legal proceedings could claim pay for periods prior to the date of judgment.

This teleological approach is also extensively used in interpreting Community legislation. Thus, in Case 9/67 *Colditz* [1967] ECR 229, concerning certain social security regulations, the Court declared that

> "the solution to this question . . . can only emerge from the interpretation of those regulations in the light of the objectives of the provisions of the Treaty (Arts. 48 to 51)."

Also, as we have seen in considering contextual interpretation, regulations and directives recite in their preambles the reasons on which they are based. This enables the

Court to invoke the objectives of the measure by reference to such recitals and to interpret it accordingly.

As part of its teleological approach the Court not infrequently refers to the principle of effectiveness (*l'effet utile*), a concept borrowed from international law which is sometimes rendered inelegantly into English as "useful effect." In Community law this has come to mean that "preference should be given to the construction which gives the rule its fullest effect and maximum practical value" (Kutscher, *op.cit.* 41). Cases in which the Court has invoked this principle of what we would term "Community efficacy" (compare the principle of "business efficacy" as laid down for English law in *The Moorcock* (1889) 14 P.D. 64) include Case 8/55 *Fédéchar* [1954–1956] ECR 245 and 292; Case 20/59 *Italy* v. *High Authority* and Case 25/59 *Netherlands* v. *High Authority* [1960] ECR 325 and 355; and Case 34/62 *Germany* v. *Commission* [1963] ECR 131.

The European way

The separating out in this chapter of the various methods or approaches which the Court brings to its task of interpreting Community law should not mislead the reader into concluding that the Court operates in some mechanical way. As we have said, interpretation is an art in which the judicial instinct looms large. Frequently the Court uses a combination of methods, much as the artist blends the primary colours of his palette. A characteristic example is provided (as we have seen) by Case 6/72 *Continental Can* [1973] ECR at 243 where the judgment states:

> "In order to answer this question (whether Art. 86 EEC applies to changes in the structure of an undertaking) one has to go back to the spirit, general scheme and wording of Article 86, as well as to the system and objectives of the Treaty."

Literal, contextual and teleological approaches are here

all mixed together to enable the Court to reach its landmark decision on the full scope of Article 86.

Finally, over the 30 years of its existence the Court has changed the emphasis of its methods, especially in interpreting the founding Treaties. The earlier reliance on literal interpretation has given place increasingly to the contextual and teleological approaches, approaches which befit a jurisdiction charged with a quasi-constitutional function as the guardian of the grand objectives laid down in the Treaties.

Pitfalls for the common lawyer

The non-civilian lawyer, be he English, Irish or Scottish, should beware of approaching Community law as if it were no different from his national law: he must heed the injunction of Lord Denning with which we began this chapter. In particular, he should not strain to apply to Community law the canons of interpretation which the common law judges have evolved over the centuries. It would be a salutary exercise for the English-speaking lawyer who has some French to make a practice of looking at the French as well as the English version of the text in issue. As illustrations of where English courts may have gone astray in interpreting Community law, see *Schorsch Meier* v. *Hennin* [1975] Q.B. 416 (Lord Denning M.R.); *R.* v. *Henn and Darby* [1980] 2 All E.R. 166 (Lord Widgery C.J.), see above, p. 152; *R.* v. *Secchi* [1975] 1 CMLR 383 (Metropolitan Magistrate), see Plender [1976] Crim. L.R. 676; Durand (1979) 4 E.L. Rev. 3 at 9; Case 131/79 *R.* v. *Santillo* [1980] ECR 1585 (Divisional Court and Court of Appeal), see Dashwood (1981) 6 E.L. Rev. 73.

Chapter 14

GENERAL PRINCIPLES OF LAW

Introduction

We have already had occasion to refer to the "general principles of law" used by the Court to supplement the written sources of Community law. But, for several reasons, the subject requires fuller treatment. Firstly, it illustrates both the character of Community law as developed by the Court and the interaction of that law with the national laws of the Member States. Second, the use made by the Court of the general principles of law illustrates, as well as does any other of its techniques, the law-making function of the Court. Third, this technique has enabled the Court to elaborate a doctrine of far-reaching importance, no less than the protection of fundamental rights in Community law.

The use of general principles of law, or something very similar in effect, is found in many legal systems. The Statute of the International Court of Justice requires that Court to apply, *inter alia,* "the general principles of law recognized by civilised nations" (Art. 38(1)). In the European Communities there is no such comprehensive direction to the Court to apply the general principles of law; and the criterion is less exacting, since the general principles need be found only in the legal systems of the Member States, and, in the Court's practice, need not be common to all nor even to a majority of them. As Advocate General Lagrange stated:

"In this way the case law of the Court, in so far as it invokes national laws (as it does to a large extent) to define the rules of law relating to the application of the Treaty, is not content to draw on more or less arithmetical 'common denominators' between the different national solutions, but chooses from each of the Member States those solutions which, having regard to the objects of the Treaty, appear to it to be the best or, if one may use the expression, the most progressive. That is the spirit, moreover, which has guided the Court hitherto": Case 14/61 *Hoogovens* v. *High Authority* [1962] ECR 253 at 283–284.

General principles of law are found, not only in international law, but also in many municipal legal systems. The principle of proportionality (below) is especially prominent in German law, where it has a status similar to that of a general principle. Although not expressly mentioned in the German Basic Law, it has been held by the German courts to be the principle underlying two fundamental Articles of the Basic Law, Articles 2 and 12. Indeed German law has made perhaps the greatest contribution to the development of the general principles of law applied by the Court, including the principle of proportionality (*Verhältnismässigkeit*) and the principle of protection of legitimate expectations (*Vertrauensschutz*) (below, p. 265).

For the English lawyer the closest analogies are perhaps to be found in the rules of natural justice in administrative law, in the common law notion of reasonableness, and in the maxims of equity; we shall see that these also are now making their mark on Community law.

The French lawyer is familiar with the *principes généraux du droit* which, especially in the field of administrative law, have much the same function as in Community law. In French administrative law, the general principles of law have a restrictive effect in relation to *règlements* or governmental decrees which they do not have on legislation, that is, *lois* enacted by the French Parliament. Similarly, in Community law, although they may be invoked to interpret the treaty provisions, the general principles cannot prevail over the express terms of the Treaty. In the *Sgarlata* case, Case 40/64 [1965] ECR 215, the applicants sought to challenge Commission regulations fixing the reference prices for lemons and other citrus fruits. Faced with the objection that the application was inadmissible under Article 173 EEC as being directed against regulations rather than decisions, the applicants argued that if recourse to Article 173 were to be refused by reason of a restrictive interpretation of its terms, individuals would be deprived of all judicial protection under both Community law and national law, which would be contrary to the fundamental principles prevailing in all the Member States. Advocate General Roemer considered that this argument would require the Court not to interpret but to amend the Treaty on this point and the Court agreed that the considerations invoked by the applicants could not be allowed to override the clearly restrictive wording of Article 173. Hence the application was inadmissible. The result would of course have been different if the measures challenged, although in the form of regulations, had been in substance decisions of direct and individual concern to the applicants (above, p. 97). This they also alleged, but were unable to establish.

While general principles of law, or their analogue, can be found in many legal systems, they play a special part in Community law, as will be seen when we look in turn at those principles upon which the Court has most often relied.

1. *Proportionality*

The earliest decisions of the Court under the Coal and Steel Treaty contain references to general principles of law such as the principle of proportionality. Mention has already been made of Case 8/55 *Fédéchar* [1954–1956] ECR 245 and 292, where the Court held (at 299) that, by a generally accepted rule of law, the reaction of the High Authority to an unlawful act must be proportional to the scale of the act. The principle of proportionality, expressed in those terms, sounds unfamiliar to the English lawyer, but he uses a similar concept when he talks of what is reasonable: see for example *R.* v. *Barnsley Metropolitan Borough Council, ex parte Hook* [1976] 1 W.L.R. 1052. The Court too has used the language of reasonableness. In another early case, it held that the High Authority must go no further than is reasonable and must avoid causing harm to the extent that it is, within reason, possible to do so: Case 15/57 *Chasse* [1958] ECR 211 at 228.

These cases illustrate the characteristic role of general principles of law as limiting the power of the administration to take measures affecting the citizen, even in the absence of any written text to this effect. Such principles were typically applied in actions for annulment under Article 33 ECSC, and subsequently under Article 173 EEC: an administrative act could be annulled as contrary to the general principles of law. If a formal justification were required for annulling measures on this ground, it could be found in the references in those Articles to infringement of a rule of law relating to the application of the Treaties. Further, the Court is required to ensure that, in the interpretation and application of the Treaties, "the law is observed" (Art. 31 ECSC, Art. 164 EEC). The reference here to "the law" is manifestly to a body of law outside the Treaties themsleves, and can only be to unwritten rules whose origin it is natural to seek in the legal systems of the Member States.

The general principles of law are thus one, but only one example of the contribution of national law to Community law. Whenever the Court is faced with a question of law which is not resolved by any written Community text, it is likely to be influenced by the laws of the Member States. The advocate general, in his opinion, will very often survey these laws and the Court in its judgment will apply the most appropriate solution. Many concepts undefined in the Treaties, such as "misuse of powers" (above p. 108), and many other legal problems, have been clarified in this way; we have seen examples of the approach in the previous chapter (p. 254).

The principle of proportionality has also played an important part in the Court's approach to the treaty provisions on the free movement of goods (Articles 30 to 36 EEC), which the Court has treated as imposing far-reaching prohibitions on national measures restricting trade between Member States: see above, pp. 249–251. While such measures may be defended by the State on public policy grounds under Article 36, a defence of this kind is subject to the important proviso that the measures do not constitute, in the words of Article 36, "a means of arbitrary discrimination or a disguised restriction on trade between Member States." In applying this proviso, the Court has used the principle of proportionality so as to declare State measures unlawful if other, less restrictive measures would achieve the same purpose: see, *e.g.* Case 104/75 *de Peijper* [1976] ECR 613. Here the principle is parallel to the doctrine of the "less restrictive alternative" applied by American courts to assess the compatibility of State legislation with the United States Constitution: the question there too is whether the State interest, however legitimate, could be achieved by a measure less damaging to free trade than the one adopted: see T. Sandalow and E. Stein, *Courts and Free Markets* (1982), Vol. I, p. 28.

2. *Non-discrimination*

Several provisions of the EEC Treaty, and many provisions of EEC legislation, prohibit specific forms of discrimination. Article 7 EEC prohibits discrimination on grounds of nationality across the whole field of the Treaty; Article 40(3) EEC prohibits discrimination in relation to agriculture; Article 119 contains the principle that men and women should receive equal pay for equal work. However the Court of Justice has taken the view that, beyond those specific provisions, the guarantee of equal treatment or the prohibition of discrimination, is a general principle of law which must be observed in the whole field of Community law: see *e.g.* Case 1/72 *Frilli* [1972] ECR 457 at 466: the rule of equality of treatment "is one of the fundamental principles of Community law."

Similarly in one of the *Isoglucose* cases the Court held that the provisions of Council Regulation 1111/77 establishing the production levy system for isoglucose "offend against the general principle of equality of which the prohibition on discrimination set out in Article 40(3) of the Treaty is a specific expression": Joined Cases 103 and 145/77 [1978] ECR 2037 at 2081.

A different form of discrimination was at issue in a staff case. Signora Sabbatini (née Bertoni) was employed by the European Parliament and benefited, under the Staff Regulations, from an expatriation allowance. On her marriage she lost this allowance since the Staff Regulations provided that an official should forfeit it if, on marriage, he did not become a head of household. Under the Regulations, a married man was classified *ipso facto* as a head of household, but a married female official was so treated only if her husband was unable to work being an invalid or seriously ill. Signora Sabbatini successfully contended that the Regulations were discriminatory on grounds of sex, and therefore contrary both to a general principle of law and to Article 119 EEC. Accepting her plea of illegality under Article 184 (see above, p. 112), the Court held that the Regulations were unlawful and annulled the decision withdrawing the applicant's expatriation allowance: Case 20/71 *Sabbatini* v. *European Parliament* [1972] ECR 345. In accordance, however, with the nature of the plea of illegality, the judgment only declared the offending Regulations to be inapplicable *inter partes*: consequently, other female officials could not rely on this judgment to bring their own claims out of time (see Cases 15–33, etc., /73 *Schots-Kortner* [1974] ECR 177, p. 147 above). The offending Regulations were subsequently amended by the Council.

3. *Protection of legitimate expectations, etc.*

Another rather exceptional case concerned the annual review by the Council of staff salaries: Case 81/72

Commission v. *Council* [1973] ECR 575. Here the Court held that the discretion which the Council enjoyed, under Article 65 of the Staff Regulations, in fixing those salaries was subject to the principle of protection of legitimate expectations so that the staff of the Community institutions were entitled to rely on the implementation of a system which the Council had adopted experimentally for a three-year period. When the Council departed from that system, after only nine months, in adopting a new Regulation on salaries, the Commission took the Council to Court, and obtained the partial annulment of the Regulation, which was promptly replaced by a Regulation made in conformity with the new system.

The judgment illustrates effectively the technique of the Court in handling the general principles of law. Although such principles were considered extensively by the advocate general and full references to national law, the principle of protection of confidence, which had not been considered by the advocate general or relied upon by the Commission, at least in that form, was adopted by the Court without reference to its origins and with only limited explicit justification.

The principle of protection of confidence applied in this case is related to a number of other general principles which have featured in the reports. This family includes the protection of legitimate expectations, the principle of non-retroactivity of legislation, legal certainty, and respect for acquired rights; these principles shade into one another, and the same case may raise one or more of them: see, *e.g.* Case 62/70 *Bock* v. *Commission* [1971] ECR 897; Case 74/74 *CNTA* v. *Commission* [1975] ECR 533, esp. at 556; Case 2/75 *Mackprang* [1975] ECR 607, esp. at 622 *et seq.*; and Case 98/78 *Racke* [1979] ECR 69. All these principles had their origin in the laws of the original Member States, particularly in German administrative law; for although the system of remedies contained in the Treaties was principally based on French administrative law, the German courts have been and remain by far the most active in referring cases to the Court of Justice, with consequent opportunities for the German lawyer to draw the Court's attention to the principles of his legal system.

4. *The right to be heard*

The enlargement of the Communities in 1973 left intact the general principles derived from the legal systems of the founding Member States, but enabled the Court to extend its sources to the laws of the new Member States. English and Scottish decisions were cited by the advocate general as early as March 1973, in the staff salaries case, and later cases contain frequent references to Danish, English, Irish, and Scots law, especially in the opinions of the first advocate general from the new Member States, Mr.J-P. Warner, and of his successor, Sir Gordon Slynn. Perhaps the best illustration is the *Transocean* case, in which Advocate General Warner invoked a close analogy in English law to the general principles of law, namely the rules of natural justice: [1974] ECR 1063.

Here the applicant Association had been exempted by the Commission from the provisions of Article 85 of the EEC Treaty, but the exemption was subject to certain conditions, one of which the applicant considered too onerous. The condition in question was a requirement that the members of the Association, who were medium-sized firms manufacturing ship paint, should inform the Commission without delay of any links between them and any other company or firm in the paint sector. The Association, which was a loosely-knit grouping designed to enable its members to compete with the big multinational manufacturers, brought an action before the Court to annul this single condition in the decision, which it considered would be difficult if not impossible to comply with. It contended that the requirement was not mentioned in the notice of objections which the Commission had sent it and that it was never given the opportunity of making its views known on the subject. It relied on

Regulation No. 99/63 which governs the procedure before the Commission and maintained that the Commission, by not giving it an opportunity to make its views known, had not followed the proper procedure.

The difficulty with that argument was that Regulation No. 99/63 was not sufficiently detailed to provide for a hearing on the particular matter to which the applicant objected. However the Court is not limited to the arguments which the parties put before it; and the advocate general took the view that the procedure had infringed, not the terms of the Regulation, but one of the rules of natural justice, the principle *audi alteram partem,* which, he said, requires an administrative authority, before wielding statutory power to the detriment of a particular person, to hear what that person has to say about the matter, even if the statute does not expressly require it. Having reviewed the scope of the principle in the laws of the Member States, the advocate general concluded that "the right to be heard forms part of those rights which 'the law' referred to in Article 164 of the Treaty upholds, and of which, accordingly, it is the duty of this Court to ensure the observance."

In its judgment the Court, while following the advocate general, stated the principle in even broader terms, referring to "the general rule that a person whose interests are perceptibly affected by a decision taken by a public authority must be given the opportunity to make his point of view known." It is doubtful, however, whether the principle is to be treated as going as far as this formulation suggests. It is characteristic of the Court's jurisprudential approach to lay down a principle in broad, even absolute terms, but to leave its application to be refined by subsequent developments in the case law.

5. *Fundamental rights*

Some of the cases cited in the previous section have what might be called a "human rights flavour." The Court has accepted general principles of law which serve to protect the individual or undertaking from the administration. In some cases, such as the sex equality cases, the same result was secured by the use of general principles as might have been achieved by an express catalogue of fundamental rights written into the Treaties. But the Treaties contain no such bill of rights, despite suggestions that they should be amended to include one. And the Court over a period of years rejected appeals to the fundamental rights protected by national laws such as the German Basic Law.

In a series of cases, notably *Stork* (Case 1/58 [1959] ECR 17), *Geitling* (Joined Cases 36–38, 40/59 [1960] ECR 423) and *Sgarlata* (Case 40/64 [1965] ECR 215), the Court refused to recognise fundamental rights as such. Perhaps its reaction is, with hindsight, explicable; the issue may have been presented to it in the wrong way. When an applicant sought to rely directly on a fundamental right protected by his own law, even by his national constitution, the Court reacted by re-asserting the supremacy of Community law over the laws, even the constitutional laws, of the Member States. The development of Community law has often naturally responded to the way in which a question has been put to it, whether by an applicant in a direct action or by a court of a Member State on a reference.

So it was only when an administrative judge in Stuttgart asked the Court whether a particular requirement was compatible, not with the fundamental rights of national law, but with "the general principles of Community law," that the Court expressly included the protection of fundamental rights within those principles. The case, mentioned above, p. 244, arose out of an attempt by the Commission to reduce the Community "butter mountain." A decision of the Commission authorised Member States to sell butter at a reduced price to persons receiving social assistance. To ensure that the cheap butter reached only those persons for whom it was intended, provision was made in the decision for them to be issued with coupons. The wording of that provision was not precisely the same in all the official language versions, and led to doubts as to whether the beneficiary was required to disclose his name to the shop assistant. As implemented by the German authorities, he was required to do so, and one such beneficiary, Erich Stauder, challenged that requirement.

The Court interpreted the provision on the basis of all the language versions and having regard to its purpose, and held that it did not require—although it did not prohibit—the identification of beneficiaries by name. Then the Court ruled that, so interpreted, that provision contained nothing capable of prejudicing "the fundamental human rights enshrined in the general principles of Community law and protected by the Court": Case 29/69 *Stauder* v. *Ulm* [1969] ECR 419 at 425.

Two linguistic comments must be made on this formula which recognises for the first time the principle of protection of fundamental rights under Community law. Firstly, the expression "general principles of *Community* law"—the term used by the Stuttgart court—must be taken as shorthand for the general principles of law recognised in the Community legal order. The term "general principles of law" is to be preferred and has been used in subsequent decisions. Second, the original French text of the judgment refers to "les principes généraux du droit communautaire *dont la Cour assure le respect.*" These words repeat the formulation of Article 164 EEC requiring the Court to ensure that in the interpretation and application of the Treaty *the law is observed.* They show that the general principles, including fundamental rights, are part of "the law" referred to in Article 164—a point which is lost in the English version of the judgment.

The recognition of fundamental rights was taken a step further in the *Internationale Handelsgesellschaft* case (Case 11/70 [1970] ECR 1125). What was stated elliptically, almost parenthetically, in *Stauder* v. *Ulm* (that the general principles of law include the protection of fundamental rights) is here put into the forefront of the judgment. This was understandable, since the Court was here faced with a direct challenge by the German courts to the supremacy of Community law. The Frankfurt administrative court had already held certain provisions of Community law, relating to the system of agricultural export licences and the deposits attached to them, to be invalid as contrary to fundamental rights protected by the German Basic Law. A German company had forfeited a deposit of about £3,000 for not using export licences for ground maize which it had been granted. On a reference from the Frankfurt court, the Court again refused to look at German constitutional law but asked instead whether there was any analogous guarantee of fundamental rights in Community law. It held that there was. The respect for such rights formed part of the general principles of law. But, having examined the provisions in question, the Court ruled that those rights had not been infringed.

The sequel is well known. The Frankfurt court, not content with this reply, referred the case to the German Federal Constitutional Court and asked whether the Community provisions were compatible with the German Basic Law. The Second Chamber of the Constitutional Court agreed with the Court of Justice on the substance. But the important question was whether the reference was admissible. Could the German courts pronounce, after a ruling of the Court of Justice, on the validity of Community law? The Constitutional Court ruled, by a five to three majority, that the German courts could. So long as Community law contained no catalogue of fundamental rights, passed by a Parliament and equivalent to the catalogue of rights contained in the Basic Law, the German courts remained competent to examine whether the acts of German authorities, although done under Community law, were compatible with the Basic Law.

The judgment of the Federal Constitutional Court has been much criticised, not least by the minority in the Court itself, and was qualified by a later judgment of the same Court: see *Steinike und Weinlig* [1980] 2 CMLR 531. But the challenge to the supremacy of Community law may at least have had the merit of reinforcing concern at the Community level for the protection of fundamental rights. The Court of Justice had already gone somewhat further. After the Council of Europe's European Convention on Human Rights had finally been ratified by all the Member States, it accepted, in the second *Nold* case, that the European Convention, and also more generally "international treaties for the protection of human rights on which the Member States have collaborated or of which they are signatories, can supply guidelines which should be followed within the framework of Community law": Case 4/73 [1974] ECR 491 at 507.

Subsequently, in its judgment in the *Rutili* case, Case 36/75 [1975] ECR 1219, the Court took further the applicability of the European Convention. Rutili was an Italian national resident in France whose trade union and political activities had incurred the disapproval of the French authorities. His residence permit was subjected to a restriction prohibiting him from residing in certain parts of France. On a reference from the administrative court of Paris, before which he had challenged that restriction, the Court of Justice considered the limitations imposed by Community law on the powers of Member States in respect of the control of aliens, in particular under Council Directive No. 64/221 and Regulation No. 1612/68. It held that these limitations were "a specific manifestation of the more general principle," enshrined in the European Convention, to the effect that (in the words of the Convention) "no restrictions in the interests of national security or public safety shall be placed on the rights secured by [Arts. 8, 9, 10 and 11 of the Convention] other than such as are necessary for the protection of those interests 'in a democratic society.' "

Here the Court appeared to come close to giving direct effect to the Convention, but in Case 118/75 *Watson and Belmann* [1976] ECR 1185, Advocate General Trabucchi considered that the *Rutili* judgment "did not involve any substantive reference to the [Convention] provisions themselves, but merely a reference to the general principles of law of which, like the Community rules with which the judgment drew an analogy, they are a specific expression."

A further development in the Court's approach can be see in the *Hauer* case, Case 44/79 [1979] ECR 3727. A Council regulation prohibiting the new planting of vines was in issue. The German administrative court, putting questions on the interpretation of the regulation to the Court of Justice, had suggested that the regulation might not be applicable in Germany as being incompatible with fundamental rights protected by the German Basic Law including the right of property. The Court of Justice sought to dispel those doubts by, not merely repeating its earlier references to "general principles," but citing specific provisions of the Basic Law and of the Irish and Italian Constitutions, as well as the European Convention on Human Rights, in order to show that the right of property was subject to limitations in the public interest and that the regulation in issue did not go beyond the limitations generally allowed. It has been suggested (by J.A. Usher (1980) 5 E.L. Rev. 209) that the unusual course taken by the Court, in referring expressly to provisions of national law, may be explained as an attempt to reassure those courts "which fear that their fundamental principles are threatened by the primacy of Community law, that in practice these principles *are* taken into account at the Community level."

From the point of view of the general principles of law, the recent judgments of the Court dealing with fundamental rights are of particular interest as showing the sources on which the Court will rely. In the *Internationale Handelsgesellschaft* case the Court refers to "the constitutional traditions common to the Member States"—a very wide term. In the *Nold* and *Rutili* cases it goes further and refers to international treaties as a source of such general principles. In the *Hauer* case it cites specific provisions of national constitutions, a practice hitherto avoided.

Despite the efforts which the Court has made to develop its case law, debate continues on whether the case law approach provides sufficient protection on this sensitive issue, or whether, as the Federal Constitutional Court suggested in the *Internationale Handelsgesellschaft* case, an enacted catalogue of fundamental rights is required (see below). The European Parliament, the Council and the Commission appeared to endorse the approach of the Court of Justice when they adopted, on April 5, 1977, a joint declaration in which they underline the paramount importance which they attach to the respect for fundamental rights and especially those derived from the constitutions of the Member States and from the European Convention on Human Rights, and declare that, in the exercise of their powers and in pursuance of the objectives of the European Communities, they respect and will continue to respect those rights.

The Commission has also advocated the adoption of a Community Bill of Rights (see *The Protection of Fundamental Rights in the European Community*, Bulletin of the EC, Supplement 5/76), but, in recognition of the difficulties inherent in such a proposal, has suggested that, as a first step, the Community should itself accede to the European Convention on Human Rights (Bulletin of the EC, Supplement 2/79). Accession also, however, raises a number of legal, political and institutional problems (see House of Lords Select Committee on the European Communities, Session 1979/80, 71st Report, "Human Rights;" and J. McBride and L.N. Brown, *Yearbook of European Law* (1981), p. 167); and the question of the place of human rights in the Community legal order is far from resolved.

Chapter 15

PRECEDENT AND THE COURT

It is a fundamental principle of the administration of justice that like cases should be decided alike. Inconsistency in judicial decisions affronts even the most elementary sense of justice. In this sense the principle of *stare decisis*, of abiding by previous decisions, figures prominently in most legal systems, including those of all the Member States of the Communities. In England, whose law, at least in some important areas, is still based largely on case-law, the principle of *stare decisis* has been elaborated and extended into a complex doctrine of precedent, to which whole books have been devoted *e.g.* Rupert Cross, *Precedent in English Law* (3rd ed., 1977). Strict rules have developed, based on the practice of the courts, as to the circumstances in which one court must follow its own decision, or the decision of another court, in a previous case. Much depends on the respective positions of the courts within the hierarchy of the legal system. According to Professor Cross's "preliminary statement" of the English doctrine of precedent (*op. cit.* p. 7), every court is bound to follow any case decided by a court above it in the hierarchy, and appellate courts (except, since 1966, the House of Lords) are bound by their own previous decisions. But a decision of the High Court, for example, is a persuasive precedent, although not of course binding, even for courts above it in the hierarchy.

In France, at any rate in theory, such a doctrine of precedent has no place; indeed, it is expressly prohibited by Article 5 of the Civil Code. In France, as in other countries sharing the civil law tradition, the predominant view is that judicial decisions are not a formal source of law at all. The reasons for this contrast between England

and France throw much light not only on the law and constitution, but also on the politics and history of the two countries: see Kahn-Freund, Lévy and Rudden, *A Sourcebook on French Law* (2nd ed., 1979), Part I. Here it must suffice to note that the French judge does not regard himself as bound by a single decision of any court; instead, he tries, with the aid of the writings of legal scholars (the *doctrine*), to discern the general trend of decisions on a particular point. Unlike the English (or Scottish) judge, he does not feel compelled to analyse or to reconcile earlier judgments, or to explain his own judgments in those terms.

Judicial decisions are of great importance in Community law, where many fundamental doctrines, as well as much of the elaboration of the texts, are the creation of the Court. However, it is a feature of the Community legal system that Community law is applied by the courts of the Member States, but can be authoritatively interpreted by the Court of Justice alone. Accordingly this chapter is divided into two parts: the first part considers precedent in the Court of Justice, the second considers precedent in the national courts.

A. *Precedent in the Court of Justice*

The Court's decisions are of course authoritative. But what does this mean? Certainly the English rules for ascertaining the principle upon which the case was decided, the *ratio decidendi*, have no automatic application to the Court's judgments. These judgments, as has already been remarked, have been strongly influenced by the model of the higher French Courts. They are abstract and syllogistic, rather than concrete and discursive like the typical English or Scottish judgment. Although they now sometimes refer to previous decisions which they are following, they rarely allude to any earlier decisions from which they may be departing. Their character has a decisive impact on the question of precedent. Firstly, it means that the judgments often start from broad propositions of law which may not be intended to be taken at face value, in absolute terms, but rather to be refined by subsequent decisions. If taken literally, these propositions are sometimes strikingly broad: we have seen an example in the general principle stated in the *Transocean* case, above, p. 267. Second, judgments of this kind do not easily lend themselves to the characteristic technique of distinguishing earlier judgments in the way of an English lawyer. But in Case 112/76 *Manzoni* [1977] ECR 1647 at 1662, Advocate General Warner did use the language of *stare decisis* and *ratio decidendi* in his opinion.

Like any other court, the Court prefers to follow its own previous decisions. For example, in Case 35/75 *Matisa* [1975] ECR 1205 at 1210, it cited its previous decision (Case 14/70 *Bakels* [1970] ECR 1001) on the authority of the Brussels Nomenclature in interpreting the Common Customs Tariff and continued: "Since there is nothing in the present case capable of leading to a different conclusion, it is proper to reply to the same effect." And, as we have seen (pp. 46 and 248, above), in the *Import Gadgets* case the Court followed, but without citing, both the earlier cases on this point.

The Court has not hesitated however to depart from its previous decisions where it thought it was necessary. Such departures may take different forms. Sometimes it is a matter of developing a particular doctrine, such as the doctrine of the direct effect of treaty provisions. Here the Court started from rather narrow criteria in deciding whether a treaty provision had direct effect, as in Case 26/62 *Van Gend en Loos* (above, p. 162). Subsequently it has taken a progressively broader view of the circumstances in which the Treaty has direct effect; this development has continued via Case 43/75 the second *Defrenne* case (above, p. 257), to the latest restatement of the doctrine in Case 8/81 *Becker* [1982] ECR 53 (above, p. 41). In this way the Court has been able to give direct effect to a far wider range of Community provisions than would have been possible if the narrower criteria had been retained. At other times the Court has appeared to overrule directly, if not explicitly, an earlier decision.

An example of the Court changing its mind was on the question whether an act had to be annulled before a claim for damages for the injury caused by that act could be successful. As we have already seen (p. 129, above), the Court's original view was that prior annulment was a condition precedent to the action for damages. This was so decided in Case 25/62 *Plaumann* [1963] ECR 95, which discouraged for several years the bringing of such actions. Then, in Case 4/69, *Lütticke* [1971] ECR 325, the Court adopted the view that the action for damages was established by the EEC Treaty as an independent form of action and could, in consequence, be brought in respect of an act that had not already been annulled. After a return to the *Plaumann* approach in Case 96/71 *Haegeman* [1972] ECR 1005, the Court finally confirmed the *Lütticke* view in Case 43/72 *Merkur* [1973] ECR 1055.

The Court thus showed that it does not regard itself as bound by its previous decisions. Although the English lawyer may find it strange that the Court should not expressly recognise that it is departing from precedent let alone give no reasons for doing so, the fact that it should have this freedom can be readily understood. A final court can only be bound by its previous decisions if the law established by those decisions can, in the last resort, be amended by legislation. Since the decisions of the Court of Justice could be affected only by an amendment of the Treaties, a practical impossibility, it is inevitable that it should be flexible in its approach to precedent. Like a constitutional court, its freedom can be explained by the finality of its decisions. But such departures from precedent are very much the exception.

The problem arises in a different form in decisions of the Chambers. The three Chambers may disagree *inter se* on a question of law, so that, again very exceptionally, there are conflicting precedents. This has occasionally happened in staff cases, but in future the wider use of a Chamber as the normal organ of judgment (see p. 25, above) will increase the danger of conflicting precedents unless care is taken to channel difficult cases to the full Court. Experience in other divided courts shows that it is often difficult to foresee such a potential conflict; fortunately, the Rules (Art. 95(4)) permit a Chamber at any time to refer to the Court a case assigned to it.

So far we have considered the authority of judgments of the Court and of the Chambers. A separate question is that of the authority of opinions of the advocates general. These may be, and frequently are, cited in subsequent cases, both by counsel and by advocates general themselves. They may be considered in three separate situations.

Firstly, they may be the only authority available on a particular point: this will be the case if the judgment has not dealt with a point on which the advocate general has expressed a view. Since the opinions are more wide-ranging than the judgments, this situation arises very frequently; there are many unsettled areas of Community law where only the dicta of the advocates general can be cited as directly in point. Such dicta might be compared with the statements of a single judge in the English Court of Appeal on an issue on which the other judges have not pronounced.

Second, the Court may have dealt with the point considered by the advocate general, but have differed from him. Should one then treat the opinion as having been, in effect, overruled; or should one treat it rather as a dissenting opinion? The answer would seem to be that, since the Court is not bound by its own decisions, it should be treated as a dissenting opinion; and here too the advocate general is, in practice, cited by counsel, although they must then of course seek to show that the judges were wrong and the advocate general was right.

Third, and perhaps most commonly, where the Court has followed the advocate general on the point in question, it may be unnecessary to refer to the opinion at all, except perhaps to strengthen the authority of the judgment. But, whether the Court has followed it or not, the opinion may help to show for precisely what proposition the case is indeed authority.

So far we have considered the significance for the Court of its own decisions. What then is the significance for the Court of national court decisions? These are not, of course, authoritative for the Court on questions of Community law; they are most frequently cited as evidence of the existence of one or more general principles of law (considered in the previous chapter). Often, as we have seen, fundamental concepts have been elucidated with the aid of comparative law. But decisions of national courts are rarely cited directly on questions of Community law, unless for purposes of comparison; and for these purposes even decisions from non-Member States have occasionally been cited, as in the American cases cited by Advocate General Mayras in the *Dyestuffs* cases, Cases 48, etc., /69 [1972] ECR 619.

Decisions of national courts may also be relevant where questions of national law have to be decided by the Court. Such cases are infrequent but three examples may be given. Firstly, in Case 18/57 *Nold* v. *High Authority* [1957] ECR 121 the Court had to consider questions of German law in order to decide whether Nold himself had the necessary capacity to bring proceedings before the Court in the name of his company, then in liquidation. Second, just as the question may arise, in a direct action, whether the applicant has the capacity to bring proceedings, so on a reference for a preliminary ruling the question may arise whether the body making the reference is competent to do so, that is, whether it is a "court or tribunal of a Member State"; and the answer to this question may, as we have seen (p. 164), depend partly on national law. Finally, national law may be in issue, not as a preliminary question but on the substance of the case, in direct actions against Member States (Chapter 5), if it is alleged that the law of that State is contrary to the Treaty: see, for example, Case 167/73 *Commission* v. *French Republic* (above, p. 81). Here the question whether a provision of national law infringes Community law is a two-part one: first, the Court must determine the rule of Community law which is allegedly infringed, and this is a question of law; secondly, the Court must determine the rule of national law under attack as infringing that Community rule, and this for the Court is a question of fact: see Audretsch, *Supervision in European Community Law* (1978), pp. 49–50.

It is significant of the relationship between the Court of Justice and the national courts that, in all these cases, the questions of national law are, for the Court of Justice, merely questions of fact, which require to be proved, just as questions of national law are questions of fact for international courts and questions of foreign law are questions of fact for national courts. In contrast, it is a fundamental principle of the Community legal order that questions of Community law are questions of law, not questions of fact, for the courts of the Member States, which must take judicial notice of the provisions of Community law. In the United Kingdom this is expressly recognised by section 3 of the European Communities Act 1972 (below, p. 283), but this is merely declaratory, and the principle is valid for all Member States.

B. *Precedent in the national courts*

Apart from the role of precedent in the Court itself, the authority of judicial decisions on Community law must also be considered from the point of view of the courts of the Member States, since, as we have seen, they too are Community courts. Three questions arise: Firstly, what is the authority, for them, of decisions of the Court of Justice? Second, what is the authority, within the national hierarchy of the courts, of the decisions on Community law of their supreme courts—for example, the House of Lords in the United Kingdom, the *Cour de Cassation* and

Conseil d'Etat in France, or the various federal supreme courts in Germany? And finally, what is the authority, within the courts of one Member State, of the decisions of the courts of other Member States?

Two overriding principles may be of guidance in attempting to answer these questions. Firstly, there is no Community hierarchy of courts. The judicial systems of the Member States remain intact. In the absence of any federal structure, the Community system respects the judicial independence of the Member States, subject always of course to the principle that the courts, like all other State organs, are bound by the obligations of the Community Treaties.

Second, while the courts of the Member States remain sovereign, subject to that principle, in the *application* of Community law, only the Court of Justice can pronounce authoritatively on its *interpretation*. So much indeed is apparent from the last paragraph of Article 177 EEC, which obliges the national courts of last instance to refer questions of Community law to the Court.

What then, in the light of these principles, is the authority for national courts of decisions of the Court of Justice?

Plainly, in a case where it has given a ruling on a question referred to it, that ruling is binding on the referring court. But is the ruling also binding on other courts in subsequent cases raising the same question? The Court itself has taken the view that, where it has already answered the question in a previous case, there is no need for even a court of last instance, which would otherwise be obliged to refer under the third paragraph of Article 177, to do so, since "the authority of an interpretation under Article 177 already given by the Court may deprive the obligation of its purpose and thus empty it of its substance": Cases 28, 29 and 30/62 *Da Costa en Schaake* [1963] ECR 31 at 38. On the other hand, the Court held in the same cases that a national court may always, if it considers it desirable, refer questions of interpretation to the Court again. Even where the same question has already been answered, it may do so if it considers for some reason that a different answer might be appropriate in the case before it. Since the Court of Justice does not regard itself as strictly bound by its previous decisions, it will be able to modify its previous ruling if necessary. Thus the conclusion would seem to be that, in a case raising a question on which the Court has already ruled, the national court has a choice: it can either apply the ruling, or seek a new ruling. But it is bound by the ruling in the sense that it cannot simply disregard it.

So far as the courts in the United Kingdom are concerned, the binding force of decisions of the Court is recognised and given effect (albeit parenthetically) by the European Communities Act 1972. Section 3(1) of the Act provides that:

> "For the purposes of all legal proceedings any question as to the meaning or effect of any of the Treaties, or as to the validity, meaning or effect of any Community instrument, shall be treated as a question of law (and, if not referred to the European Court, be for determination as such in accordance with the principles laid down by and any relevant decision of the European Court)."

It would seem to follow also, from what has been said, that, no matter what the national rules of precedent may provide, the lower courts of a Member State cannot be bound by any decision of a higher court in that State on a question of Community law. It could only be so bound if the higher court had obtained a ruling from the Court of Justice on the point in issue; and even then the lower court would be bound by that ruling rather than by the higher court's decision. And it would remain free to refer any new question of Community law.

This point was established by the Court in Cases 146 and 166/73 the *Rheinmühlen* cases [1974] ECR 33 and 139, which were episodes in a long legal battle between a

German cereal exporter, Rheinmühlen-Düsseldorf, and the German intervention agency for cereals. The Hessisches Finanzgericht had decided that Rheinmühlen was not entitled, under Community law, to any refunds on the export of certain consignments of barley. On appeal the Federal Finance Court (Bundesfinanzhof), having obtained a preliminary ruling on certain questions of Community law (Case 6/71), quashed this judgment and ruled that Rheinmühlen was at least entitled to a refund at a lower rate. The case was accordingly sent back to the Hessian Court to decide certain questions of fact.

Under German law the Hessian court was bound by the Bundesfinanzhof's ruling on the point of law. However, the court considered that that ruling raised a new question of Community law, which it accordingly referred to the Court (Case 146/73). It also asked whether it is permissible for a lower court to make a reference only when the case comes before it for the first time or whether it may do so also when reconsidering the case after the judgment of a lower court has been quashed by a higher court.

This reference by the Hessian court was challenged by Rheinmühlen in the Bundesfinanzhof, which then itself made a further reference (Case 166/73). It asked whether a lower court has a completely unfettered right to make a reference or whether Article 177 leaves unaffected rules of national law under which a lower court is bound on points of law by the judgment of a higher court.

On this question the Court of Justice ruled that the power of a lower court to make a reference cannot be abrogated by such a rule of national law; and it gave the same answer to the Hessian court. Advocate General Warner went further, arguing that the discretion of a lower court to make a reference cannot be fettered by any rule of national law, and he concluded from this that the Treaty does not allow appeals against a decision to refer. The Court held, however, that Article 177 does not preclude an appeal of a type normally available under national law. But the Court's judgments on the two references do establish that, although a lower court may be bound under national law to follow the ruling of a higher national court, it remains free to refer a new question under Article 177, and to follow the ruling given by the Court in reply. To that extent any national rule concerning the binding force of a higher court's decision upon a lower court, whether in the same litigation (as in *Rheinmühlen*) or *a fortiori* under the doctrine of precedent, is displaced by Community law.

Finally, what is the authority of decisions of courts of other Member States on questions of Community law? Again, it seems clear that such decisions can in no sense be regarded as binding, although any rulings given by the Court of Justice on references in such cases will be followed unless a new reference is considered necessary. In the absence of a reference, the authority of the national decision will be at best persuasive.

CHAPTER 16

FUTURE OF THE COURT: CONCLUSIONS

We have seen, in previous chapters, the ways in which the Court has carried out its task, under Article 164 EEC, of ensuring that, in the interpretation and application of the Treaty, the law is observed. The Communities themselves are creatures of law, and are governed by law in every aspect of their operations. The reader may be left to judge for himself the extent to which the Court has succeeded in preserving the rule of law, and in ensuring that on the judicial level, at least, European integration is being progressively realised.

Here we shall attempt, instead of a retrospective survey of the 30 years or more since the setting up of the Coal and Steel Community in 1952, a brief look forward into the future as well as a critique of the present.

As we said in our first edition, it would of course be rash to venture firm predictions on the future of the Court, which must largely depend upon the unpredictable future of the Communities themselves. The Communities are volatile structures which, if they do not progress, are liable to slip backwards: like a man walking a tight-rope, they need momentum if they are not to fall. Being relatively young and artificial creations, they cannot be left to fend for themselves but need constantly to be nurtured in order to survive. Yet, plagued as they are both by economic difficulties and by political weaknesses, their future development must remain a matter of conjecture. At best we can only base ourselves on a number of hypotheses.

Enlargement of the Communities

Already, since our first edition, the Communities have been enlarged by the addition of Greece. The inclusion of

Spain and Portugal may not be far off. Such enlargement must have an immediate practical impact on the working of the institutions, and especially of the Court of Justice.

In the first place, as happened with Greek entry, the composition of the Court would have to be increased to include a judge of the new Member States. The increased work-load would require at least one additional advocate general: the likelihood would be that Spain would join the four larger Member States in permanently having one of its nationals as advocate general.

In the second place, the enlargement of the Court might reinforce the tendency for the Chambers to become the normal organ of judgment and for the Court to sit in plenary session only exceptionally. We have seen above that this pattern is already beginning to develop, but a larger Court would permit, either the creation of four instead of three Chambers, or the creation of divisions with a quorum of, say, five or seven judges, so that the Court sat regularly in two divisions. When a plenary session was still necessary, it might be desirable to retain for the enlarged Court the present quorum of seven judges rather than to increase it, although normally, say, nine judges would sit.

Perhaps English experience in judicial administration in the wake of the Beeching Commission does have something to teach Europe about the conservation of that most precious commodity, "judge-power."

Another question of practical importance is the problem of languages, which the enlargement of the Communities would inevitably aggravate. Within the Court it seems an inescapable requirement, at least in preliminary rulings, that any of the national languages of all the Member States should be available, but it may become necessary to restrict the choice of languages for other purposes. The principle of linguistic equality may be in danger of becoming the Community's sacred cow impeding the path of justice.

Again, the addition of a new legal system will, if past

experience is a guide, encourage the Court to resort extensively to national law in developing the general principles of law, the role of which we have explored in Chapter 14.

Developments in the Court's Jurisdiction

Other developments, apart from the enlargement of the Communities, may affect the Court's work-load. There are likely to be developments in its jurisdiction. Some of these have been mentioned in previous chapters; for example the jurisdiction to give advisory opinions (Chapter 10) and to interpret Conventions concluded between Member States (Chapter 9). The latter jurisdiction might be further extended to include other international agreements in the economic field which have not been entered into pursuant to the Treaties but which may nonetheless require uniform interpretation in the different Member States. Conversely, the work-load in staff cases may eventually be lightened as a result of the proposals mentioned at the end of Chapter 8.

The net result of such developments, when coupled with enlargement, is likely to be a substantial increase in the Court's work. There may then be suggestions for establishing a separate court or courts to share the work, or specialised divisions within the Court for such matters as patents, bankruptcy and others. But the importance of preserving a uniform structure, and the principle of "unity of jurisdiction," are likely to be stressed as objections to such suggestions. The Court itself, as we shall see, has emphasised the importance of these factors.

To assist its task the Court has made frequent pleas, especially to the Council, for more generous staffing, and, as we have seen (Chapter 3, above), the establishment of legal secretaries has been doubled since 1980 and the total number of staff has increased from 244 in 1977 to some 440 in 1982.

Such growth in personnel, however, has its dangers.

Professor Vining of Michigan has warned that the American federal court system is becoming a "depersonalized bureaucracy" as judges increasingly rely on the growing cadre of law clerks to write a major share of their opinions, which then cease to be authoritative reflections of the workings of a single legal mind or the joint efforts of judges accurately to reflect the dialogue that produced the collegiate decision (26 *Law Quadrangle Notes*, Ann Arbor, 1981, no. 1, 5).

Another, but not dissimilar danger, if the Court becomes overloaded, has been stressed by Professor Cappelletti of Florence. He points out that "constitutional decision-making demands that kind of careful consideration which it is unrealistic to expect from courts which are submerged under thousands of cases they are obliged to decide; it requires a high degree of creativity and of policy-oriented balancing of interests and values which bureaucratic and routine-oriented judges can hardly provide" (*Festschrift für Konrad Zweigert* 1981, p. 391).

The 1980s have brought increasing signs that the Court is indeed becoming over-burdened. To give only one example: if a national court has now to wait some 12 months for a ruling on its preliminary reference (in our first edition, the period was six months), this may well be intolerable: in practice, justice delayed may mean justice denied. How then to lighten the load at Luxembourg and cut down delay? As well as the suggestions referred to above for subdividing the Court of Justice or creating a separate court or courts for certain specialised matters (such as staff cases), could one envisage purely routine cases proceeding direct to judgment without the benefit of any advocate-general's opinion or with a merely formal opinion deferring to the wisdom of the Court? French administrative courts have adopted or are contemplating such reforms to relieve their backlog of cases.

Another common device for easing congestion and one very familiar in common law systems is the filter provided by leave to appeal (or the application for judicial review made subject to leave, as too in *certiorari*). But such a filter is incompatible with the terms of Article 177 EEC. Its only use might be in direct actions, including staff cases and appeals against fines, so as to stop unmeritorious applications *in limine* where a single judge refused leave.

Comparisons, however, with a fully fledged federal legal system are not entirely apt when describing the Court as the Community's supreme constitutional court. For the Community legal system is one in which any national court or tribunal may rule upon constitutionality of its national law in relation to Community law: if the national (*i.e.* State) judge elects to decide such a "federal" question instead of referring it to Luxembourg under Article 177, he is usually free to do so (only a final court *must* refer). To this extent, the burden of adjudicating upon constitutional issues is shared by the Court with the national judiciary.

European Union

At the "summit conference" held in Paris in October 1972 the ambitious but obscure objective was fixed of "transforming, before the end of the present decade and with the fullest respect for the Treaties already signed, the whole complex of the relations of Member States into a European Union." Specific proposals with a view to achieving this "European Union" were made by the Community institutions, and Mr Leo Tindemans, Prime Minister of Belgium, when invited to define what was meant by this term, duly presented a report to the European Council (Bulletin of the European Communities, Supplement 1/76).

The following section of the Tindemans report deals with the Court:

> "The Court of Justice stressed in its report on European Union that the Community constitutes a 'state of law' (*Rechtsstaat*) and that this characteristic

must be maintained within the Union. This is an essential factor conferring legitimacy upon our undertaking which leads me to formulate the following:

(a) In the new sectors covered by the Union, the Court must have powers identical to those which it has at present, so as to be able to interpret the law of the Union, to annul the acts of the institutions not in accordance with the Treaties and to point out when the Member States fail to comply with their obligations;

(b) Individuals must also be able to appeal directly to the Court of Justice against an act of one of the institutions of the Union infringing their basic rights;

(c) Once European Union has gained its own momentum we should examine whether the Community's current legal system can be improved or extended: the Court has made proposals about this."

A number of specific proposals for strengthening the jurisdiction of the Court were made in the reports of the Commission and of the Court (Bulletin of the European Communities, Supplements 5/75 and 9/75). The Court emphasised, however, and the Commission agreed, that a single court should be preserved: "Because of the need to ensure uniform application of the law in all the Member States, it is of fundamental importance that the judicial system should be subject to a single supreme court." But the reference to a "supreme court" does not imply the creation of a supreme court on the lines of the United States Supreme Court, a model which would be appropriate only in a federal Europe. None of the reports on European Union went as far as this; on the contrary they sought to preserve, with relatively minor modifications, the judicial structure in substantially its present form, in which the Court of Justice and the national courts cooperate in the administration of Community justice.

In retrospect, the hopes of the Paris summit were dashed by the deepening economic depression of the past decade, and the Tindemans report remains only a blueprint of what might be achieved if there were the political will.

The Protection of Fundamental Rights

Apart from the possible accession of the Community to the European Convention on Human Rights (see p. 274 above), it may also prove necessary to review the mechanisms for the protection of fundamental rights which are divided between the Court on the one hand, and the bodies set up under the Convention (the European Commission and Court of Human Rights) on the other. For at present the acts of Member States are subject to review by the Convention bodies in Strasbourg, and the acts of the Community institutions by the Court of Justice in Luxembourg, while the possibility cannot be excluded that measures taken by Member States in implementation of their Community obligations may be open to challenge in both Strasbourg and Luxembourg, with perhaps conflicting results.

If the field of activity of the Community institutions continues to widen, more matters may fall outside the competence of the Convention bodies. Although the Court of Justice will have the power to ensure that Community action complies with respect for fundamental rights, its paramount concern may be the promotion of integration and the standards it applies may not be the same as those of bodies whose main function is to preserve the rights of the individual.

Again, various proposals have been made to overcome these difficulties. In a different context, the suggestion has been made that the Court of Justice should be empowered, when faced with a question of interpretation of the Convention, to seek a ruling from the European Court of Human Rights (see the opinion of Advocate General Warner in Case 130/75 *Prais* v. *Council* [1976] ECR 1589).

Defiance of the Court and Other Criticisms

The plea made by President Giscard d'Estaing at the Dublin summit in 1975 "to do something about the Court and its illegal decisions" did not fall on deaf ears in his own country. As we have seen (p. 171, above) the Conseil d'Etat later went out of its way, in *Cohn-Bendit*, to confront the Court with an uncompromising rejection of its case law on the doctrine of direct effect of directives. It is to be expected that governments in the Member States may sometimes, under political pressure, be slow to comply with Community law. But defiance by the national judiciary is a more alarming phenomenon which, if it were to spread, would be the death-knell of that doctrine of judicial co-operation which is the hallmark of the procedure under Article 177. The German Federal Finance Court has now been equally defiant: see p. 4, above.

The reaction of the Court has been deliberately restrained and low key. Recent judgments have defined more clearly the limits upon the direct effect doctrine; judicial conferences have continued to bring national judiciary to Luxembourg to become better informed about the Court and to improve mutual understanding under the mellowing influence of wine and good cheer; and the great majority of national judges have loyally accepted the supremacy of Community law and its concomitant, the authority of the Court's rulings and decisions.

Falling far short of defiance of the Court, there has been informed criticism of its procedures and decisions in the Member States, notably by the House of Lords Select Committee on the European Communities, which reviewed the Court's procedures and recommended that there should be formal collaboration between the Court and practitioners on questions of procedure, with consideration being given to the establishment of a Joint Committee (House of Lords, Session 1979–80, 23rd report, p. 18).

Certainly, the Court has shown itself responsive to criticism, some of it, indeed, self-criticism. Thus, in the *Sugar Cartel* cases (Cases 40–48, etc., /73 [1975] ECR 1663), it reformed its procedure for taking evidence of witnesses so as to expedite consideration of the factual issues before it; in its longest judgment (to date) the Court demonstrated its ability to deal with complicated facts, every point of fact and every argument of the parties being given due consideration in the decision. Nevertheless, this was only achieved after prodigious expenditure of effort and time. In the *Pioneer* case (Cases 102–103/80) now before the Court, even more voluminous evidence will fall to be examined, a daunting prospect.

A criticism of the Court that has not been met is that it frequently adjudicates on points (usually of law but sometimes of fact) which have not been argued before it. This inspires more objection in common lawyers, accustomed as they are to an adversarial process of trial in which the court makes up its mind according to the ebb and flow of argument by counsel: the judge who engages in his own research is hardly playing the game. The civil lawyers, by contrast, have been conditioned to accept that the judge may turn inquisitor.

A particular aspect of this problem is the lack of general provision in the Rules of Procedure to permit counsel to comment upon the advocate-general's opinion, even though this raises new issues upon which no argument has been presented. Only exceptionally will the Court order the re-opening of the oral proceedings: see Case 155/79 *AM & S* [1982] 2 CMLR 264, above, p. 205; and even then, counsel are in no better position in relation to the *second* opinion. The House of Lords Select Committee proposed that the Court should give parties a right to submit, within a limited period, written comments on statements of fact in an advocate-general's opinion, and should be willing to re-open the oral procedure where it is alleged that the advocate general has introduced a new point of law.

Cross-Fertilisation of National and Community Legal Systems

Finally, we turn to what may be, in legal terms, the most significant future development: the cross-fertilisation of Community law and the national legal systems. This is a two-way process.

Firstly, in previous chapters, and especially in Chapter 14, we have seen examples of the impact of national law upon Community law. Until 1973 Community law was largely a product of the relatively homogeneous laws of the Six: only competition law reflected outside influence, that of the United States. But, since the first enlargement, the distinctive legal families of the British Isles and of Scandinavia have added their important contribution, to be joined recently by Greek law. The scope for comparative legal research at Luxembourg is now obviously immense, and we have seen how well equipped are the various services of the Court for this purpose. The fruits of this research emerge in the opinions of the advocates general and more indirectly in the Court's decisions. Moreover, by a kind of process of osmosis, common law concepts and modes of thought now permeate the Court by the mere presence there of British (and Irish) lawyers, whether as judge, advocate general, member of the Commission's Legal Service, or counsel for the parties.

Second, Community law, as it becomes more widely known, will have an increasing influence upon national law. So far as the United Kingdom is concerned, two developments in particular may already be remarked in this direction. The first relates to the principles of interpretation (which we have examined in Chapter 13) applied by the Court and applied also now by United Kingdom courts to provisions of Community law. These principles, as they become increasingly familiar, are having some impact in our own courts' approach to domestic legislation: see *e.g.* the judgment of Lord Denning M.R. in *Macarthys* v. *Smith* [1979] 3 All E.R. 325, C.A.; also the judgments of the Court of Appeal in

James Buchanan & Co. v. *Babco*, judgments with which
the House of Lords pointedly disagreed in favour of the
traditional English methods of construction: [1978]
A.C. 141, H.L. In the longer term, the Community
methods may influence also the style of our own legislative
drafting.

Third, the wider basis of judicial review in the Community legal order (discussed in particular in Chapter 6)
throws into relief the more restrictive approach of our
own law, although in recent years English administrative
law has been revitalised through the twin principles of
reasonableness and fairness. Judicial review as effected at
Luxembourg for constitutionality has also prompted
English reformers, such as Lord Scarman, to propose a
United Kingdom Bill of Rights by reference to which our
judges would invalidate offending legislation.

Parallel developments may occur in the field of procedure, a subject to which we have adverted in Chapter 11.
The simplicity, flexibility, and relative speed of the
Court's procedures may in the course of time have some
effect on the reform of national court procedure, at least
in the higher courts and in cases concerned primarily with
questions of law. For the determination of questions of
law, the Court's methods have proved themselves effective and have made savings in time and in costs which are
hard to quantify but must be very great. Conversely, the
practitioner accustomed to English methods may find
cause for concern in the Court's methods for resolving
issues of fact. Here the English lawyer will feel that there
is scope for contributions from his own practices to the
working of the Court: since 1973 there have already been
changes in the hearing of witnesses.

Improvements can obviously be made in both direc-
tions; in any event, the greater exposure of judges,
practitioners and students (the practitioners of tomorrow)
from the Member States to the Luxembourg method can
only be salutary.

An increasing convergence of ways of thinking and of

practices, both in law and procedure, would thus be of mutual benefit. Beyond the development of Community law itself, this may lead to a wider integration within the Community. For as Mr Roy Jenkins reminded the European Parliament in his inaugural address as President of the Commission on January 11, 1977: "In all our activities, we must remember our underlying political purposes. Our means are largely economic, but our end is and always has been political. It is to make a European Union." Since these words were spoken, the nature of such Union may have become more shadowy and its fulfilment more distant, but the purpose remains, and to that purpose the Court of Justice remains constant.

SELECT BIBLIOGRAPHY

Note. This bibliography is confined to a selection of recent English-language publications giving special emphasis to the Court of Justice.

Books

H. Audretsch, *Supervision in European Community Law* (North Holland 1978).

Lawrence Collins, *European Community Law in the United Kingdom* (Butterworths, London, 2nd ed. 1980).

T. C. Hartley, *The Foundations of European Community Law* (Oxford University Press, 1981).

A. J. Mackenzie Stuart, *The European Communities and the Rule of Law* (Hamlyn Lectures, Sweet & Maxwell, London, 1977).

Henry G. Schermers, *Judicial Protection in the European Communities* (Kluwer, Deventer, Netherlands, 2nd ed. 1979).

Articles

Ami Barav, "Preliminary Censorship? The judgment of the European Court in Foglia v. Novello" (1980) 5 E.L. Rev. 443.

Gerhard Bebr, "Preliminary rulings of the Court of Justice, their authority and temporal effect" (1981) 18 C.M.L. Rev. 475.

A. A. Dashwood, "The Advocate General in the Court of Justice of the European Communities" (1982) 2 *Legal Studies* 202.

Elizabeth Freeman, "References to the Court of Justice under Article 177" [1975] C.L.P. 176.

Christine Gray, "Interim measures of protection in the European Court" (1979) 4 E.L. Rev. 80.

Christopher Harding, "The impact of Article 177 of the EEC Treaty on the review of Community action" (1981) 1 *Yearbook of European Law* 93.

T. Koopmans, "*Stare Decisis* in European Law," *Essays in European Law and Integration* (eds. O'Keeffe and Schermers, Kluwer, Deventer, Netherlands, 1982), p. 11.

Jeremy McBride and L. Neville Brown, "The United Kingdom, the European Community and the European Convention on Human Rights" (1981) 1 *Yearbook of European Law* 167.

A. J. Mackenzie Stuart, "The 'non-contractual' liability of the European Economic Community," Maccabean Lecture in Jurisprudence *Proceedings of the British Academy* 1975; "The Court of Justice of the European Communities and the control of executive discretion" (1974) *Journal of the Society of Public Teachers of Law* 16.

M. H. Mendelson, "The European Court of Justice and human rights" (1981) 1 *Yearbook of European Law* 125.

J. D. B. Mitchell, "Sed quis custodiet ipsos custodes?" (1974) 11 C.M.L. Rev. 351.

Peter Oliver, "Limitation of actions before the European Court" (1978) 3 E.L. Rev. 3.

Eric Stein, "Lawyers, judges and the making of a transnational Constitution" (1981) 75 Am. J. Int. Law 1.

M. Waelbroeck, "May the Court of Justice limit the retrospective operation of its judgments?" (1981) 1 *Yearbook of European Law* 115.

J.-P. Warner, "Some aspects of the European Court of Justice" (1976) *Journal of the Society of Public Teachers of Law* 15; "The relationship between European Community Law and the national laws of Member States" (1977) 93 L.Q.R. 349.

Reports presented to a Judicial and Academic Conference, Court of Justice of the European Communities, Luxembourg, 1976.

House of Lords, Select Committee on the European Communities, Session 1979/80, 23rd Report, "European Court of Justice"; Session 1979/80, 71st Report, "Human Rights."

INDEX

Actions,
  annulment, for, 93 *et seq.*
  contractual, 119, 120
  inactivity, for, 110–112
  joinder, 212
  judicial statistics, 187 *et seq.*
  Member State, against, 75 *et seq.*
  non-contractual, 121 *et seq.*
  tortious, 121
Advisory jurisdiction, 179 *et seq.*
Advocates General, 54 *et seq.*
  appointment of, 31, 56
  biographical backgrounds, 61–63
  contribution of, 59
  independence of, 32, 57
  national origin, 61
  number of, 61
  opinions, 57 *et seq.*, 64 *et seq.*, 204, 279, 294
  role of, 54 *et seq.*
Annulment,
  actions for, 93 *et seq.*
  effect of, 109, 110
  grounds for, 104 *et seq.*
  interest to bring action, 96 *et seq.*
  limitation period, 103, 104
Appeal, 212–214
Audience,
  right of, 225 *et seq.*, 267, 268

Barristers,
  right of audience, 227, 228

Case reports, 19, 20
Cases. *See* Judicial Statistics.
Chambers, 16, 25–27
  assignment of cases to, 25, 26, 200, 287

Chambers—*cont.*
  disagreement between, 278
  presidents of, 35
  staff cases, hearing of, 148
Commission,
  actions against Member States, 75 *et seq.*
  work of, 7, 8
Community acts,
  interpretation of, 94, 95
  judicial review of, 91 *et seq.*
  preliminary rulings on, 163
Community institutions, 1 *et seq.*
  competence to negotiate treaties, 181, 182
  positioning of, 10
  relationships between, 3, 7, 8
Community servants,
  acts of, 134–136
  immunity of, 135
Comparative law,
  influence of, 295, 296
  interpretation influenced by, 252–254
Costs, 208, 209, 217
Council of Ministers, 6
Counsel,
  notes for the guidance of, 218–220
  See also Lawyers.
Courthouse, 27–29
Court of Justice,
  composition of, 37
  creation, 1, 2
  jurisdiction and function, 8, 15, 16, 71 *et seq.*
  members of, 15, 16, 288
  organisation of, 15 *et seq.*
  precedent in, 276 *et seq.*
  work-load, increase in, 288, 289

Damage,
　　causation and liability, 130 *et seq.*
　　proof, 131
Direct actions,
　　articles 93, 169 and 170, under, 75 *et seq.*
　　judicial statistics, 188, 190
　　procedure, 197
Directorate of Administration, 23
Documentation Service, 20

Enforcement,
　　judgment, of, 85 *et seq.*, 207
Enlargement,
　　Community, of, 286
European Council, 6
European Parliament, 5
European Union, 290–292
Evidence,
　　taking of, 201
Execution,
　　judgment, of, 207

Fault,
　　concept of, 124, 125
　　Member State, 136–138
Fundamental rights, 268, 292

General principles of law,
　　fundamental rights, 268 *et seq.*
　　national legal systems, in, 261, 266
　　non-discrimination, prohibition of, 264, 265
　　proportionality, 261, 262–264
　　protection of legitimate expectations, 266
　　right to be heard, 267, 268
　　source of Community law, 260

Human rights, 272–274, 292

Illegality,
　　plea of, 112 *et seq.*

Immunity,
　　community servants, 135, 136
　　judicial, 36
Inactivity,
　　actions for, 110–112
Information Office, 22, 23
Institutions. *See* Community institutions.
International court,
　　role as, 72, 73
International Federation for European Law, 222
Interpretation,
　　approaches to, 239
　　common law rules, 259
　　comparative law influence, 252–254
　　contextual, 248 *et seq.*
　　historical, 244 *et seq.*
　　literal, 240 *et seq.*
　　plurilingual dimension, 238, 239
　　teleological, 254 *et seq.*
Interpretation Division, 22
Intervention,
　　third parties by, 212

Joinder of actions, 212
Judge-rapporteur, 201, 203
Judges, 16, 30 *et seq.*
　　appointment of, 31
　　biographical backgrounds, 41 *et seq.*
　　dismissal, 34
　　immunity, 36
　　incompatibility with office, 36, 37
　　number of, 31
　　oath taken by, 33
　　qualifications, 32, 33
　　resignation, 34
　　salaries, 36
　　term of appointment, 33, 34
Judgment,
　　appeal against, 212–214
　　collegiate character, 206, 234
　　declaratory, 76
　　delivery of, 205
　　enforcement, 85 *et seq.*, 207

Judgment—*cont.*
  example of, 46 *et seq.*
  form of, 38–40
  publication of, 206
  ratio, 276
  style of, 40, 41
Judicial legislation, 233
Judicial personnel, 15
Judicial review, 71, 91 *et seq.*
  actions for inactivity (article
    175), 110–112
  actions to annul (article 173), 93
    et seq.
  competence, lack of, 105
  grounds for, 104 *et seq.*
  infringement of law, 107
  infringement of procedure, 105,
    106
  limitation period, 103, 104
  locus standi, 96 *et seq.*, 102, 113,
    114, 116
  misuse of powers, 108, 109
  plea of illegality (article 184),
    112 *et seq.*
Judicial sittings, 29
Judicial statistics, 187 *et seq.*
Judicial style, 40, 41
Jurisdiction, 8, 15, 16, 71 *et seq.*,
    288, 291
  advisory opinions, 179 *et seq.*
  article 88 (ECSC) procedure, 76
  article 93 procedure, 83–85
  article 169 procedure, 75 *et seq.*
  article 170 procedure, 82 *et seq.*
  conflict of, 158
  developments in, 288–290
  international court, as, 72, 73
  judicial review, 71, 91 *et seq.*
  non-contractual actions, 121 *et
    seq.*
  plenary, 118 *et seq.*, 147
  preliminary rulings, 72, 151
  remedy, nature of, 129, 130
  staff cases, 144 *et seq.*

Language,
  choice, restriction of, 287

Language—*cont.*
  court, before, 16, 17, 216
  decision as to, 199
Language Divisions, 21
Lawyers,
  qualifications required, 222, 225
  representation of parties, 224,
    225
  right of audience, 225 *et seq.*
  role of, 221 *et seq.*
  technique, 222
Legal aid, 229–231
Legal secretaries, 23, 24, 58
Liability,
  damage for, 124
  legislation, arising from,
    126–128
  non-contractual, 121 *et seq.*
  vicarious, 135, 136, 137
Library, 20
Limitation period,
  article 173 actions, 103, 104
  article 215 actions, 128, 129
  judicial review, 103, 104
Locus standi,
  actions for judicial review, 96 *et
    seq.*, 102, 113, 114, 116, 211
Luxembourg Accords, 6

Member States,
  actions against, 75 *et seq.*
  competence to negotiate
    treaties, 181, 182
  compliance with obligations, 85
    et seq.
  courts of, what constitutes, 163
    et seq.
  defiance of Court, 293
  enforcement of judgments
    against, 85 *et seq.*
  fault on part of, 136–138
  intervention by, 211
  judicial systems of, 282
  sovereignty of, 85, 175, 176, 282
  tribunals of, what constitutes,
    163 *et seq.*

National courts,
  Community law applied in, 10,
    152, 155
  conflict of jurisdiction, 158
  co-operation with, 169, 170
  decisions of, 280
  exclusive jurisdiction of, 119
  precedent in, 281 *et seq.*
  question referred, formulation
    of, 160–162
  referral from, 158, 160, 167, 285
  remedy in, 138 *et seq.*
Normative injustice, 126–128, 134,
  142

Opinions,
  advocates general, of, 57 *et seq.*,
    64 *et seq.*, 204, 279, 294
  external relations, on, 179 *et
    seq.*

Plenary jurisdiction, 118 *et seq.*,
  147
Power,
  misuse of, 108, 109, 243
Precedent, 172, 173, 275 *et seq.*
  Court of Justice, in, 276 *et seq.*
  departure from, 277, 278
  national courts in, 281
  opinions of advocates general,
    279
  reversal of decisions, 3, 4
Preliminary ruling, 151 *et seq.*, 214
    et seq.
  Community law, questions of,
    163
  decision to refer, 158–160
  effects of, 172 *et seq.*
  interpretation of Community
    law, 155, 156
  legal aid for, 230
  national courts, co-operation
    with, 169, 170
  nature of, 152
  obligation to refer, 167–169
  origins of, 157
  procedure, 156, 214 *et seq.*

Preliminary ruling—*cont.*
  validity of Community law, on,
    153, 154
President of Chambers, 35
President of the Court, 18, 35
Procedure, 193 *et seq.*
  administrative meeting, 201,
    202
  admissibility, 199, 200, 211, 216
  article 88 (ECSC), under, 76
  article 93, under, 83–85
  article 169, under, 75 *et seq.*
  article 170, under, 82 *et seq.*
  article 228 opinions, 183
  defence, filing of, 199
  developments in, 296
  evidence, taking of, 201
  infringements of, 105
  interim relief, 209, 210
  investigation, 200
  judgment, delivery of, 205, 206
  lawyers' addresses, 204
  oral proceedings, 203–205
  preliminary ruling, 156, 214 *et
    seq.*
  preparatory inquiry, 200
  preliminary objection, 200
  Rules of, 194
  staff cases, in, 148–150
  witnesses, hearing of, 201, 202
  written proceedings, 198–200

Rapporteurs,
  assistant, 24
  See Judge-rapporteur.
Referral,
  preliminary ruling, for, 158 *et
    seq.*, 167
Registrar, 15, 17–19
  appointment, 17
  residence, 17, 18
  responsibility, 18, 19
Registry, 15, 17–19
Relief,
  interim, 209, 210
Remedies. *See* Judicial review and
  Jurisdiction.

Representation,
  legal, 224, 225

Salaries, 36
Secretaries,
  legal, 23, 24, 58
Servants. *See* Community
  servants.
Sittings, 29
Solicitors,
  right of audience, 227, 228
Sources of law, 4, 233, 260, 267,
  275
Staff cases, 143 *et seq.*
  costs in, 208
  jurisdiction of Court, 144 *et seq.*
  plenary jurisdiction of Court,
    147
  procedure in, 148–150

Staff Regulations,
  jurisdiction of Court, 144
  legality of, 146
Stare decisis doctrine, 275
  And see Precedent.
State aids,
  enforcement procedure, 83–85
Summit meetings, 6

Third parties,
  intervention by, 211
Translation Directorate, 21, 22
Travaux préparatoires, 246, 247
Treaty-making powers,
  review of by Court, 179 *et seq.*

Validity,
  preliminary rulings on, 153, 154

Witnesses, 149, 201